NEW YORK
NOTES

Whitney Balliett

NEW YORK NOTES

A Journal of Jazz, 1972-1975

A DA CAPO PAPERBACK

FOR NANCY

Library of Congress Cataloging in Publication Data

Balliett, Whitney.
New York notes.

Reprint of the 1976 ed. published by Houghton
Mifflin, Boston.
1. Jazz music—New York (City) I. Title.
ML3561.J3B247 1977   785.4'2   76-51396
ISBN 0-306-80037-3

ISBN 0-306-80037-3

First Paperback Printing 1977

This Da Capo Press paperback edition of *New York Notes* is an
unabridged republication of the first edition published in Boston
in 1976. The material in that book is reprinted by arrangement
with Houghton Mifflin Company. Originally published by the
New Yorker.

Published by Da Capo Press, Inc.
A Subsidiary of Plenum Publishing Corporation
227 West 17th Street
New York, N.Y. 10011

NOTE

THIS JOURNAL is a highly selective record of what has gone on in New York in the world of jazz during the past four years. I have only written about what seemed important to me — the final dissolution of the Modern Jazz Quartet; the deaths of Duke Ellington, Harry Carney, Ben Webster, Jimmy Rushing, and Mahalia Jackson; the founding of *two* jazz repertory companies in the city; the issuing by no less than the Smithsonian of a recorded history of jazz; that annual parade and extravaganza, the Newport Jazz Festival-New York; and the resurgence of such musicians and singers as Helen Humes, Anita Ellis, Ellis Larkins, Earl Hines, and Jimmy Rowles, as well as the continuing value of such musicians and singers as Gerry Mulligan, Charlie Parker, Joe Turner, Charlie Christian, and Mabel Mercer. The music appears to be in good health. Indeed, there are probably more people of all ages playing jazz than ever before, and, even more, the young are listening again.

Most of this journal appeared in *The New Yorker* but in somewhat different form. It is astonishing how easy it is in a workaday record of this kind to repeat oneself and commit other blunders—shortcomings that I hope have all been spotted and removed.

I would like to thank for their kindness and even inspiration Alec Wilder, James T. Maher, and Charles Bourgeois. Each of them — to recall an observation that the trombonist Benny Morton made about his colleague Vic Dickenson — "has ears like a vacuum cleaner."

W. B.

1972

JANUARY 4TH: THE CONDITION OF JAZZ remains parlous but persuasive. Night clubs and concerts appear for the moment to have stopped dwindling, and the music has even surfaced at such unexpected spas as the St. Regis-Sheraton and Delmonico's as well as at Barney Josephson's Cookery, which has become the pleasantest place in the city to hear jazz. New recordings, though greatly reduced in the past five years, form a steady trickle, and several impressive reissue programs are under way. Victor has released six LPs given over to Lionel Hampton, Hot Lips Page, and assorted small groups and singers, and six more will be out in April. Columbia, winding up its monumental Bessie Smith project, now talks of reissues by Billie Holiday, Count Basie, and Charlie Christian. And Prestige, a small, worthy New York company that has been bought by a West Coast label, Fantasy, has just released ten two-record sets — some of them classic — made mainly in the fifties by Charlie Parker, Miles Davis, Thelonious Monk, Eric Dolphy, John Coltrane, Sonny Rollins, Charlie Mingus, and the Modern Jazz Quartet. (Unfortunately, two other reissue programs, begun a couple of years ago by Decca and Blue Note, have apparently gone by the board, and their disappearance

freshet

raises a spectre. The two labels have been swallowed by
conglomerates, and it is entirely possible that their catalogues
will in time simply be destroyed or lost; consider the hopeless
limbo of such invaluable labels as Keynote and Dial. Such
documentary material should be acquired by the Library of
Congress or the Smithsonian and made available to the public
on reasonably priced tapes, and royalties should be set aside
for the musicians involved. Such a plan would eliminate
pirated recordings, from which musicians get nothing.) There
has also been a freshet of books on jazz during the past year or
so. Among them are three volumes on Louis Armstrong, the
best of them an interview done by Richard Meryman for *Life* in
1966 (*Louis Armstrong*, Eakins Press); the memoirs of the
pioneer bassist Pops Foster (*Pops Foster: The Autobiography
of a New Orleans Jazzman*, University of California Press),
which has illuminating chapters on the early days in New
Orleans; a stolid but sure collection of critical essays by Martin
Williams (*The Jazz Tradition*, Oxford); a collection of ingenuous, backslapping reminiscences of some of his peers by Rex
Stewart (*Jazz Masters of the Thirties*, Macmillan); and a
gossipy, second-hand account of the great days of Fifty-second
Street by Arnold Shaw (*The Street That Never Slept*, Coward,
McCann & Geoghegan). Most of the books share one quality:
they are full of remarkable photographs. One of them, in
Meryman's book, is astonishing. Jack Teagarden and Louis
Armstrong loom over a hospitalized, critically ill Pee Wee
Russell. Russell's eyes are closed, and his aquiline face is
bone-tight and waxen. His mouth is slightly open and he is
apparently whispering, for Teagarden and Armstrong, their
faces pained and attentive, are only inches away. Armstrong's
right hand lies on the pillow by Russell's head, and looks as if it
were about to smooth his brow. Russell recovered, of course,
but the picture, taken in 1951 by Wayne Miller, stands as a
great photograph of death at bay.

1 st time —

And I learned tonight, at a press conference held in the
Rainbow Grill by George Wein, the producer of the Newport
Jazz Festival, that for nine days jazz will fare better in New
York this year than it has since the late fifties. Wein announced that the festival, for various reasons, will be held in
New York, and from all indications it will be the biggest show
since the White Fleet. It starts on July 1 and ends on July 9,
and there will be twenty-seven events, involving over six
hundred musicians. They will play at concert halls and at
Yankee Stadium, on a Hudson River boat, in parks and on the
street, and at Radio City Music Hall. There will be every kind
of music, from the Preservation Hall Jazz Band to Cecil Taylor.
There will be a midnight dance, presided over by the bands of
Duke Ellington, Count Basie, and Sy Oliver, and there will be
two midnight jam sessions. There will be seminars and a
gospel concert. Thus, on the busiest day, Monday, July 3, one
will be able to attend a seminar that morning at Lincoln Center
at ten-thirty, an avant-garde concert at one in an unspecified
hall, a five-o'clock Stan Kenton-with-alumni concert at Carnegie Hall (to be repeated at nine), a nine-o'clock Philharmonic
Hall concert (a repeat of one given at five) by Cecil Taylor,
Ornette Coleman, and Charlie Mingus, and, at midnight, one of
the jam sessions, at still another unspecified place. Depending
on the length of the jam session, it may be possible to soak up
fourteen hours of jazz, and, after a catnap, to start again at
noon next day with the Hudson River boat ride.

JANUARY 7TH: DOWN TO THE COOKERY to hear Marian McPartland, who, because of the steady widening and sharpening of
her skills, has become an irresistible pianist. She does not, in
the way of such mandarins as Thelonious Monk and Earl
Hines, have a Style; she is a highly compact, highly charged
distillation of her contemporaries and of the best pianists who

& pianist

came before her. One can hear in her solos intelligent echoes of Art Tatum and Bud Powell and Red Garland and Bill Evans, and behind them murmurs of Fats Waller and Hines. (It is good, once in a while, to go back and listen to Hines' first solo recordings. Their originality and invention are amazing. Hines still wows one now, but he was, in 1929, a singular example of youth and art locked perfectly together.) Marian McPartland is a lively, growing repository of jazz piano playing, and, more important, of the emotions that made Hines and Tatum and Powell masters. A handsome, elegantly groomed woman who makes her blue-haired contemporaries look like galleons, Mrs. McPartland (she is the former wife of the fine Bix Beiderbecke cornettist Jimmy McPartland) sits at the keyboard — her long English face and long English chin swaying impassively back and forth — as if she were pouring tea. But the image is deceptive. She is a rigorous, two-handed pianist who can move in a measure from a passage suggesting the traceries of winter branches to one recalling booming summer sunsets. She is a chordal pianist whose harmonies sometimes rival Tatum's, and a clean, fluid, single-note player whose lines are full of surprising runs and freshly accented notes. She swings very hard, and her sense of time, whether in a stop-time chorus or in one of Tatum's bedazzling arhythmic whirlpools, is faultless. And she has an encyclopedic repertoire.

On the way home, I walked over to the Village Vanguard to hear Dizzy Gillespie, who doesn't appear much in New York anymore. Gillespie is always brilliant, even when he is loafing. Tonight, though, he worked, and two of the numbers he played with his quintet (Mike Longo on piano, Al Gafa on guitar, Alex Blake on bass, and Mickey Roker on drums) were superlative. The first was an attractive slow blues by Longo, and in it Gillespie fashioned a long, muted solo, jammed with unbelievable skipping-stone runs, flag-raising double-time excursions, and legato blue notes. The second was his old anthem from

whats a blue note - outside?

bebop days, "I Can't Get Started." The song is a marvelous success in spite of itself, for its serious, even stately Vernon Duke melody is at complete odds with its inseparable, funny Ira Gershwin lyrics. But Gillespie managed to walk a line midway between these poles by playing high, inflated, godlike phrases, funny off-notes, and reverential melodic passages.

JANUARY 18TH: BUCKY PIZZARELLI AND GEORGE BARNES have been playing rewarding guitar duets for almost a year in the tiny St. Regis Room — they sit on an eyebrow-size bandstand against one wall and share a single amplifier — and they have come to be known simply as "the guitarists." Barnes is a stiff, somewhat chunky player, who started in the thirties, before Charlie Christian, and Pizzarelli, younger, is a Christian graduate. But they are good foils. Pizzarelli provides excellent support on his bass string for Barnes' hopping, singsong solos, and Pizzarelli's lean, melodic lines scud along over Barnes' sharp two-and-four, two-and-four accompanying chords. Their ensembles, sometimes in unison and sometimes loosely improvised, are intricate, amusing chats. They appeared in fine form tonight when I stopped in, but after one set something went wrong. Between numbers, the two men muttered audibly at each other. Their playing began to go out of sync, and when their brief last set was over, they parted without a word or look. True Gilberts and Sullivans, they had, their manager informed me, gradually come to detest one another, and they were, as of tonight, splitting up. It was a rare, seriocomic occasion, for jazz musicians generally sheathe whatever hostilities they may have when they pick up their instruments. The guitarists' swan set was played not on their instruments but on each other.

JANUARY 28TH: MAHALIA JACKSON died yesterday, in Chicago, at the age of sixty. She was an unalterably majestic performer, no matter whether, at Newport in 1970, she was clowning around the stage with Louis Armstrong and shouting "When the Saints Go Marching In," or whether, at an Easter Sunday concert in 1967 at Philharmonic Hall, she was standing still as stone, her long, birdlike hands endlessly turning and smoothing and easing her words. Her curving contralto never lost its fullness or agility (she was recuperating from an illness when she did the Easter concert, and her voice had sunk to a whisper, but by the time of the Newport appearance she had regained her powers, and she gave one of her most stirring performances), and she remained, despite her materials, a great jazz singer. But more than Mahalia Jackson is gone, for she was the only mirror — in person and voice — that we had of her childhood idol, Bessie Smith. Their whole giant, soaring, secret black world is gone, too.

FEBRUARY 4TH: ALL COMEDIANS COVET HAMLET and all tragedians Falstaff. Charlie Mingus, who has spent his career with small groups, covets big bands, and tonight, in a concert at Philharmonic Hall given over to his music, he had one. There were twenty-odd musicians on hand, including Lee Konitz, Gerry Mulligan, Julius Watkins, Milt Hinton, Eddie Bert, and Gene Ammons. But the band was muscle-bound. The ensembles, with the exception of a few characteristic cacophonous Mingus passages, were massive yet meaningless (the orchestrations were by Sy Johnson, and many of the compositions were conducted by Teo Macero, who looked like a burglar emptying drawers), and the rhythm section, despite Mingus and Milt Hinton, sagged. But the soloists — in particular Mulligan, Bobby Jones, and Konitz — offered some relief, and there was more when James Moody sat in for a flute solo and

Dizzy Gillespie scatted several choruses with Bill Cosby, who was the m.c. It was puzzling, for Mingus has often used exciting contrapuntal ensembles in which as many as eight or nine horns roar along their own paths — a device that seems to point the way out of the military box that big bands have been stuck in since Fletcher Henderson.

As an antidote, I went to hear Teddy Wilson's last set at the Cookery. Wilson, who will be sixty this year, is a marvel, and we must not take him for granted. There are certain songs he has come to own over the years — "Stompin' at the Savoy," "Love for Sale," "I Only Have Eyes for You," "Sweet Lorraine," "Tea for Two" — and he played them tonight with a stunning ease and grace. The famous style was in place — the feathery arpeggios, the easy, floating left hand, the impeccable rhythmic sense, the intense clusters of notes that belie the cool mask he wears when he plays. If Tatum and Monk and Hines sometimes suggest painters, Wilson suggests a superb watercolorist, whose textures and colors and draftsmanship are an unfailing delight.

MARCH 2ND: THERE HAVE BEEN, since jazz really got itself together fifty years ago, less than a dozen groups that, by building new houses with the best stones their predecessors left behind, have distinctly helped push the music forward. But one of them — the Modern Jazz Quartet — has done even more. It has unimpeachable taste and a self-charging musical imagination. It is sensitive but not precious, subtle but powerful, controlled but swinging, stirring but not sentimental. Indeed, it is more resilient and adventurous than when it was formed. In many ways, it is the finest of all jazz groups, and it is certainly one of the phenomena of Western music. In recent years, the quartet (John Lewis, piano; Milt Jackson, vibraharp; Percy Heath, bass; and Connie Kay, drums) has appeared mostly in concert; the settings have a becoming dignity, but they tend to keep the group under glass. So a rare event is taking place, for the group — at its own request — is at the Village Vanguard. If the way it performed tonight is any indication, the gig will be not only a rare event but a high-water one; I had never heard the quartet exhibit such fervor and brilliance. It played several fine new pieces, including "In Memoriam" (for a revered piano teacher), which turned out to be one of Lewis' most graceful melodic carvings since "Django" (also played). It played old gems like "England's Carol," "True Blues," "Home," "Bag's Groove," and "Pyramid," and it played tunes it rarely touches, among them Charlie Parker's "Confirmation," Thelonious Monk's " 'Round Midnight," and "Willow Weep for Me." It tossed off about ten blues, and they were stunning. Jackson went on chorus after chorus, with Lewis attentively paving the background with glistening medallions, and then Lewis went on and on. Heath was witty and ingenious, and time after time Kay developed that singular singing four-four beat that he learned so well from his master, Sidney Catlett. By one o'clock, the Vanguard seemed like a ship at sea — tossing and swinging and plunging — and the exultant atmosphere led its captain, Max Gordon, who is a master of the *sous mot*, to observe, "This place has a nice disarray tonight."

MARCH 19TH: THE SLOW, PURPOSEFUL, PAINFUL GAME of hide-and-seek that Sonny Rollins, the masterly forty-two-year-old tenor saxophonist, has long played with his public appears to have finally ended. It began in 1959, when Rollins, who had become the most famous and influential tenor saxophonist since Coleman Hawkins and Lester Young, abruptly retired. He returned two years later, and was greeted with hosannas and a ninety-thousand-dollar Victor recording contract. But

the scene had changed. The vacuum created by his absence
had been filled by two revolutionary admirers — Ornette
Coleman and John Coltrane. The three men jostled briefly for
position, but Coleman himself began stepping in and out of
little self-imposed oblivions, and Rollins' bonus-baby Victor
records were not his best work. Coltrane, who had already
built a commanding style out of borrowings from Coleman and
Rollins, surged into the lead, which he held firmly until his
death, in 1967. No one, though, abhorred the vacuum Coltrane
had left: Coleman remained out of sight, and in 1969 Rollins
again disappeared. Then, recently, he surfaced like a whale at
the Village Vanguard with a new quartet. He talked tonight
between sets about his second return: "I had got into a very
disillusioned attitude by 1969, a despondent attitude. The first
time I dropped out, it was to write and study. This time it was
disillusionment with the music scene. I started playing again
in public last summer, at a festival in Norway, and it was a
nice, inauspicious way to begin. I'm going to make my little
contribution, whatever it might be. There'll be no more
hiatuses for me from now until the end, which isn't that far
away when I consider the time I have left. Time. It's a
dimension I don't understand at all. I look in the mirror and
study myself and I see that my face is changing, that it's aging,
but inside I'm still little old me."

Rollins' new Coming at the Vanguard has been exhilarating.
His style — volcanic, acerb, funny, wildly inventive — is
absolutely intact; indeed, his playing, polished and shorn of the
extraneous "new-thing" hooliganisms that he tacked on to it in
the sixties, is more imposing than ever. (Rollins has also
consolidated himself. He emerged from his first retirement
with a shaved head and a goatee, and he looked like a genie.
Now he wears a normal head of hair, shades, and a modest
beard.) Rollins did a singular thing in the fifties: He bent
together the best elements of his two idols, Coleman Hawkins

and Charlie Parker. He extracted the muscle from Hawkins' tone, lopped off Hawkins' famous vibrato, and sharpened Hawkins' method of melodic playing by parodying it. He learned Parker's teeming disregard of bar lines, Parker's way with rhythm (the oddly placed notes, the silences, the avalanches of thirty-second notes), and Parker's trick of mixing surreal melodic passages with bursts of improvisation. And over all this he superimposed a witty garrulity that made his immensely long solos seem, paradoxically, like endless strings of epigrams.

Rollins played just two sets tonight, and each one had just three tunes. But each set went on for an hour and a half, and some of the tunes lasted fifty minutes. It was an extraordinary display of energy, an all-at-once attempt to loose three years of dammed-up brilliance. Rollins' very first number turned out to be untoppable. It started out at a breakneck tempo as Charlie Parker's "52nd Street Theme," and it ended in half tempo, fifty minutes later, as "Three Little Words." His twenty-minute solo bridged the two parts, and it was a furious creation, full of twisted fragments of melody, rough staccato passages shoulder to shoulder with serene behind-the-beat ones, mad Parker runs, and vinegary interpolations of melodies like "Moonlight in Vermont." Rollins' pianist, Al Dailey, who has absorbed both Art Tatum and Bud Powell, soloed well, and he was followed by Rollins' fine, sound bassist, Larry Ridley. Then the rhythm section fell silent, and Rollins went softly into one of his celebrated ten-minute cadenzas. It became encyclopedic and demonic. There were splinters of "Three Little Words," "Humoresque," and Chopin's "Funeral March," chaise-longue legato meditations, and sprinting double-time sections. The rest of the evening — a couple of ballads: "Easy to Remember" and "In a Sentimental Mood"; a couple of blues: "Sonnymoon" and "Blue Monk"; and a merengue — was anticlimactic Rollins but par for anyone else. Almost as phenomenal tonight as Rollins was his new and young drummer, David Lee. Rollins' non-stop methods have felled countless drummers, but Lee, beautifully under every Rollins phrase, demonstrated perfect time, dynamics, and a refreshing sense of taste.

Pianist

MAY 6TH: WHEN EARL HINES CAME East from Oakland eight years ago to give his celebrated concerts at the Little Theatre, he was in precarious condition. He had lost favor in much of the jazz world, both because he had been out of sight and mind and because jazz itself had changed a good deal in the decade since he had gone West. Always a supremely confident musician and showman, he had fallen prey to self-doubt; he was, in fact, thinking of quitting music altogether and going into shopkeeping with his wife. But two things put Hines back on his feet: his longtime friend and amanuensis the English critic Stanley Dance, who had kept after him by long-distance telephone and had set up the concerts; and the concerts themselves, which, deservedly, received a rousing response. Within a year or so, Hines' life had turned completely around. He had made half a dozen recordings, he had had a triumphant European tour, and he had appeared at the Newport and Monterey Festivals — occasions that have not always signified musical conquests but that nonetheless are always News. Suddenly, he was everywhere: in night clubs, on television, at festivals, on record after record, at Duke Ellington's seventieth-birthday White House party. But the excitement at having one of the great masters of jazz back in currency tended to obscure the fact that he was *playing* harder than he ever had and that year by year his style was growing denser and more complex and more exhilarating. No less than five unaccompanied solo recordings recently released — "Hines '65" and "Earl Hines Plays Duke Ellington" (Master Jazz Recordings), "Earl Hines at Home" (Delmark), "My Tribute to

critics

Louis" (Audiophile), and "Quintessential Recording Session:
Earl Hines" (Chiaroscuro) — document this brilliant growth.
Indeed, the "Quintessential" album, supervised by Marian
McPartland, is one of the great jazz piano recordings.

For a long time, the revolutionary style that Hines first
exhibited in the late twenties in Chicago was hidden under
Louis Armstrong's bushel. Hines' "trumpet-style" piano, as it
was called, was said to be derived almost wholly from
Armstrong's playing. But it is now clear that Hines and
Armstrong borrowed from each other, and that Hines' style, a
fusion of his own genius and what he had absorbed in
Pittsburgh, where he grew up, was pretty well formed when he
got to Chicago. It was and is an inventive wonder. Unlike
such Eastern stride pianists as James P. Johnson and Willie the
Lion Smith and Fats Waller, who were still oompahing their
way out of the intricate straitjacket of ragtime, Hines was
completely fresh. He used tenths or sudden single-note stabs
in his left hand and a mixture of chords and long, single-note
lines in his right hand. The stride pianists were locked in
seesaw rhythms, but Hines did anything he chose with the
beat. He would break up passages with double-time or
out-of-tempo explosions, all the while implying a metronomic
beat. And he covered these inventions with subtle and ingenious decorations. He often ended his phrases with little
tremolos that had the graceful effect of a vibrato on a
vibratoless instrument, and he had a continually undulating
sense of dynamics. He would accent the central notes of
certain phrases, back away for a measure or two, then
underline several more notes, and all of this suggested breezes
bellying across flat water.

Then, over the next twenty years, a variety of things
happened to Hines. He became the leader of a succession of
good big bands, and his playing, though "featured," took a
secondary place. (He once said, "I never considered myself a

piano soloist anyway, so I was happy to just take my little
eight bars and get off. It's the public that's pushed me out and
made me a soloist.") At the same time, a group of masterly
admirers began appearing — among them Art Tatum and
Teddy Wilson and Mary Lou Williams and Nat Cole and Erroll
Garner — and the great originator, obscured by these attentive
encircling saplings, no longer seemed as startling and fresh.
Even the handful of piano solos he recorded in the thirties and
forties sounded discursive and mechanical, as did the random
small-band recordings he made throughout the fifties.

Hines will be sixty-seven this year, and his late-inning
renaissance is unequaled in jazz history. (Other venerable
musicians, such as Pee Wee Russell and Red Allen, turned in
marvelous, new-look last decades, but they were younger
when they did.) Hines' style has become involuted, rococo,
and subtle to the point of elusiveness. It unfolds in orchestral
layers, and its continual surprises demand intense listening.
Despite the sheer mass of notes he now uses, his playing is
never fatty. Hines may go along like this in a medium-tempo
blues: He will play the first two choruses softly and out of
tempo, unreeling placid chords that safely hold the kernel of
the melody. By the third chorus, he will have slid into a steady
but implied beat and raised his volume. Then, using steady
tenths in his left hand, he will stamp out a whole chorus of
right-hand chords in between beats. He will vault into the
upper register in the next chorus and wind through irregularly
placed notes, while his left hand plays descending, on-the-beat
chords that pass through a forest of harmonic changes. (There
are so many push-me-pull-you contrasts going on in such a
chorus that it is impossible to grasp it one time through.) In
the next chorus — bang! — up goes the volume again, and
Hines breaks into a crazy-legged double-time-and-a-half run
that may make several sweeps up and down the keyboard and
that are punctuated by off-beat single notes in the left hand.

Then he will throw in several fast descending two-fingered glissandos (fat boys tearing down a slide), go into an arhythmic swirl of chords and short, broken runs, and, as abruptly as he began it all, ease into an interlude of relaxed chords and poling single notes. But these choruses, which may be followed by eight or ten more before Hines has finished what he has to say, are irresistible in other ways. Each is a complete creation in itself, and yet each is lashed tightly to the next. Hines' sudden changes in dynamics, tempo, and texture are dramatic but not melodramatic; the ham lurking in the middle distance never gets any closer. And Hines, in a way I find unique, is a perfervid pianist; he gives the impression that he has shut himself up completely within his instrument, that he is issuing his chords and runs and glisses not merely through its keyboard and hammers and strings but directly from its soul.

Most of the Hines records at hand are full of these beauties. The main exception is "Hines '65." It was made in London when Hines was still reconstituting himself, and it has a static, I-wish-I-could-get-going quality. There are traces of the mechanical mid-period Hines and strong suggestions of what is to come, but the crossing-over is not yet complete. It is good Ph.D. stuff. The four other records, made within the past two years or so, are the new Hines. "Earl Hines at Home" is of particular interest, for it was recorded in his living room on a fantastic Steinway built in 1904 and given to him by an editor of the San Francisco *Chronicle.* The instrument has the wise sound of seasoned first-rate pianos, and it is obvious that Hines relishes every tone. Listen to his slow reading of "You'll Never Know." Hines makes a stately rhapsody out of it, padding around richly and comfortably in the lower registers — a series of distant booms — and then leaping into the highest octave, where the notes are round and alabaster. Hines is again at a superior Steinway in the "My Tribute to

Louis" album. He was meditating on his old colleague, for
there are two affecting versions of "When It's Sleepy Time
Down South" — the first bravura and rumbling and the second
wistful and sad. There is a scattershot "Struttin' with Some
Barbecue," and a wild, springing "A Kiss to Build a Dream
On." The "Hines Plays Ellington" album is, barring two
selections, an interesting instance of an improviser's being
buffaloed by Ellington's sheer melodic strength as a composer.
In "Sophisticated Lady," "Warm Valley," and "Come Sunday," Hines attempts to turn the melodies into his own
channels. But they won't move, and he ends up encasing them
in flourishes and embellishments — like Colonial houses
engulfed in gingerbread trimmings. "C Jam Blues" and "Mood
Indigo" are different. Both are free, plunging Hines; listen, in
particular, to the opening and closing sections of "Mood
Indigo," in which he coasts along out of tempo, developing a
set of chords whose philosophical harmonies Ellington himself
would admire. The "Quintessential Recording Session" album
is precisely that. Hines reworks all eight of the tunes he set
down on the famous 1928 QRS sides, and, unlike the revisions
of their early work that elderly authors indulge in (Henry
James' eccentric New York edition of his novels), each one of
these is a masterpiece. Note how he drifts sidewise into "A
Monday Date," and how, through a gradually rising volume
and more and more complex figures, he eventually constructs
a castle of sound; how, in the opening section of "Chimes in
Blues," he plays a series of delicate out-of-tempo chords; how
the very fast "Chicago High Life" nonetheless gives the effect
of slow motion; and how the harmonies in "Off Time Blues"
flex and unflex, changing back and forth from triads to
cumbrous flatted ninths. The recording, with its knotted
intensity, its imaginative brilliance, and its richness and control, appears to be a climactic achievement. But Hines may
fool us again.

JUNE 9TH: JIMMY RUSHING, the great blues singer, died yesterday, at the age of sixty-eight. He was a short, joyous, nimble,
invincible fat man who shouted the blues as if he were wearing
kid gloves and carrying a swagger stick. His diction was
faultless; in fact, it had an elocutionary quality, for his vowels
were broad and sumptuous, his "b"s each weighed a pound,
and he loved to roll his "r"s. His lyrics had a pearl-gray,
to-the-manor-born cast to them. His voice — light, tenorlike,
sometimes straining — was not much, but it was hand-
polished and it could be, despite his dandyish style, extraordinarily affecting, as in the mourning, deep blue "How Long
Blues" he recorded in memory of his friend Hot Lips Page. But
most of the time Rushing's blues were elegant, lifting celebrations of life, and he sang them that way — his voice finally
threadbare — until almost the day he died.

JUNE 15TH: CHARLIE CHRISTIAN was an altruist. He literally
gave his life for his art, and in the process all but vanished
himself. Not much is known about his background. He was
born in Dallas, in 1918 or 1919, and was raised in Oklahoma
City. His father, a blind guitarist and singer, apparently taught
him the guitar, and as a child Christian was a member, along
with his father and two brothers, of a strolling group that gave
sidewalk musicales in white districts. He started profession-
ally as a bassist with the Alphonso Trent band well before he
was twenty, and in the next several years he jobbed around the
West, possibly getting as far east as St. Louis and as far north
as Bismarck, in North Dakota, where he was heard, with
astonishment, by the teen-aged Mary Osborne, who later
became an ardent Christian disciple. He had heard Lester
Young as early as 1929, but his own playing seems to have
sprung whole from the rich soil of the Southwest. Then, in
1939, word about Christian got to John Hammond, the remark-

able discoverer and shepherd of jazz talent. Hammond, on his way to the West Coast, looked up Christian, and, at Hammond's behest, Benny Goodman hired him. He stayed with Goodman just under two years, but in that time he became one of the few great jazz musicians to achieve fame in a commercial setting. Fame, that is, as a musician, for little else of him survives beyond his recordings, and they number only around fifty. (Goodman treasured Christian as much as the celebrated master egotist was able to treasure any of his sidemen, and we are indebted to him for the thirty-odd records he allowed Christian to solo on. Christian's solos were never more than two choruses long, but it doesn't matter. His intense originality, which was in every bar he played, long ago upstaged his boss.) A handful of photographs survive, too, all but one showing a slight, dapper, serious young man wearing rimless glasses and a keep-out! expression. The exception is remarkable. It must have been taken at a *Metronome* "all-star" recording in 1940. Christian, seated next to Gene Krupa, is wearing a top-heavy high-crowned felt hat on the back of his head, an open double-breasted jacket, and a sports shirt, and he looks like a child in adults' clothing. But he doesn't have his glasses on, and his face, lean and flat and tight, is startlingly old. And there are Mary Lou Williams' recent recollections: "I think I was the one really got him to join Benny Goodman. I used to jam with Charlie in a little club in Oklahoma City when we passed through town with Andy Kirk's band, and one night in 1939 I asked him if he was going to take the Goodman job. I don't think he wanted to leave Oklahoma City, and I don't think his family wanted him to leave, either — maybe because they already knew about his sickness. All he said was 'Mary, I'll join if you'll join, too.' There *was* some talk about my going with Goodman, but I told him go ahead anyway, and he did. Later, whenever I was in New York with Kirk, I'd look Charlie up and we'd go to a basement room in the Dewey Square

Hotel, usually around ten in the morning, and sometimes we'd jam, just the two of us, until eleven at night. It smelled down there and the rats ran over our feet and only ten keys on the piano played, but we didn't pay any attention. All those little figures that later became the famous riff numbers that Goodman recorded would come out [Christian rarely received credit for them], and after we'd played a couple of hours he'd put down his pick and play classical guitar and things like 'Rhapsody in Blue.' It was beautiful. He wasn't a swellheaded person at all. He was very sweet and easygoing — a sweet, thin, easygoing person. Fact, I only saw him mad once. At one of our sessions, he said, 'Mary, can't you call Benny and tell him to stay out of my solos? He keeps coming in in the middle of them, and I think if he doesn't quit I'm going back to Oklahoma.' Of course, he never did. The last time we played together, he must already have been quite sickly, because the only thing he wanted to eat was ice cream." What else survives of Christian? Such matters as his inveterate, debilitating, all-night jamming uptown with such other remarkable juveniles as Dizzy Gillespie, Charlie Parker, and Thelonious Monk; his tuberculosis, which hospitalized him permanently in 1941; and his death — a moth extinguished by his own flame — in a Staten Island hospital on March 2, 1942.

Christian was not the first great jazz guitarist. He was preceded, in the mid-thirties, by the masterly Belgian eccentric Django Reinhardt. Christian knew Reinhardt's work, and, the legend goes, could play some of his solos note for note, but that is as far as the admiration went. He applauded vigorously, then went his own way. (One wonders what Reinhardt thought of Christian's recordings, if, indeed, he knew them at all. He never heard Christian in the flesh, for he visited this country only once, in 1947, and Christian never got to Europe. What a marvel they would have been in a duet — Washington and Lincoln breaking bread!) Reinhardt was mainly an acoustical guitarist, and Christian was the father of the electric guitar. He never indulged himself by playing too loud or by hiding under the shimmering surface of his instrument. Instead, he used it as it was meant to be used — as an electronic catapult for what is basically a soft and secret instrument. At the same time, he was the first guitarist to transcend the guitar; that is to say that, in the manner of all great jazz musicians, what he *played* became more important than the instrument itself. (Lesser musicians remain locked within their instruments.) His style was a model of clarity and design and order. It had the wastelessness and purpose of geometry, the flow and logic of Albers. But the laconic exterior was frequently ruffled, for Christian freely transmitted the emotions that drove him — those unfathomable, nameless emotions that compel all first-rate music — and he did it without ever disturbing the master plan each solo seemed to follow. He was an astonishing technician, and at the age of twenty he had already learned a seminal secret about jazz improvisation that few players twice his age know — the value of silence. He rounded his phrases, which ran anywhere from one to ten or more bars, with little rests — some of them a beat in length, some a whole measure. They had a pleasant shock effect, and they allowed the listener to catch up with what had gone before and to ready himself for what was to come. (One of the strangest things about Christian's legion of imitators is that almost to a man they have completely ignored this brilliant aspect of his style. Indeed, they play thousands and thousands of notes non-stop, as if sheer musical poundage would raise them to Christian's stature.)

Christian loved the blues, as all Southwestern musicians do, and several of his choruses went like this: He'd start with a descending two-note phrase, repeat it quickly two or three times, and pause. He then reversed the notes, added several others, went into a behind-the-beat legato passage, a drifting-with-the-current passage, and paused again, briefly, climbed into fast, on-the-beat eighth notes that surged up and down the scale, and ended in a rocking, offbeat chord. An ingenious riff popped out at the beginning of the next chorus, and he repeated it several times, achieving a concentrated, singsong effect. Then he abruptly broke out of the riff, passed through a silent clearing, fashioned a descending phrase full of odd notes, and kept compounding the phrase past the end of the second chorus and halfway into the third. He then went limp and legato again, and, remembering the riff, repeated it once, lightly, and made way for the next soloist, who almost invariably began with a paraphrase of Christian's last measure. Christian's rare recordings of slow ballads were tropical delights. He pushed the melody straight before him, allowing it to swell sumptuously here and sink easily there, then took the melody, and, in a passage resting on long-held notes, turned it gently inside out before returning to direct melodic ruminations. His ballads became sensuous slow-motion dreams that filled the listener's mind. Christian's imagination, no matter the tempo or the materials, seemed to have no limit, and it is a pity that Goodman *did* step on his heels most of the time.

But how fine that we do have a handful of recordings — made by amateurs in night clubs — in which Christian stretches out and sounds as if he could play a hundred straight choruses without repeating a phrase. Three of these on-the-spot treats are now available, for the first time, in a Columbia release, "Solo Flight: The Genius of Charlie Christian." They are extended versions of "I Got Rhythm," "Stardust," and "Tea for Two" — all of them recorded by a disc jockey in a club in Minneapolis in September of 1939. The first number, a fast one, has four Christian choruses (spliced from two different versions); the second has two slow, singing choruses; the last has three perfect statements. Also on hand are Jerry

Jerome (a middling tenor saxophonist who was with Goodman
at the time), a pianist named Frankie Hines, and the bassist
Oscar Pettiford. Everything of Christian is here — the rests,
the little riffs, the funny interpolations, the charging, on-the-
beat phrases, the way-out notes and chords that were to be
part of the cornerstone of the bebop movement, and, above all,
the transcendant authority. The rest of the LP consists mostly
of sides made with Benny Goodman — two of them with the
big band and the rest with small groups. A third of the latter
are alternate takes that have never been released before ("I've
Found a New Baby," "Royal Garden Blues," "Wholly Cats,"
and "All Star Strut" among them), and in "Breakfast Feud"
four Christian choruses, three of them lifted from unissued
takes, have been spliced. Also included are two long studio
warmup numbers, in which Christian, along with Georgie
Auld, Cootie Williams, Johnny Guarnieri, Artie Bernstein, and
Dave Tough, rambles around comfortably in the blues. (One of
them, "Waitin' for Benny," has a relaxed and brilliant open-
horn Williams solo.) Not included, though, are the ten or so
other Goodman-Christian efforts, and it's too bad; we would
finally have had their complete œuvre at hand. Most of the
small-band sides among the present recordings have long been
considered classics, but they would not be so without Christian. Listen to the pre-Christian Goodman small-band records
and to the ones Goodman made after Christian — who had
barely said hello to the world — was gone.

JULY 1ST: THE EIGHTEENTH NEWPORT JAZZ FESTIVAL, removed
for sociological and economic reasons from the great, gentle
slope above Newport Harbor where it resided for eleven years,
began in Carnegie Hall at five o'clock this afternoon as the
Newport Jazz Festival-New York, and it was, for a time, a
dislocated occasion. The Festival made Newport hum. It

packed its narrow streets and roads with cheerful rivers of cars and people. It provided Newport kids with their one big whoopee of the year. It brought people out on their lawns in the evening to ogle the swells from New York and Illinois and Colorado. It filled the merchants' coffers. It caused hotels and motels to sprout. It even put the weather on the *qui vive*, so that we invariably had one spectacular each weekend — a smashing thunderstorm, a woollen fog, a hellish heat wave, or a cannonading rain. It made Newport, twice famous before — in Colonial days and at the turn of the century — famous again, and the town, despite the grumbling of its officials, who were indulging in the classic love-hate behavior that the residents of all New England resort towns display toward tourists, enjoyed that. So Newport hummed, but New York, stripped of the furniture of automobiles and pedestrians by a record Fourth of July exodus, looked naked and empty today. Even Carnegie Hall was less than half full this afternoon, and I had the feeling at the outset of the concert that I was in the wrong place — that the real Festival was going on somewhere else, perhaps in Newport. But the first group, the Modern Jazz Quartet, set things immediately right with six flawless numbers, among them a blues, "Valeria," that had a sorrowing, gentle melodic line, played sotto voce by Milt Jackson; John Lewis' beautiful "In Memoriam"; and a swinging, spinning "Bag's Groove." The high point of the quartet's performance came during Jackson's first solo chorus in "Bag's Groove," when Lewis pushed a simple, ascending background figure so close to Jackson's melodic line it threatened to get entangled in his spokes. But it didn't; it merely boosted Jackson up and into several superlative choruses. Stan Getz then floated serenely by on a powerful rhythm section that served to introduce the heralded twenty-one-year-old Philadelphia bassist Stanley Clarke. He may well be the most accomplished and exciting bassist to come along since Charlie Mingus. He has an extraordinary technique (he does not pluck his strings but brushes his fingertips over them), he already realizes the dramatic value of silence, his ideas are vigorous, and he has a huge tone.

During the evening concert at Philharmonic Hall (for the first six days of the Festival, there will be a five-o'clock concert and a repeat nine-o'clock concert at both Carnegie and Phil-harmonic Halls), Billy Eckstine demonstrated that he still has his celebrated bass voice but that he no longer can get it to the right place at the right time, Sarah Vaughan practiced her arabesques, and the Giants of Jazz (Dizzy Gillespie, Kai Winding, Sonny Stitt, Thelonious Monk, Al McKibbon, and Art Blakey) came to life just once, and that was in Monk's solo in a fast blues, in which he kept repeating a complex and funny phrase, making it higher each time, until it simply trailed off the end of the keyboard and into thin air.

JULY 2ND: THE FESTIVAL BEGAN in earnest today. In addition to the double Carnegie and Philharmonic stands, we were offered a 1 P.M. affair at Carnegie Hall (the first of six this week at that hour and place) and a midnight dance in the main ballroom of the Commodore Hotel. The one-o'clock concert included an indifferent performance by the J.P.J. Quartet (Budd Johnson, Dill Jones, Bill Pemberton, and Oliver Jackson); a surprisingly pale one by Mary Lou Williams, a devout Catholic who is so sensitive to her surroundings when she plays that she has been known to feel bad vibrations even when there were half a dozen vigilant priests in the audience; a predictably tumultu-ous, driving one by Rahsaan Roland Kirk, who, with his customary galaxy of instruments slung around his neck, resembles a walking pawnshop; and a classic solo perform-ance by the pianist Cecil Taylor. Taylor, as is his wont, played just one number, but it lasted forty minutes. It was full of his usual devices — the slamming chords, the agitated staccato passages, the breathtaking arpeggios, the blizzard density — but it had two new qualities: lyricism and gentleness. Again and again, after Taylor had launched one of his tidal waves, his hands going up and down like driving rods, he slipped into clear lagoons where shadows of melody glided just below the surface. The audience, a full house made up mostly of kids, was transfixed, and it rewarded Taylor with what may have been the first standing ovation of his fifteen-year career.

Big bands dominated the rest of the day. At the five-o'clock Philharmonic concert, Bobby Rosengarden's group from the Dick Cavett Show appeared, and it was good to hear such an impeccable and swinging band stretch out and to hear its two best soloists — the high-voltage trombonist Bill Watrous and the fine reedman Eddie Daniels — at length. Billy Taylor's twelve-piece group, from the defunct David Frost talk show, was porous in comparison, and was dominated by its leader's effusive piano. The chomping, barrel-chested Thad Jones-Mel Lewis band closed the proceedings.

Count Basie's band opened the nine-o'clock concert at Carnegie Hall with over a dozen brassy, expert numbers that contained vocals by Joe Williams and by Al Hibbler, who sang a hand-carved tribute to Jimmy Rushing. They also contained a couple of self-effacing delights — eight solo choruses by Basie in a medium blues, and the bells-and-flowers sound of Basie and his master guitarist, Freddie Green, behind Hibbler and behind Williams' "In the Evenin'." The next band was a surprise. Assembled for the Festival by Benny Carter, who wrote the arrangements and three of the numbers, it included eighteen alumni from the bands of Basie, Cab Calloway, Erskine Hawkins, Duke Ellington, and Carter — among them Buddy Tate, Benny Morton, Dickie Wells, Harry Edison, Taft Jordan, Teddy Wilson, Milt Hinton, and Jo Jones. The band played with precision and verve both in the ensembles and the solos, the most striking of which were taken by Edison, Morton, Wells, Wilson, and Carter himself, who fashioned a brocaded "I Can't Get Started." A trio from the band also accompanied Maxine Sullivan in five numbers, and everything about her — the pixie features, the tipped-up chin, the motionless stance (her right arm hanging loose and her left poised lightly at her waist), the tissue-paper voice — was in balance and proportion. Carter's arrangements were full of those long, creamy, supple saxophone passages, and the only flaw was a Jo Jones drum solo in the middle of "Sleep." The number was arranged as a graceful, fleeting dream — it hums along at a terrific speed — and Jones' contribution, though very good, broke it in half.

Count Basie's band and Sy Oliver's bouncy Jimmy Lunceford group presided at the dance. The ballroom is long and narrow and tacky, and chairs, instead of tables, were arranged around its edges. Basie's band was sluggish and Oliver's peppy, and one missed the easy, coasting, middle ground that the best big dance bands invariably developed in the course of an evening. But it was instructive to watch the faces of the scattering of kids on hand when the Lindy Hop broke out; they looked as if they were seeing a ritual dance from the court of King Tut.

JULY 3RD: DON BURROWS, a clarinettist and flutist from Australia, opened the 1 P.M. concert, and he was as affecting as anyone who played all day. The chief reason — he is only a fair clarinettist, in the mold of Tony Scott and Buddy De Franco — was his sheer pleasure at being where he was. Most foreign musicians regard the Newport Festival as the Summit, and it was clear that Burrows felt that way. Several of his numbers had a fascinating folk flavor — a Down Under funk — and all his solos, including one on a tiny flute, were impassioned. Lee Konitz, an underrated alto saxophonist who long ago skimmed the cream off the styles of Charlie Parker and Lester Young, followed, and he was at his best in an ingenious reworking of Louis Armstrong's "Struttin' with Some Barbecue," in which he and the trombonist Marshall Brown used Armstrong's opening and closing statements from the Hot Five recording as their ensembles, and in which Konitz took a masterly solo, complete with darting melodic lines and superbly placed off notes.

During the 5 P.M. concert at Carnegie Hall, Elvin Jones, in company with a couple of reedmen and a bassist, was unusually restrained, and Bill Evans, supported by Eddie Gomez and Marty Morrell, played six inward-looking numbers that nonetheless flashed with Evans' taste and inventiveness. The nine-o'clock Lincoln Center concert was a King Kong production. Stan Kenton, the Paul Whiteman of his day, erected half a dozen or so numbers, their tops lost in the clouds, and then accompanied a brittle and unsure June Christy. Woody Herman's newest band was as volcanic as Kenton's (whatever happened to that velvet quality, that squeeze-me sound, which big bands used to offer in between their flag-wavers?), but it was more up to date, for there were fancy time signatures and snatches of gospel and rock. Such Herman old grads as Zoot Sims, Red Norvo, Flip Phillips, and Chubby Jackson were brought out at the end of the evening, and all of them managed to swing without lifting a single decibel.

The first of two midnight jam sessions at Radio City Music Hall was carried out by three different groups, which included such as Bobby Hackett, Roy Eldridge, Vic Dickenson, Norvo, and Teddy Wilson (first group); Stan Getz, Max Roach, Kenny Burrell, Mary Lou Williams, Dizzy Gillespie, and Milt Jackson (second group); and Herbie Hancock, Tony Williams, James Moody, Dexter Gordon, Harry Edison, Zoot Sims, and Rahsaan Roland Kirk (final group). It lasted three hours, and some

lights were lit, notably by Hackett, Eldridge, Wilson, Mary Lou
Williams, Getz, Tony Williams, Harry Edison, and Kirk, who
completely dominated his group by choosing the numbers,
determining background riffs, and playing immense solos. The
sound in the hall was badly distorted. (It was discovered later
that the microphones were hooked up to the wrong set of
speakers.) But the hall itself — the inside of a giant armadillo
— was a good spot for such a free-for-all. Its vastness seemed
to provoke the brave little groups onstage, which looked from
the upper balconies like shipwrecked crews, and the full house
responded with lots of standing ovations and enthusiastic
billows of cigarette and pot smoke. For the first time in its
existence, Radio City Music Hall jumped. But it would have
jumped even more with one addition — Count Basie on the
great organ.

JULY 4TH: JAZZ SPENT A LOT OF TIME on rivers in the teens and
twenties, and today it spent some more. A Staten Island ferry
loaded with three traditional groups — Papa Bue and the
Viking Jazz Band, Papa French and the Original Tuxedo Band,
and Kid Thomas and the Preservation Hall Band (the first is
Danish and the two others are from New Orleans) — plied its
way up the Hudson three times to the George Washington
Bridge and back, via the Statue of Liberty. A bandstand had
been set up in the center of the middle deck, and huge
loudspeakers were placed throughout the boat, making the
music audible everywhere. The best place on board, though,
was not by the bandstand, which was packed to the point of
suffocation, but at the railing on the upper deck, where, the
music washing along in the background, one could marvel at
the skyline, the swinging gulls, and the surprising jungle that
covers much of Manhattan's western shore.

Charlie Mingus' big band performed onshore at five o'clock

at Philharmonic Hall, and it sounded far better than it did several months ago. Particularly impressive among the five numbers was Mingus' "Ecclusiastics," a slow, beautiful gospel-flavored piece arranged in a succession of huge ensemble chords, which were divided by solos, double-time passages, and brief cacophonic bursts. The number used a big band as it should be used: every instrument was essential, the massed sounds proved new melodic and harmonic points, and a majestic aura was achieved. The second half of the program was given over to the American première of Ornette Coleman's forty-minute concerto grosso "Skies of America." The solo parts were played by Coleman, Dewey Redman (tenor saxophone), Charlie Haden (bass), and Ed Blackwell (drums), and the written sections by the American Symphony Orchestra. The piece marked one of the few times that jazz and symphonic techniques have been successfully wedded. The composed sections sounded like Coleman improvisations, and the improvised parts were instantaneous Coleman compositions. The soloists and the orchestra continually fed one another. Coleman and Redman would work their way through a difficult contrapuntal section, and then Coleman, who played superbly, would solo, and after a time the orchestra would come in behind. Coleman would finish, the strings would state a theme (often lovely), and Redman would solo, with the orchestra backing him. Then everybody would lay out and Coleman would solo, his notes ringing in the void, and the orchestra would rush in again with thumping, widely spaced chords. And so it went, with Coleman conversing endlessly with himself in the many tongues and tones he made available on the stage. The composition was orchestrated by Coleman in a purposely thin, high-pitched fashion, and at first it was distracting. But perhaps Coleman is right. The alto saxophone is a lightweight instrument, and it would founder in the rich orchestral gravy of, say, Berlioz.

The evening concert at Carnegie Hall was notable for what didn't happen. Miles Davis, scheduled for both the afternoon and the evening, failed to appear. (He told the press that he wasn't being paid enough and that he had never agreed to do the concerts in the first place, but the real reason may well have been fear, for he has played little in recent months, and a trumpeter's chops, if not used, can deteriorate in a week.) Davis was replaced by the trumpeter Freddie Hubbard, who got off a vacuous set, and then Sonny Rollins came on with his quartet and pretended that he wasn't there, either. During his three numbers, he walked ceaselessly in and out of the wings, pausing occasionally as he passed along the back of the stage to deliver a short cadenza, to play one chorus of the melody of "In a Sentimental Mood," or to ruminate briefly on "There Will Never Be Another You." His sidemen — Al Dailey, Larry Ridley, and David Lee — played some of the longest solos of their careers, all the while peering anxiously over their shoulders like Bo-peeps.

JULY 5TH: THE HALFWAY POINT OF THE FESTIVAL was marked today by two cheerful events — Dizzy Gillespie was awarded the Handel Medallion by the city, and Eddie Condon, in company with some of his old helpmeets (Lee Wiley, Wild Bill Davison, Georg Brunis, Max Kaminsky, Buzzy Drootin, Bobby Hackett, and Benny Morton), officiated at a delightful evening concert at Carnegie Hall. Two bands, padded with such non-Condon musicians as Joe Thomas, J. C. Higginbotham, Barney Bigard, and Dick Hyman, played six spirited evergreens. They were memorable for Davison's swearing, hell-bent lead cornet, for Brunis' short solos, still intact, note for note, thirty-five years after he invented them, for Bigard's loop-the-loop flights, and for a magnificent four-bar break delivered late in the evening by Hackett. Lee Wiley, long in

retirement, sang midway through the concert. Her style, a
subtle concatenation of Billie Holiday and Mildred Bailey,
remains absolutely on keel, and it was pointed up in almost
every phrase throughout her dozen numbers by her accompanists, who included Hackett, Teddy Wilson, Bucky Pizzarelli,
George Duvivier, and Don Lamond. Indeed, they unob-
trusively provided the most gracious and inventive backing I
have ever heard a singer receive. The World's Greatest
Jazzband rounded out the concert. Vic Dickenson and Yank
Lawson played a duet in "Colonial Tavern," Bob Wilber and
Bud Freeman went through their funny, acrobatic "Just One of
Those Things," Billy Butterfield and Lawson did "Baby, Won't
You Please Come Home," Butterfield played a gorgeous flugel-
horn version of "She's Funny That Way," and Ralph Sutton
got off an expert revitalization of Meade Lux Lewis' "Honky
Tonk Train Blues."

Gato Barbieri, a young Argentine tenor saxophonist who
spends much of his time on the fringes of the avant-garde, gave
a typically puzzling performance at the midday concert. He
has a sweet, throaty tone, and most of his solos are made up of
sustained, singsong planes of sound. But every once in a
while, as if embarrassed by such a pounding-heart approach,
he breaks into giant shrieks and wails, destroying the structure
and mood he has so carefully developed. (The virtuoso bassist
Stanley Clarke reappeared in Barbieri's group and again
demonstrated his gifts.) Eubie Blake, who will be ninety next
February, brought his splendid time machine onstage and took
us directly back to 1900 in five numbers, three of them new
creations, including a willowy waltz written for his wife and
titled "Valse Marian."

The five-o'clock concert at Philharmonic Hall was a wash-
out. Charlie Byrd played several static numbers, and Lionel
Hampton's band ba-boomed around and then backed some
creditable solos by Teddy Wilson and Roy Eldridge.

JULY 6TH: EVERY CULTURE WORTH ITS SALT has its counter-
culture, and the Festival's is the so-called New York Musicians
Jazz Festival, which started last Friday and will continue
through next Monday. It is being held in churches and parks
and studios and theaters around the city, and, despite its
attempt to be rebellious, it appears to be merely an inevitable
overflow from the Newport affair. In fact, some of the
musicians in it (Sun Ra, Archie Shepp, Wilbur Ware, Bill
Hardman, Milford Graves, Rashied Ali, Jimmy Garrison, and
others) have appeared at earlier Newport festivals and/or will
appear at this one. It's also interesting that many of the
prominent members of the only real anti-Newport festival,
given in Newport at the Cliff Walk Manor Hotel in 1960, have
long since packed away their war paint and are ensconced in
the Festival establishment, among them Max Roach, Charlie
Mingus, Ornette Coleman, and Charlie Haden.

Dizzy Gillespie celebarted his new medal at one o'clock at
Carnegie Hall by playing four first-rate numbers with his
sextet, which has an irresistible, rocking rhythm section
(Mickey Roker on drums, Big Black on conga drums, Gary
King on bass, Al Gafa on guitar, and Mike Longo on piano); by
introducing a passel of visitors from his home town, Cheraw,
South Carolina — among them a former teacher, the mayor,
and Gillespie's twin nephews, Wesley and Presley; by singing
"Sometimes I Feel Like a Motherless Child" in his high,
aching, potatoey voice; by dancing and telling jokes; by
playing several of his compositions with the New York All-City
Choir, an admirable body conducted by another Cherawian,
John Motley; and by taking a solo in his final number,
"Manteca," that included a seven-or-eight-measure run as
brilliant as anything Gillespie or any other trumpeter has ever
played.

Following desultory performances by the Cannonball Adderley Quintet and by Oscar Peterson, *tout seul,* Mahavishnu, a

rock-jazz group made up of two Americans (the violinist Jerry Goodman and the drummer Billy Cobham), a Czech (the pianist Jan Hammer), and an Englishman (the guitarist John McLaughlin), held forth at the 5 P.M. Carnegie Hall concert. It operated at well above the hundred-decibel level, and it was curious to hear improvisation so highly magnified. It was like walking through a garden full of Maillol nudes. At nine o'clock, in Lincoln Center, the New Orleans bands from the Staten Island ferry reappeared, and were joined by Harold Dejan and the Olympia Brass Band, as well as by the country-blues singer Robert Pete Williams and by a solo pianist, Bob Greene. Williams, not the most agile of the backwater singers resurrected in recent years, moaned and cracked his way through several blues. But Greene was startling. He is a Jelly Roll Morton scholar, and he played four Morton tunes, including "Tiger Rag," a piece derived from an old quadrille, which he delivered straight before jazzing it up. He has mastered all the nuances of Morton's style, and, if one closed one's eyes, it was Morton himself onstage. The New Orleans bands did not fare as well, but they rarely do outside their habitat. They have become dependent on the trappings and the moods of the French Quarter, and exhibiting them separately is like plunking a good 1710 banister-back chair down in a Scandinavian room. There was one exception, though. Ellyna Tatum, the New Orleans singer and street dancer, sang "Just a Closer Walk with Thee" with the Olympia Brass Band and then danced behind the band as it marched through the audience. She has no bones or joints, and her dancing is one long, uninterrupted fluid motion. Her elbows fly in and out, as if she were pumping a bellows, her legs bend slowly and then shoot her upright, her trunk undulates continuously, and her head whips wildly back and forth. She is a supreme freeform dancer, and it is too bad that she wasn't let loose onstage, where more of the audience could see her.

George Wein's second Radio City Music Hall jam session
took place tonight. Two different groups, made up of the likes
of Elvin Jones, Gerry Mulligan, Nat Adderley, Sonny Stitt,
Jimmy Smith, and Gary Burton, played buoyantly and well.
Then the third and final group, which consisted of, among
others, Buddy Tate, Charlie Mingus, Milt Buckner, Cat Anderson, Jimmy Owens, and Charlie McPherson, swept through a
good fast blues before settling into a slow blues that had two
astonishing solos. The first was by the young trumpeter
Owens, and it was a series of stately choruses, each more
intense and daring than the last, and the second was by
Mingus, who has played very little solo bass in public in recent
years. It turned out to be a masterpiece of jazz improvisation.
He played heavy, arching notes (the sound system was nearly
normal tonight), endless weird runs that skirted the edge of
tonality, deep double-stops, broken, deliberately staggered
connective passages, and double-time flights that moved faster
than the ear. He ran through the emotional spectrum of the
blues and, for that matter, of jazz. Even Mingus, puffing and
sweating afterward in the cathedral-like backstage, was
pleased.

JULY 7TH: THE ONE-O'CLOCK CONCERT was an interminable
demonstration of the new abstract jazz. It is made up mainly
of free rhythms, deafening volumes, electrified soloists who
may play at length two or three times in one number, wild
ensembles, little discernible thematic material and little discernible form, and percussionists who work from tables laden
with bells, bones, gourds, gongs, and the like. And it is
resolutely humorless. Only Archie Shepp's group appeared to
enjoy itself. During one long number, he shouted rudely while
his trombonist soloed, a poem was read to thunderous accompaniment, and a little girl in a white party dress sang in a flat

voice and was backed up by a fat trumpeter in a floor-length
blue gown. Shepp has always been an avant-garde dresser,
and I wonder if his costume today was a bellwether one, for he
was wearing a rumpled business suit and a plain white shirt
with an open collar.

The double concerts at Carnegie and Philharmonic Halls
have ended, and tonight, at seven, the Festival moved to
Yankee Stadium. It was a mistake. The audience was small
and the acoustics were horrible, it rained, and Nina Simone got
laryngitis and didn't show up. The audience sat along the
third-base line, and the musicians played in a small covered
bandstand behind second base. But jazz musicians have a way
of breasting perversity, and one at least sensed good performances by Dave Brubeck, who had Paul Desmond and Gerry
Mulligan with him; by B. B. King; and by Ray Charles, who
turned in hi-jinks renditions of "Take Me Out to the Ballgame"
and "Indian Love Call."

JULY 8TH: YESTERDAY, THE *TIMES* RAN a recent picture of the
bandstand at Festival Field in Newport. It was standing
knee-deep in grass, and it looked desolate and forlorn. It made
me homesick, and tonight, instead of going back up to Yankee
Stadium, where a predictable concert by Roberta Flack, Lou
Rawls, Les McCann, and the Giants of Jazz was scheduled, I
went to the New York Cultural Center to see the Bert Stern
documentary "Jazz on a Summer's Day," which was shot
during the 1958 Festival. There were fine, if mud-colored,
glimpses of Anita O'Day, Jimmy Giuffre, Bob Brookmeyer,
Louis Armstrong, Jack Teagarden, Thelonious Monk, Big
Maybelle, Mahalia Jackson, Buck Clayton, and Dinah Washington. They all played and sang well (especially Giuffre and
Brookmeyer), Newport looked wonderful, and the movie
should have cheered me up, but all it did was remind me that

Teagarden and Armstrong and Mahalia and Dinah Washington
and Big Maybelle are dead, and that Buck Clayton is suffering
from an apparently incurable case of trumpeter's block, a
weak lip.

The last of the one-o'clock Carnegie Hall concerts was built
around Duke Ellington and Bobby Short. The program, some
fourteen or fifteen numbers long, was pretty much de rigueur,
but it was performed beautifully (Cootie Williams, in "C Jam
Blues," "Take the A Train," and "Satin Doll," played with that
great primitive ferocity he now has; it is, indeed, a weird
throwback by a trumpeter who was once among the most
sophisticated of his generation to what the very first jazz must
have sounded like), and it included a ballad, "Happy Reunion,"
played fervently by Paul Gonsalves, and a reworking of
"Harlem," a "tone parallel," as Ellington calls it, written
twenty years ago. It opened with a stunning primeval trumpet
call by Williams, went through several complex ensemble
passages, taken at different tempos and enclosing brief solos,
and ended with a long conversation between bass clarinet, alto
saxophone, and two regular clarinets. The instruments, played
by Harry Carney, Norris Turney, Harold Ashby, and Russell
Procope, were truly people talking in the evening on a Harlem
street corner, just as other parts of the piece suggested
beautiful women strutting down Seventh Avenue or people
shouting out of windows to passers-by. The work has a
denseness and tension that have largely disappeared from
Ellington's composing, and it was a treat to hear it again. Near
the end of the program, Bobby Short, thin as a pole and
sporting a log-sized mustache, sang five songs associated with
Ivie Anderson — three with the band and two at the piano —
and they *did* summon up Miss Anderson, particularly "I Got It
Bad and That Ain't Good," which Short sang with unerring
plaintiveness and delicacy. Ellington closed the afternoon by
bringing out a remarkable and beautiful Rumanian soprano

named Aura, who hummed and scatted "Mood Indigo," pushing her voice up almost beyond hearing and never missing a
note or losing pitch. The concert was the best swatch of
Ellingtonia we have had in a long time.

JULY 9TH: THE FESTIVAL ENDED in an anticlimactic fashion,
which was suitable, for it left the many excellences of the past
week standing clearly in the mind. A gospel program was held
at 9 A.M. in Radio City Music Hall, and because there were
seven groups and just two hours for them to perform in (way
had to be made for the regular twelve-o'clock show), no one
could do much more than warm up his pipes. Gospel music is
not just lyrical; it is a music of possession and frenzy, which
take time. But it was a pleasure to finally hear the Birmingham
singer Dorothy Love Coates. She has a fine contralto and a
spacious, magisterial way of phrasing; she is ready for Mahalia's shoes.

Later in the day, I at last got to see "Miss Truth," which had
been playing all week at the Carnegie Recital Hall. It is a
drama with music and dance based on the life of a slave,
Sojourner Truth, who was born in Ulster County, New York, in
1797, and who, after she gained freedom, became an activist
and feminist. Written and composed and acted in by Glory
Van Scott, it is a charming and funny curiosity that particularly delighted the children in the audience. It would do well
touring schools.

AUGUST 19TH: IT IS TIME someone made a study of the effects
of environment and climate on jazz. Herewith some notes:
New Orleans jazz, nurtured in that easy, moist city, was a
legato, flowing music propelled by the undemanding two-four
beat. The instrumentalists had spacious tones and generous

vibratos, and the music was largely collective, which suggested casualness and bonhomie. (New Orleans musicians are
apt to greet one another by saying, "How you be? I see you
brought yourself today.") When New Orleans jazz moved to
Chicago, in the twenties, it tightened up. Arrangements were
increasingly used, and so was the four-four beat. Soloists, by
nature godlike and anti-social, came to the fore, and collective
music waned. The legato attack gave way to an on-the-beat
one, and even to staccato phrasing. The first generation of
Chicago-born musicians carried these changes further by
converting the music of their New Orleans models into a wild,
winds-of-Chicago attack, full of breaks and surprising dynamics. (Some of the fastest jazz records ever made have come out
of Chicago.) When New York took over as the capital of jazz,
in the early thirties, it affected the music the way it affects
everything: It made it grow up. Corners were smoothed,
vibratos controlled, and tempos modulated. Rhythm sections
began to swing for the first time, and the music became more
and more subtle. Duke Ellington's music became New York
music, and as he went so went the musical community — until
the arrival, that is, of a kind of jazz that had been bypassed
in the New Orleans-Chicago-New York trek. It was the music
of the Southwest, and of Kansas City in particular, and when it
was brought to town, in the late thirties, by Count Basie and Jo
Jones and Charlie Christian and Lester Young, it turned
everything around.

Not much was known about Kansas City jazz in New York;
it had been geographically isolated and it had not been widely
recorded. Indeed, its importance in the shaping of jazz was
not fully understood until the last decade. Its irresistible and
original characteristics seemed to imply endless spaces and
crazy weather and the howdy openness of Southwesterners. It
was laconic and at the same time highly charged. It swung
very hard, but in a look-ma-no-hands fashion. It was a

face-to-face music, yet it often implied more than it said. It
had a unique, misterioso quality — a longing for distant hills
and deep woods. The Southwestern horn players had big
tones, and they transmitted emotion generously and in a
variety of ways. Consider the opposite approaches of the
Southwest's two most famous tenor saxophonists, Lester
Young and Herschel Evans. Young, with his light, almost
colorless tone, used laissez-faire melodic lines that tipped their
hats to the melody, that applauded it with soft hands. He was
gracious and accommodating and oblique. But Evans had a
heavy, keening tone, a rich-soil tone, and his phrases, which
were short and annunciatory, were continually shaded by bent
notes and sad November inflections. Evans mourned the
world in every chorus. The Southwestern musicians were also
indefatigable, for they had been weaned on the legendary
nonstop Kansas City jam sessions, which thrived in a city that
literally never closed. (These sessions sometimes went around
the clock, and they virtually wore out whole rhythm sections.)
Kansas City jazz was a blues-soaked music. Blue notes and
husky timbres infused every type of song, and the blues
themselves were enriched in a way not known in jazz before.
They were either light and happy — but never tongue-in-
cheek, in the manner of many Eastern musicians — or
brooding and majestic. There are countless instances of these
approaches in the work of Basie and Joe Turner and Young
and Buck Clayton, and now we have still another in "John
Hammond's Spirituals to Swing: Thirtieth Anniversary Concert (1967)" (Columbia). The three best numbers in the album
are blues performed by Turner, who, backed by several of his
old Kansas City colleagues, is in superlative form. In fact, one
of these blues is possibly the finest he has recorded.

In many ways, Turner, who is now sixty-one, is the epitome
of Kansas City music. More than that, he encompasses all
blues singing, from Blind Lemon Jefferson to B. B. King. When

one listens to Turner, it is immediately clear that *this* is the way the blues should be sung, *this* is what his countless predecessors and contemporaries have been striving for. Everything about Turner is outsize and seignorial. He is well over six feet and heavily assembled, and he has a big head and mountain-encircling arms. His voice matches. It is deep and muscular and booming; it is a bear hug of a voice. But Turner never spends it all; one has the impression that he is using only two-thirds of his powers, that if he wanted he could blow the house down. He is also a master of inflection and dynamics, and his rhythmic control is flawless. He can amble thunderingly along behind the beat, ride it lightly, or push it mercilessly. And he has a rich dramatic sense (all blues singers should have it, but few do). When his lyrics are concerned with diurnal, domestic matters, he sings in a gray, offhand way — he sometimes gives the effect of almost yawning — but when he delivers a line like "But I want the sun to rise, the wind to blow" his voice becomes huge and commanding. The sun *rises*, the wind *blows*. When the lyrics are funny, his voice is mocking and implacable, as in this reverberating, almost frightening stanza:

> Don't the moon look pretty shining
>   down through the trees,
> Don't the moon look pretty shining
>   down through the trees,
>   . . . my baby look good walking
>   out on her knees.

Turner will go at a slow blues this way: He spreads out the first phrase behind the beat, and he uses just two notes (Turner is not a melismatic singer) — one for the first and last words of the phrase, and one for its middle section. Then he pauses a full measure, goes on to his second phrase, pauses again, briefly, and completes the line. He repeats the line, with slight melodic variations, subtracting one of the pauses and re-arranging the lyrics in an almost sleight-of-hand way, as in:

> That one record, particular, baby   [pause],
> *always* sticks in my mind,
> That one little song, particular darlin',
> always sticks in my mind.

In the third line of the stanza he raises his volume and moves up slightly on the scale, then swoops abruptly down. He jams the first eight words of the first line of the next stanza together, and finishes the line by planting the remaining words six inches apart. The second and third lines are gap-toothed all the way through. Two more stanzas pass, and then, his words demanding intensity, he italicizes them and even repeats them, hammering away at the beat and at the inevitable woman he is imploring. He subsides again, and in the final stanza he goes up on the mountaintop. His voice rings, he inserts an iron blue note, and suddenly the hall he is singing in is filled with trumpeting winds. He repeats a key phrase in this stanza at the close of the third line, in the manner of announcing a victory, and then, as is his wont, lets loose a booming Bronx cheer to tell us that it is time to set foot on earth again. Turner's diction at slow tempos is intelligible in a drawling, backhanded fashion, but in a fast blues he doesn't have time for niceties. He flattens his words, and they become planes of sound that climb and fall and bend away, and it doesn't really matter what he is singing about. He has become a joyous, shouting, hornlike wash of melody and rhythm and emotion.

The Columbia album was recorded at a concert given five years ago in Carnegie Hall to celebrate the two great, pio-neering concerts that John Hammond engineered there in the late thirties. On hand, along with Turner, are the gospel singer Marion Williams, the guitarist George Benson, the alto saxophonist John Handy, the blues singer Big Mama Thornton, and Count Basie's band. Big Mama Thornton is the only performer who comes close to matching Turner. She shrieks and yodels and moans and shouts with great authority, but there is a hysterical, overweening quality in her singing (the blues tend to melt away when they are pressed so hard), and I suspect that the surroundings unnerved her. Turner is extraordinary. Listen to the way he crowds his words together at the opening of the second stanza of his single slow blues, "I'm Going Away to Wear You Off My Mind," the way he beseeches his baby at the start of the fourth stanza, and the way, in the final stanza, with his accompaniment lifting behind him mightily, he turns into Zeus. His two other blues, "Roll 'Em Pete" and "Blues for John," are medium-fast, and they are brilliant exercises in hill-and-dale non-articulation. His accompaniment in "Blues for John" is handled in a slapdash way by the Basie band, but in "Roll 'Em Pete" and "I'm Going Away to Wear You Off My Mind" he is backed by a remarkable group made up of Buck Clayton (his lip still healthy), Buddy Tate, Edmond Hall, Ray Bryant, Milt Hinton, and Jo Jones. (Pete Johnson, who had been retired for years and who died not long after the concert, was added in "Roll 'Em Pete," and it was a misty moment when he went onstage. He and Turner had come to New York to appear at Hammond's first "Spirituals to Swing" concert, and before that they had worked together for years in the Sunset Café, in Kansas City. Johnson had led the house band, and Turner had been a singing bartender who occasionally stepped out on the sidewalk and shouted a blues that could be heard five blocks away.) Clayton is unbelievable throughout. His two solo choruses in "I'm Going Away to Wear" are celestial, and so are his obbligatos, particularly in the final majestic stanza, where he becomes a hallelujah alter-voice to Turner. Hall (*he* died not long after, too) and Tate and Jones and Bryant are admirable as well. They must have known,

from the moment Turner started to sing, that magnificence
was abroad that night.

OCTOBER 28TH: FOR TWENTY YEARS, Gerry Mulligan, the forty-
five-year-old baritone saxophonist, arranger, and composer,
has been celebrated for his forward-looking arranging and
composing and for the unusual instrumentations of his various
groups, but these innovations, though witty and graceful, have
rarely been startling, and sometimes they have seemed inconclusive. And he has been celebrated as a player, but he has
failed to dim the imperishable luster of Harry Carney or the
impassioned caperings of the late Serge Chaloff. He has also
become a celebrated Person, and this has been apt. He is a tall,
thin, mordant, nervous, funny Irishman with red hair, a boyish
smile, and a commanding presence. And he has nurtured his
image carefully. When it was seemly, he was a bonelike figure
who wore a crewcut and madras jackets; now, in his mod
clothes, long hair, and huge, fiery beard, he looks like a
patriarch. But Mulligan's pervasive presence and occasional
musical rockets have long obscured the fact that he is an
inspired and often ingenious conservationist who has spent
his career pursuing and reshaping the traditional beauties of
jazz. His arranging and composing are excellent and illuminating recastings of Count Basie and Duke Ellington and
Gil Evans, and his playing is a finely carved set of variations
on the best of such forebears as Lester Young and Coleman
Hawkins.

Mulligan came to the fore as a member of the famous and
beautiful nonet assembled by Miles Davis in 1948. The group
recorded twelve 78-r.p.m. sides for Capitol in 1949 and 1950,
and Mulligan, in addition to playing in all of them, arranged
and/or composed four of the numbers. They were remarkable
records for several reasons. The most complex small-band

efforts yet made, they employed an unorthodox instrumentation (trumpet, trombone, French horn, tuba, alto and baritone
saxophones, and a guitarless rhythm section) and the equally
unorthodox visions of the arranger Gil Evans (B.A., Duke
Ellington U., circa 1940) to distill and control the melodic and
harmonic inventions of bebop. They also set the rhythmic
discoveries of bop in perspective for the first time, and they put
together, for an unforgettable group musical think, such future
movers and shapers as Davis, Evans, Lee Konitz, J. J. Johnson,
John Lewis, Max Roach, Gunther Schuller, and Mulligan, all of
whom have brought tablets down from the mount. And the
records provided the chief inspiration for the cool jazz that
flourished in Los Angeles in the fifties. But the nonet, a
prophet without honor, got little work, and in 1950 it dis-
banded. Mulligan wandered west, ending up in 1951 in Los
Angeles, where, after some scuffling, he hit on his first and
probably best-known group — a pianoless quartet made up of
his horn, a trumpet, a bass, and drums. It was an attractive
group, and it made Mulligan famous. Most of what it played
consisted of a pair of melodic lines that moved seemingly at
will through a carefully preserved silence broken only by the
discreet sounds of the bass and drums (almost always wire-
brushed). The ensembles were in unison or in a gentle
counterpoint, and when one horn soloed the other noodled
around in the background. It was a witty, agreeable music
that asked little of the listener. It achieved a new delicacy in
jazz.

In 1953, Mulligan fleshed out his quartet with trumpet,
trombone, French horn, tuba, alto saxophone, and another
baritone saxophone — pretty much the makeup of the Miles
Davis group — and made eight sides, again for Capitol. They
nod continually in the direction of the Davis sides, and there is
some fine, dense ensemble writing by Mulligan, particularly in
"A Ballad" and "Simbah." Then Mulligan temporarily set

aside his quartet (it was never out of sight long, for it reappeared, with a trumpet or trombone as Mulligan's alter-horn, many times during the next decade), and in 1955 put together the best group he ever had. It was a sextet, and it was made up of trumpet, tenor saxophone, trombone, Mulligan, bass, and drums. It took up where his quartet left off, and it was a refreshing attempt to restore the collective ensemble to jazz in a time when the music, lured on by the apparently limitless time of the LP recording, consisted of little more than endless solos enclosed by dull unison ensembles. A typical Mulligan number went this way: The theme was stated by the horns, in unison or in harmony; solos followed, often backed by organ chords or by Ellington counter-melodic lines; a light, Basie walking-bass interlude came next; then the horns closed ranks for a long collective passage, partly written and partly improvised. When everything jelled, these ensemble passages, which drew indirectly on the collective efforts of King Oliver's Creole Jazz Band as well as on some of the pioneering small-band sides done in the thirties by the bass saxophonist Adrian Rollini, were enormously exciting. (Unfortunately, the sextet made only two LPs, both now out of print and both pale representations of the momentum the group was capable of.) But Mulligan is an impatient man, and when the group failed to take hold he abandoned it and returned to his quartet. In 1960, casting back again to the Miles Davis sides, he organized a thirteen-piece "concert band." It included, at various times, Bob Brookmeyer, Clark Terry, Zoot Sims, and Mel Lewis, and it foreshadowed such current bands as those led by Terry and by Lewis and Thad Jones. It was an immaculately drilled band, but it was bland and it rarely swung. And Mulligan wrote very little for it, preferring to use such neophyte arrangers as the late, lamented Gary McFarland. The band lasted a couple of years, and then Mulligan, apparently closing the door for good on his adventurous years, entered his present now-you-see-me, now-you-don't period — one he has spent as solo performer at countless jazz festivals and concerts, as sideman with Dave Brubeck and Charlie Mingus, and as companion and husband to the actress Sandy Dennis, whom he married in 1965. It is a period that is pretty well summed up in the first record Mulligan has made under his own name in seven years — "Gerry Mulligan: The Age of Steam" (A & M Records). On hand are nine horns — among them Harry Edison, Bud Shank, and Bob Brookmeyer — and a large rhythm section made up of piano, guitar, bass, drums, and the percussionist Emil Richards. All eight numbers were written and arranged by Mulligan, and they are full of ghosts from the Davis days, the quartet days, the sextet days, and the concert-band days. Indeed, most of the numbers seem sketches for long-ago-finished oils. This is true even of "Grand Tour," a striking and original composition that abruptly ends in midsentence. A brooding, melancholy, arhythmic lullaby-hymn, in which Mulligan and Shank and Brookmeyer move along on different levels, stating and restating its plainsong melody, it is a mysterious and affecting piece that is quite unlike anything Mulligan or anyone else has recorded in jazz, and it is a pity that he did not carry it to the conclusion it suggests within itself — a further elaboration of its sorrowing melody, capped by a gradually intensifying polyphony.

So it is good to go back to Mulligan's "Jeru," an album recorded for Columbia in 1962 and reissued a year or two ago, for it offers, in a direct, uncluttered way, the Mulligan who will probably outlast all the other Mulligans — the baritone saxophonist. His style was fully formed when he was twenty, and it has changed little since. (There is, though, a peculiar chameleon side to Mulligan's playing, for when he works with musicians he admires enormously he tends to take on their coloration. This happened most noticeably in a series of duets he recorded ten years ago with Ben Webster and Johnny

Hodges and Thelonious Monk. The last one turned out to be disastrous, for the rhythmic approaches of Mulligan and Monk are very different, and Mulligan played as if he were Monk's partner in a three-legged race.) His style, like that of every baritone saxophonist, is continually challenged by his instrument, which, with its sheer size and weight and its bulky tone, threatens to engulf all comers. But he has met the challenge well. His tone is light, but his bottom notes have a suitable dropped-boulder effect. He moves around the horn with ease, and he almost invariably has enough energy left over to apply the icing of lyricism. His solos tend to be perfectly structured — indeed, form sometimes subdues content — and he rarely jars the listener, the way a Dickie Wells or a Pee Wee Russell does. The unexpected turns in Mulligan's improvisations appear in proportion to the level of intensity he reaches, and when he becomes red hot — he has always swung — he swaggers back and forth between octave notes and uses surprising high notes, smears, or intervals. In "Jeru," this happens in "Get Out of Town," a tight little Cole Porter melody that he limbers up and eventually turns inside out, as well as in the eight perfect choruses of blues he plays in "Blue Boy," the third consisting of one unbroken melodic line and the fifth of those swaggering intervals, and in his two choruses on "Lonely Town," the first dreaming and the second a fully conceived alter-melody to Bernstein's tune. Mulligan's accompaniment, which is flawless, is handled by Ben Tucker on bass, Dave Bailey on drums, Alec Dorsey on conga drums, and Tommy Flanagan on piano. Mulligan, above all, loves to play. He has fooled around with the soprano saxophone in recent years. Once, after dinner at a country restaurant he had never been in before, he took out his soprano, sauntered unannounced into the packed bar, where a mediocre pianist and drummer were holding forth, and played for an hour with such fervor that there was not a sound in the room. When he finished, he sat down at the bar, laughed, had a drink, and listened attentively while a woman offered him seventy-five dollars to play for her party in an adjoining room. Then he broke up.

One wonders what might have happened to Mulligan if Serge Chaloff, who was three years his senior, had not died, in 1957. Possibly nothing, for Mulligan had replaced Chaloff in all the baritone saxophone polls by 1953, apparently bringing Chaloff's powerful five-year sway to a close. Born in Boston of classically trained professional musicians (his father was in the Boston Symphony and his mother taught at the New England Conservatory), Chaloff worked his way unobserved through every kind of big band (Tommy Reynolds, Shep Fields, Ina Ray Hutton, Jimmy Dorsey, Georgie Auld, Boyd Raeburn) and then, in 1947, became part of the celebrated Four Brothers saxophone section in Woody Herman's Second Herd — a section that included Herbie Steward, Stan Getz, and Zoot Sims. He left Herman in 1950, after making an indelible mark on the band — he was as resounding an ensemble player as Harry Carney — and spent most of the rest of his life in brilliant, painful decline in Boston, where he died of cancer at the age of thirty-three. Sadly, there were those among his colleagues who did not bemoan his premature passing, for he was a drug addict whose proselytizing ways with drugs reportedly damaged more people than just himself.

In 1944 or 1945, Chaloff, who had learned his instrument at the feet of Harry Carney and Jack Washington, came under the influence of Charlie Parker, and by the time he joined Herman he had fully transferred Parker's inventions to the baritone. But he was not a copyist. His magnificent tone gave Parker's ideas a new dimension, he dared runs and complex passages that not even Parker had thought of, and he developed a *passion* in his playing that remains unequaled by any other saxophonist. His ballads were sumptuous. He never strayed too far from the melody, and he stated his variations in a battery of voices — cupped, whispering phrases; sudden declarations; cramped, sotto-voce runs; stuttering asides and divalike codas, in which his vibrato moved up and down in slow motion. At fast tempos, Chaloff somehow made the baritone saxophone a slip of a thing. He used gliding half-time phrases (his tone feathery and light), quick, reconstituting pauses, and preaching, triplet-ridden announcements, those now-listen-congregation! bursts with which Parker loved to preface his solos.

Fortunately, Chaloff is with us again, on the just reissued "Serge Chaloff: Blue Serge," which he made for Capitol a year before he died. He is accompanied with sensitivity by Sonny Clarke on piano, Leroy Vinnegar on bass, and Philly Joe Jones on drums. There are seven numbers, and there are good things in all of them — his soft easing into the melody of "A Handful of Stars" and his two contributions to the exchange of four-bar breaks near the end of the tune, both of them delivered in meteoric runs; the furious attack on the very fast "The Goof and I"; the full-palette treatment of "I've Got the World on a String"; and the thorough and beautiful reconditioning he gives "Thanks for the Memory." There are occasional weak moments in the album — "Stairway to the Stars" is too slow and tends to sag under the weight of Chaloff's heavy, whispering tones and threatening vibrato, and he misses notes here and there — but on the whole it remains a superior, perhaps even classic, testament.

It is fascinating to hear Mulligan's "Jeru" album and Chaloff's "Blue Serge" in succession. The two men are very different champions. Mulligan is elegant, lucid, thoughtful, and inventive, while Chaloff is blowzy, wild, inchoate, and brilliant. It is too bad they never recorded a duet album.

*

NOVEMBER 9TH: THE OLD HALF NOTE, down among the sheltering warehouses hard by the Holland Tunnel, was a crazy place. It seemed perversely inaccessible, and it resembled, with its cramped, terraced levels, its narrow, trestlelike bandstand, and its lowering ceiling, a set in a German Expressionist movie. Its piano was beyond belief: Even when it was in tune with itself, the keyboard might be a third or a quarter tone off, forcing the horn players to perform prodigious feats of transposition. (Zoot Sims declared one night, after a particularly trying set, that he had just played in several theretofore unknown keys.) But the place had an inexplicably fertile atmosphere, which generated some memorable music; in its way, and despite the piano, it appeared to do half the musicians' work for them. The new Half Note, on West Fifty-fourth Street, is 4-H Club in comparison. A big, well-lit, paneled rectangle, it has a bar in one corner, banquettes, rows of close-together tables, and an expandable bandstand with a backdrop of pleated raspberry curtains (a Victorian touch that recalls the seedy red draperies that enclosed two sides of the bandstand at the Three Deuces, on Fifty-second Street, in the early forties, and that admirably set off such jewels as Sid Catlett, Billie Holiday, Ben Webster, and Art Tatum). The old Half Note, operating on a budget of buttons and bones, rarely had more than one group at a time, but the new one offers two, and tonight they were led by Earl Hines and Bobby Hackett. Hines, who had Tiny Grimes on guitar, Hank Young on bass, Bert Dahlander on drums, and a Roberta Flack singer named Marva Josie, revealed that there are now two of him — the night-club Hines, who, lamps flashing and tongue wagging, gives coasting, vaudeville-tinged performances, and the recording-studio Hines, who, generally (and properly) unencumbered by accompaniment, plays empyrean piano. Night-club Hines gave a treading-water version of "Second Balcony Jump," played and sang "My Ship," let Dahlander and Grimes loose for long, inconsequential solos, and accompanied his singer in six or seven numbers. Hackett's vagaries are limited to gaining or losing a second. Playing with a pickup rhythm section, he was lyrical, arithmetical, and affecting, particularly in "You Stepped Out of a Dream," "New Orleans," and "I Can't Get Started." The Half Note was jammed tonight, as it reportedly has been since it opened. Nonetheless, there has been grumbling about its prices. There is a three-dollar-a-head admission charge on weekdays and a five-dollar one on weekends, and drinks, which are optional, are two dollars apiece. But that still beats Broadway and most of Off Broadway, to say nothing of the opera and the Philharmonic and the discothèques. Pound for pound, jazz has long been absurdly cheap.

NOVEMBER 15TH: JIMMY RANEY, the forty-five-year-old guitarist and composer, came up in the late forties and early fifties with Woody Herman, Buddy De Franco, Stan Getz, and Red Norvo. He was one of a fleet of guitarists, among them Tal Farlow, Bill DeArango, Chuck Wayne, Billy Bauer, Wes Montgomery, Joe Puma, and Barney Kessel, who, combining the teachings of Charlie Christian and Charlie Parker, developed a new way of playing the electric guitar. It was a sleek, florid style that left no note unturned and that grew wearying in its garrulity. But Raney always had a slight edge on the others. His tone was more delicate, there *were* pauses in his melodic lines, and he demonstrated an almost unceasing inventiveness. In semi-retirement in Louisville in recent years (he is Kentucky-born), Raney, who has a wandering, sad, wood-carved face, is at Bradley's, and it is an auspicious occasion. His style, in the manner of so many jazz musicians who survive the watershed of forty, has become deeper and richer. Two of his sets tonight were full of nearly non-stop lines ("Yardbird Suite," "Autumn

in New York," "Body and Soul") that were broken by lyrical
swatches of melody and by cooling pauses, and as the evening
went on the center of his improvisations moved farther and
farther into the heart of each number. He stated the melodies
of his tunes in already altered, improvised figures, and his
solos were improvisations on improvisations. Working in
astonishing closeness with Raney is Michael Moore, a young
bassist who has played a good deal with Marian McPartland.
Moore is still another of the extraordinary corps of solo
bassists spawned by Charlie Mingus and Ray Brown — among
them Steve Swallow, the late Scott LaFaro, Eddie Gomez,
Richard Davis, and Stanley Clarke. He has a big tone (he uses
amplification, and at times he threatens to engulf Raney), his
melodic lines are succinct, and he imparts to each note a
bearded gravity. Both his soloing and the counter-melodies he
played behind Raney had considerable eloquence.

NOVEMBER 17TH: SEVERAL TIMES A YEAR, the Overseas Press
Club offers late-afternoon jazz concerts in its quarters, and
some of them have been notable affairs — especially one at
which Mary Lou Williams, Bobby Hackett, and Dizzy Gillespie
played with remarkable collective and individual steam. (Their
efforts are preserved in a recording called "Giants," released
last year by Perception.) This afternoon's concert was loosely
designed as a celebration of the seventy-two-year-old banjoist
Elmer Snowden. On hand with Snowden, who was the leader
in the early twenties of what became the first Duke Ellington
band, were Earl Hines, Doc Cheatham, Sonny Greer, Dickie
Wells, Ray Nance, Louis Metcalf, and Jo Jones. Snowden
remains a fine, clear, swinging banjoist who has a guitarlike
tone, but the best moments were provided by Hines, who was
wearing his recording-session hat, and by Cheatham, Wells,
and Jones. A tall, smiling patrician, Cheatham has a subtle,

precise style that consists of miniature sprays of staccato notes, big intervals, a gentle vibrato, and legato phrases that form handsome, almost parenthetical alter-melodies. His solos, in fact, are shaped more like a series of polite questions than outright statements. "How about this, is it all right?" each phrase seems to ask as his solos go along. Cheatham is rarely on view (he has subsisted for years in Latin bands), and it was a treat to hear the five faultless numbers he played. A decade ago, Wells appeared to have lost most of his magnificent powers. He now holds down a day job and plays in his spare time; perhaps this new stability had something to do with his playing today. All the old Wells was there — the wild shouts, the sly off-notes, the brazen smears, the humor, the husky tone, and the dodging rhythmic patterns. One generation of trombonists has already sat at his feet, and it is time for a second to gather round. Jo Jones, also erratic of late, took charge for the last three numbers of the concert, and everything fell into place. He was especially appealing in a medium-tempo "Them There Eyes," in which he soloed with sticks on his snare rims: the solo was at once a tap-dancer working hard and a genial tribute to the ailing Zutty Singleton, who sat beaming in the front row. But Hines was the champion. Each of his solos, with its belling upper-register notes, perilous arhythmic interludes, and intense, involuted swing, was masterly.

NOVEMBER 29TH: SINCE MUSIC IS INVISIBLE and since television is largely a visual medium (the sound systems in most TV sets suggest wind-up Victrolas), it has not paid much heed to jazz, or to any other good music. But there have been memorable exceptions. The first was a weekly half-hour show on N.B.C. in 1949 and again in 1950, on C.B.S. Eddie Condon was the host, and it was a woolly, funny program that included, in addition to Condon's regulars, Louis Armstrong, Jack Teagarden, Sidney Bechet, Buddy Rich, and Sid Catlett. (One of its nonmusical events was provided by Armstrong's vocalist, the late Velma Middleton, whose configuration suggested massed melons, when she appeared for her first number in a hypnotic low-cut gown; for her second, a large napkin had been tucked into her bodice, which had the effect of a hastily drawn blind.) Jazz reappeared on TV in the late fifties. Indeed, one of the shows, "The Sound of Jazz," which was shown live (and was filmed) in 1957 on C.B.S., has become a classic. The level of the music was extraordinary (Vic Dickenson played a solo in an up-tempo big-band number that was one of the greatest he or any other trombonist has ever fashioned), and so were the direction (Jack Smight) and the photography. A few shots stay firmly in mind — a close-up of Rex Stewart taking his horn from his mouth and grinning after a particularly felicitous phrase, and one sequence, which took place during Billie Holiday's singing of "Fine and Mellow." Her accompanists (Roy Eldridge, Ben Webster, Lester Young, Dickenson, and Gerry Mulligan) soloed between stanzas, and when Young's turn came (he was in poor shape that day and didn't play well), the camera, staying on her face as she listened to her old friend, caught in split-second succession expressions of love, gentleness, and ruefulness, all of them coolly accented by a Madonna smile and her slowly rocking head. Some of the least estimable of the late-fifties shows were offered by Timex (they tended to be semi-popular catchalls), and so tonight's Timex show, on N.B.C., was a surprise — in fact, a double surprise: It existed, and it had some handsome music. Of special note were four numbers by Ella Fitzgerald, who, slim and newly bespectacled and schoolmarmish, sang with a plaintiveness and lack of ornamentation she has not shown since the forties, and three numbers by the reassembled Benny Goodman Quartet (George Duvivier was added as anchor man), which, despite the slight unsteadiness of Goodman and Gene Krupa, was swept gracefully along by Teddy Wilson's solos in "Avalon" and "Ding Dong Daddy." The rest of the fun came during two brief numbers by the Ellington band, with imposing statements from Cootie Williams and Harry Carney; two choruses of solo blues by Count Basie; and a tribute to Louis Armstrong that included short but brilliant excursions by Dizzy Gillespie (a muted, searching, high-noted "Basin Street Blues") and Bobby Hackett ("Blueberry Hill"). Basie's blues, which closed the program, formed the background for some impromptu and expert ballroom dancing by Ella Fitzgerald and Gillespie, one of the world's premier dancers.

DECEMBER 10TH: THE ONLY SURPRISING THING about the movie "Lady Sings the Blues" is the chameleon adeptness with which Diana Ross, who plays Billie Holiday, catches the more mannered aspects of the great singer's style. Beyond that, the movie, a strangely misshapen affair, has little to do with Billie Holiday herself. Indeed, parts of it — in particular, one of its principals, Piano Man — are embarrassing. Presumably modeled on Lester Young, Piano Man is an updated Stepin Fetchit and an insult to Young, who was a mysterious, funny, eloquent fool-poet. Pauline Kael rightly suggested that we expunge Diana Ross' Motown reproduction of Billie Holiday's singing by going back to her records, and, fortunately, there are three fine new reissues to soak in. "Billie Holiday / God Bless the Child" (Columbia) contains twenty-eight sides made between 1936 and 1942, when the union ban on recording went into effect and arbitrarily terminated her first great period of recording activity. Seven of the sides had never been reissued until now, among them "Jim" (1941), "Loveless Love" (1940), "Havin' Myself a Time" (1938), and "If My Heart Could Only

Talk" (1937). "Havin' Myself a Time" is the young Billie Holiday at her best; she is light-voiced, slightly sardonic, and amazingly agile rhythmically. But there are rewarding things all through the album; viz., "Love Me or Leave Me" and "I Hear Music," which are total improvisations, and four consummate sides — "Let's Do It," "Georgia on My Mind," "Romance in the Dark," and "All of Me" — done in 1941 with Lester Young. By 1942, her style had begun to harden. Her voice was deeper, and she fell into certain mannerisms — dying notes and a perhaps too conscious articulation of lyrics — that tended to get between her and her materials. Some of that Holiday — the Holiday that Diana Ross goes after so well — is present in "Billie Holiday: Strange Fruit" (Atlantic), which includes the twelve numbers she recorded for Commodore Records in 1944. (Also present are the four Commodore sides she made in 1939, three of them devoted to the celebrated, if stagy, "Strange Fruit," a spectacular version of "I Gotta Right to Sing the Blues," and the stunning "Fine and Mellow.") She never quite gets off the ground in "I'm Yours" and "Embraceable You" and "How Am I to Know," but the old, lilting push is very much in evidence in "I'll Get By," "Sunny Side of the Street," "I'll Be Seeing You," and "Billie's Blues" (a slightly longer take than the one first released). She surprises us in the third reissue, "Lady Love: Billie Holiday" (United Artists). Its nine numbers were recorded in concert during a 1954 European tour, and one of them, a long "Billie's Blues," is uncanny. Her voice by this time was half gone. It was full of boozy huskiness, her intonation was shaky, and her rhythmic deftness had slowed to a lumber. The great well of Holiday emotion was still there, though its walls were crumbling. But in "Billie's Blues" she miraculously puts everything together again, and we hear the Billie Holiday of 1939. Her voice is smooth and her pitch perfect. Her phrasing has that languorous quality she gave the blues. And her feelings are unavoidably clear, just below the skin of the melody. It was an astonishing rejuvenation.

DECEMBER 16TH: MORE AND MORE JAZZ CLUBS are opening rather than closing in New York. Among the most recent arrivals are Two Saints, at Eighth Street and Third Avenue, and Soerabaja, on Seventy-fourth between Lexington and Park. Two Saints is the new name for the old Five Spot, and the place, with its red ceiling and spacious dimensions, looks much as it did when it closed, five or six years ago. It has no cabaret license yet, so the music, provided tonight by Warren Chiasson on vibraphone, Joe Puma on guitar, and Midge Pike on bass, is perforce hornless and drumless. Chiasson, a young French-Canadian who has worked with George Shearing, is a fluent and articulate performer, as is Puma. Soerabaja consists of two small, shadowy, high-ceilinged rooms on the second floor of a former town house (there is a restaurant on the ground floor), and the atmosphere has more to do with a living room than with a night club. Each room has a fireplace, and there are no microphones and no bandstand; the performers — the guitarist Bucky Pizzarelli and the singer Marlene VerPlanck — were simply situated tonight in medias res, near the archway that separates the rooms. Pizzarelli moved gracefully between jazz-oriented pieces and (on acoustic guitar) brief classical offerings, and his accompaniment for Miss VerPlanck was gossamer and perfect. Small and red-haired and birdlike, she is an ivory-voiced singer who, though almost styleless, sometimes suggests Anita O'Day minus the fretwork. It was, in its way, an eighteenth-century evening, in which the music was not so much played as gently summoned from its native silence.

1973

JANUARY 6TH: ELLIS LARKINS, the shy, brilliant, semitransparent pianist, started out life in clear view. He made his début as a classical pianist at the age of eight, in Baltimore, where he was born and grew up, and his début as a jazz pianist at the age of nineteen, in New York, where he now lives. The second début was at Café Society Uptown in 1942, and during the next ten years he slipped back and forth between there and the Blue Angel and the Village Vanguard as the leader of his own trio, as a sideman with the clarinettist Edmond Hall, and as an accompanist of such singers as Mildred Bailey, Anita Ellis, Jane Harvey, Maxine Sullivan, Eartha Kitt, Georgia Gibbs, and Harry Belafonte. Then, turning to teaching, vocal coaching, and occasional radio, TV, and recording dates, he disappeared. He came up for air in the late fifties, at the Village Gate, with the harmonica player Larry Adler, and he surfaced again in the sixties, as an accompanist of Joe Williams. And last year he began an unlimited engagement at Gregory's, a *boîte* on the noisy southwest corner of Sixty-third Street and First Avenue. But several things belie his presence at Gregory's: his elusive, feather-touch style; his sliverlike shape, which is further de-emphasized by big glasses, a generous mustache, and invariably dark clothes; and his method of communication, which lies somewhere between the spoken word (not really spoken but cast forth at random, soft and half-articulated) and an ingenious and vigorous sign language.

Gregory's consists entirely of a small bar separated from the street by a glassed-in gallery. Larkins, accompanied by his bassist, Al Hall, sits at a small upright midway between the bar and the gallery, and he is an island of serenity besieged on one side by the din of his admirers, who tend to be fervent and numerous, and on the other by the din of traffic. But none of this appears to bother him, for there he sits — his body a modest parenthesis and his long, tuning-fork fingers touching the keys so lightly they seem only to suggest the tones that emerge — and spins out his fragile, luminous solos, solos that have the oblique light of de La Tour's famous candlelight paintings. There are intimations in Larkins' style of Count Basie and Fats Waller and Art Tatum, but beyond these his playing appears to be his own. It is a style — delivered conspiratorially by hands never more than inches apart — that celebrates silence and space: when no note is needed, none is played. Its spare, equally quiet dynamics range from a whisper to a murmur. Larkins' mixture of chords and single-note figures is ingenious. At first hearing, he appears to issue little more than a neat legato parade of chords that occasionally catch up to and embrace the beat, and, indeed, he will play a whole chorus of blues by repeating a simple riff. But much of the time his chordal passages are varied by surprising, almost half-hidden single-note lines that are brilliant synopses of Tatum's arabesques. His solos continually revolve, displaying at one moment silken single notes and at the next angora chords, and they are kept slowly spinning by his loping, urgent way of swinging.

When I discovered that Larkins, in addition to his duties at Gregory's, was in the midst of recording seven largely solo LPs under the supervision of the producer Ernest Anderson (historic, pioneering jazz concerts in New York and Boston in the forties; publicity work of various kinds in England ever since), I went to Larkins' apartment, which is catercornered to Gregory's, to find out how he was surviving this encyclopedic task. Freely decoded, this is what he told me: "I was the second of six children, and my mother, who died just last year, did housework and played piano and sang [*opens mouth, as if singing*]. My father, who died in 1942, was a cook and caterer and janitor, and he played violin [*rapid violin-playing motions*] with the Baltimore City Colored Orchestra. He taught me piano until I was six, and he was strict [*piano-playing gestures with both hands, followed by two emphatic forefinger stabs at a piano standing against one wall of his living room*]. Then I studied with Joseph Privett, then with *his* teacher, Austin Conradi, and with Pasquale Tallarico, and finally with Gladys Mayo. I went to the Peabody Conservatory, in Baltimore, when I was fifteen, and at seventeen, after graduating from high school, got a scholarship to Juilliard, which I attended for three years [*holds up three fingers*]. I had to give a little dissertation before I graduated, but I knew I couldn't get up there and talk. I was standing on a corner of Madison Avenue, on my way to the event, when what I'd do came to me [*hits his right temple with his right hand*]: demonstrate the similarities between the melodic lines of Bach and boogie-woogie. The teacher told me afterward that he knew that I'd made up the whole thing on the spot [*pulls an object out of the air and shapes it into a ball*] but that I'd done it very well. My touch on the piano is probably God-given [*looks up at the ceiling*], just as being able to improvise is. If you play a well-constructed tune, you go along with it, you ride with it, but if it leaks, you patch it and remake it. It's like improving a house by decorating it and adding wings and windows and such [*painting and hammering gestures with both hands*]. My idols

in classical music were Chopin and Mozart and some Beethoven, and I still play them for my own pleasure. My idols in jazz
were Fats Waller and Teddy Wilson and Art Tatum and Earl
Hines [*steady piano-playing motions*]. I'm enjoying Gregory's,
which I hope I can use as a home base. If it gets too noisy
when I'm playing, I just stop and turn on the jukebox, which
I've had stocked with records by Nellie Lutcher, Ellington,
Basie, and Charlie Barnet. The kids — twenty-one, and even
younger — are coming in, and they're listening [*cups right
ear*]. Ernie Anderson gives me complete freedom at the
recording sessions, and I don't have any idea [*shrugs shoulders
and holds out hands, palms up*] what I'm going to play before I
sit down at the piano. We're finishing up LP No. 3 tonight, at
the studio over on West Forty-eighth. At seven. Come by
[*beckoning motions with both hands*]."

Larkins was already there when I arrived. He greeted me in
the control room by holding one finger in the air, cocking his
head, and saying, "Don't tell me where we've met," and
laughed — a prolonged, almost inaudible sigh. Larkins' wife,
Crystal, introduced herself, and so did Ernest Anderson, who is
white-haired, trim, and bespectacled. "I'm doing this project
simply because I want to register some of the great neglected
players before it's too late," he told us. He and Larkins went
over a list of the tunes Larkins had already recorded, and Mrs.
Larkins, a short, forthright woman, told us that she and
Larkins had known each other since they were seven, that he
had accompanied her singing when they were eight, and that
they had been married only a year, owing to previous mar-
riages on both sides. Al Hall, who played with Larkins in the
Café Society days, arrived, and was followed by another C. S.
alumnus, the trumpeter Joe Thomas, and his wife, the singer
Babe Matthews. Larkins went into the recording studio by
himself, played some chords, so that the engineer could get his
balance, and immediately started a slow version of "Who Can I

Turn To?" He slipped into the control room when the take was
finished, and the tape was played back. The first chorus went
by, and Larkins made an abrupt stop signal with his right hand
and said, "That's it." He returned to the studio, and Anderson
said, "He's done just about everything in one take, but he did
make two of Mercer Ellington's 'Things Ain't What They Used
to Be,' and they're so beautiful and so utterly different that I'm
going to use them both." Al Hall joined Larkins in the studio,
and they did "The Lady's in Love." Larkins reappeared, and
said to Joe Thomas, "Well, you brought your horn. Want to do
'Little Girl'?"

Thomas looked puzzled. " 'I Want a Little Girl'?" he asked.
"I don't think I know that. Anyway, what key would you play
it in?"

Larkins made flat, conciliatory motions with his hands, and
said, "I'll play it with Al and then you come in and we'll do
something else."

" 'Talk of the Town'?" Thomas said.

Larkins made the O.K. Ballantine sign with his right hand.
He and Hall played "I Want a Little Girl," and he and Thomas
and Hall did "It's the Talk of the Town" and "Blue Moon."

"I think I can translate what just happened," Anderson said.
"Thomas didn't *want* to play 'Little Girl,' which, of course, he
knows like the back of his hand. He wanted to play something
that every other trumpet player hasn't recorded. Ellis got the
message right away."

By this time, the control room was bulging. Billy Moore, a
guitarist, who had been Larkins' first boss at Café Society
Uptown, arrived with his wife, and after them came a songwriter and a singer named Emme Kemp. A small bar set up on
one side of the control room was being supervised by a
raggedy-mustached man in a tweed overcoat and a fur hat,
identified only as Freddy. Because of the reflection of the
crowd in the glass that separates the studio and the control

room, Larkins had become less and less visible. But his music was forcefully and elegantly present. "Sentimental Journey," "Rose Room," a ballad with lyrics by Mrs. Larkins, and two takes of "Sweet Sue" went by. Joe Thomas, a stocky, heavy-voiced man, let loose six "Beautiful!"s and an "I *hear* you!" during "Sweet Sue." It was nearly ten o'clock, and Larkins, who hadn't been visible at all during the last two numbers, closed the session with "Solitude." I found him outside the recording studio afterward, and thanked him and said I would stop by Gregory's soon. He nodded, and clapped his hands soundlessly.

JANUARY 10TH: JOHNNY MERCER, a marvelous jazz singer, who is also our finest practicing lyricist (at his best, he is a very good light poet), gave a concert this afternoon at Town Hall, and it was a choice occasion on several counts: Mercer rarely sings in public anymore (he often sang in the early thirties with the likes of Paul Whiteman and Benny Goodman); the material was all his own; he was in generally excellent voice; and he was accompanied by the superb California pianist Jimmy Rowles, whom he introduced as "the ofay Ellis Larkins." Mercer has a quiet, husky baritone that falls between Jelly Roll Morton and Jack Teagarden. He is a legato singer whose accents are Southern (he is Georgia-born), whose diction is surprisingly clear, and who gives the impression, no matter the tempo, that he is paddling downstream on a warm, moonlit night. This was particularly true in the first half of the concert, which was given over to largely unfamiliar ballads ("My Mother's Love," "You Grow Sweeter As the Years Go By") and to equally obscure nonsense songs ("Jamboree Jones," "Spring Spring Spring," "Pineapple Pete," the last two of which included such inspired rhymes as "Even the bobolink is merrily wobolink" and "He ate so many starches he flattened both his arches"). In the second half, Mercer poured smoothly through a medium-tempo medley of a dozen of his best-known efforts, among them "Goody Goody," "That Old Black Magic," "One for My Baby," "Autumn Leaves," "Laura," "Dream," and "Moon River," leaving to the imagination such other celebrated songs of his as "Blues in the Night," "Jeepers Creepers," "Lazy Bones," "Skylark," "Too Marvelous for Words," and "Come Rain or Come Shine." Dressed in a seaman's cap, a sweater, and red-and-white checked slacks, Mercer was funny, nonchalant, and urbane. Rowles was just as much of a treat. He is as remarkable a soloist as he is an accompanist, and it was a pity there was time for only one solo offering, a moody, manifold reading of the non-Mercer "Body and Soul."

JANUARY 17TH: THERE HAVE BEEN MANY STAN GETZES: the cadaverous, green seventeen-year-old playing in fast company on Fifty-second Street in the mid-forties; the Woody Herman sideman of the late forties, who set a lyrical high-water mark in jazz with his short, rending solo in "Early Autumn"; the hugely successful bossa nova player of the early sixties, who seemed to have lost his improvisational edge; the perennial poll-winner; and the new, tough-minded, hard-playing middle-aged Getz. This Getz first appeared a year ago at the Rainbow Grill, with an astonishing rhythm section that had two or three percussionists (one of them the drummer Tony Williams), Chick Corea, and Stanley Clarke. And he was at the Rainbow Grill again tonight, being accompanied by another mad rhythm section, made up of Richie Beirach on piano, Dave Holland on bass, and Jeff Williams on drums. For many years, Getz had soft spots in his style; his vibrato tended to govern him, he played a compulsive number of notes, and he had a high, sweet-tooth tone. Sometimes his solos never seemed to get beyond adolescent yearning. But much of this appears to have changed. The yearning has hardened into middle-aged sadness. His tone is fuller, his vibrato has been curbed, and there is a hardwood quality to his playing. He uses fewer notes, and his solos are shorter and to the point. All this was clear tonight in firm readings of "Autumn Leaves" and "Lush Life" and in a very fast number written by the bass player called "Vortex." And it is equally clear in Getz's new album, "Stan Getz: Communications '72" (Verve), in which he plays ten numbers written by Michel Legrand, who also did the arrangements and conducts the chorus and a sizable orchestra. There is every sort of mood and music: a rolling, fervent medium-tempo blues, in which Getz gets off close to a dozen brilliant choruses; a Bartók-like piece, in which he plays a difficult, almost acrid melodic line nearly straight; a couple of hymn-ballads; and a piece in which he exchanges Bach figures with the orchestra and chorus. The orchestrations are ingenious, if somewhat showy, but Getz is paramount throughout — in turn lyrical, declamatory, fleet, and wholly original.

JANUARY 22ND: THE ROOMS that make up the mansion of Woody Allen have, with one exception, long been generously open to the public. That room, sumptuously furnished in the Edwardian mode, has been on view only occasionally in recent years: In it, with knitted brow and deadly serious, he plays jazz clarinet. This part of Allen has been visible on Monday nights at Michael's Pub for some months, and it is startling. He is enveloped on the bandstand in a cone of silence — he does not speak to, acknowledge, or even look at his audience, most of which comes to ogle rather than to listen — and, accompanied by a sure cornet-trombone-piano-banjo-tuba-drums band, made up of stockbrokers, admen, teachers, and so on, he plays the clarinet exactly as it would have been played in New

Orleans circa 1910 by such pioneers as Alphonse Picou, George Baquet (whom he admires), Big Eye Louis Nelson, and Lorenzo Tio, Jr. He has the warm, humid tone characteristic of New Orleans clarinettists, and a generous, leafy vibrato, and he favors the chalumeau register. His solos, made up of short, springy phrases, are concise, and his ensemble playing is properly vinelike. Best of all, his playing is clearly a safety valve for the well of emotion that nourishes all his endeavors and that he conceals with such consummate cool.

JANUARY 26TH: DICK CAVETT devoted his show tonight to Ray Charles, but there was very little talk. Instead, Charles, accompanied by the Raeletts, his own piano, and Bobby Rosengarden's band, gave a miniature concert, which included, among other things, "Georgia," "I Can't Stop Loving You," "Eleanor Rigby," a nonsense blues, and an affecting "America, the Beautiful." In the last, he yodeled, cracked his voice, inserted slippered asides, and moved with somber, legato strides. He took the entire song apart and put it back together in the rocking, keening way he once did with "Ol' Man River." He found colors and lights and textures beneath its schoolroom varnish that surely even its composer never imagined.

FEBRUARY 2ND: FOR THE PAST SEVERAL YEARS, Dave McKenna, the huge, stooped, anvil-shaped forty-two-year-old pianist, has been molting away in a Cape Cod roadhouse, where, bowed down by requests for "Raindrops Keep Falling on My Head" and "The Impossible Dream," he rarely reveals what an astonishing pianist he is. But that's exactly what he's doing at Michael's Pub. His fathers are Earl Hines and Art Tatum and Fats Waller, and, like them, he is a dazzling orchestral pianist who needs no accompaniment. (He had a bassist tonight, who was superfluous.) A great many jazz musicians of the middle generation consider him the best pianist alive, and it is easy to understand why. He is a peerless *musician*. His harmonic reach is extensive and original, he has an eggshell touch, he never misses a note or slurs an arpeggio, he rarely repeats himself, he can play "pretty" piano (strangely, a much coveted knack among jazz pianists), and he has an unerring sense of time. But his sense of time is more than just that; it is a passionate rhythmic engine. He warmed up tonight with a series of "room" tunes ("A Room with a View," "Blue Room," "Rose Room"), all of which led one to wonder what *House Beautiful* visions were passing through his mind, and with such placative Cape Cod offerings as "Moon River" and "Days of Wine and Roses." But then he roared into up-tempo versions of "I Found a New Baby," "Rosetta," and "Chero-kee," and the rhythmic impetus he developed summoned up highballing freights. He built his rhythms brilliantly. He'd come down hard on the second or third or fourth note of a phrase, not breaking the flow of his notes but emphasizing it; he'd insert rocking offbeat chords with his left hand while his right hand fashioned descending, hanging-garden chords; and he'd pause for split seconds here and there. But his slow numbers tonight were just as hypnotic, for they offered listeners the chance to see how he does it in slow motion.

FEBRUARY 4TH: THE CHOICE PLATOON OF TAP-DANCERS that has been floating around town off and on for the past ten years is visible again. Every Sunday evening, they assemble at the New York Jazz Museum, and, for forty-five minutes, stage an exhilarating tap jam session. On hand tonight were Chuck Green, L. D. Jackson, Buster Brown, John T. McPhee, and the Master himself, Baby Laurence. Jackson is a curious, sly, mercurial dancer, who, built like a toothpick, seemed to intimate his steps rather than actually perform them. The dancing of Brown, another diminutive man, resembled the racing, feathery flow of Bunny Briggs. McPhee, a large man, moved in a calculated, boxlike way. And Green, a staccato, precise dancer, ticked through his patterns. But Laurence was the champion. He paraded all his best routines — wing steps, in which he rapidly scraped the outside edge of one shoe with the instep of the other; hammering, flat-footed steps passed back and forth from foot to foot; and spins delivered with arms out, one leg in the air, and one foot chattering on the floor — and ended the session with a spectacular chorus that knocked out even his compeers. It should be pointed out that the dancing was preceded by a dreary, largely amateur jam session, which was enlivened briefly by Mary Lou Williams, the clarinettist Rudy Rutherford, and a young and gifted pianist, and protégé of Willie the Lion Smith's and Duke Ellington's, named Brooks Kerr.

FEBRUARY 24TH: IT IS IRONIC that the first good biography of Bessie Smith (*Bessie*, Stein & Day) should have been written by a white. Ironic, but hardly surprising, for blacks were just as responsible as whites for the stigma that jazz dragged after it for so many years. The black middle class was embarrassed by what it felt was the music's ignorant, low-down origin, and the black church, so pervasive until the present generation, regarded jazz as the work of the Devil. Only recently have black writers — LeRoi Jones and A. B. Spellman among them — begun looking closely at their own music. *Bessie* is by Chris Albertson, a Danish jazz scholar who emigrated to this country fifteen years ago. Albertson has managed a triple feat: he has written the first estimable full-length biography not only of Bessie Smith but of any black musician; he has successfully immersed himself in a black world that has almost vanished; and he has at last removed from Bessie Smith the myths that have enclosed her for almost four decades.

The mythical Bessie Smith was the creation of both blacks and whites. The first black American stars came to the fore after the First World War, and they considered her very rough timber; it is doubtful whether Josephine Baker and Florence Mills would even have broken bread with her. Liberal, well-meaning whites completed the image. They made her death, supposedly the result of a racial situation, a tragic celebration: it was one more unforgivable instance of the white man's cruelty to the black man. Other, and more minor, encrustations accumulated through the years: that her drinking eventually ruined her career; that her magnificent gifts began to diminish around 1930, and that, anyway, she was hopelessly démodé by the time of her death, seven years later; that toward the end, she no longer appeared in New York and had been reduced to being a singing hostess in Philadelphia dives; that she was bilked of a fortune by her husband, Jack Gee, and eventually became destitute; that she was an Uncle Tom; and that she was an unappreciated genius in her own time.

Albertson, by dint of heroic original research, snuffs out these notions one by one. Bessie Smith was a hard, periodic drinker all her life, but her occasional binges did not significantly impair her career. Like John Barrymore, she could still perform almost dead drunk. By the mid-thirties, she had pretty much switched from blues singing, which had lost its currency, to pop singing, which had become fashionable, and her voice was in admirable shape. (Witness her final recordings, made in 1933, with the likes of Frankie Newton, Jack Teagarden, and Chu Berry as her accompanists; they are in many ways her best.) In common with most entertainers, black and white, she suffered lean times during the worst years of the Depression, but by 1936 she was landing first-rate gigs, in particular at the Apollo and at Connie's Inn, at Broadway and Forty-eighth, where she replaced an ailing ingénue named Billie Holiday. (Their paths had nearly crossed once before: Billie Holiday's first recording date and Bessie Smith's last one occurred in the same studio just three days apart. One wonders if they ever met — the mother and her spiritual daughter. Albertson doesn't say.) Jack Gee spent a lot of Bessie Smith's money, but it was freely given him; she was almost wickedly generous, and she completely supported two households of relatives during the last ten years of her life. (She and Gee had no issue, but Albertson has discovered an adopted son, Jack Gee, Jr., who is still alive.) Bessie Smith's attitude toward whites was exacting, reserved, and occasionally rough. Thus, Albertson's excruciating description of how Bessie Smith, after singing at an illustrious soirée at Carl Van Vechten's apartment in New York in the twenties, literally flattened Van Vechten's wife when she attempted to give the singer a farewell embrace. Indeed, Albertson's restoration of Bessie Smith is almost painfully complete. Her sexual habits were free to the point of the open practice of bisexuality. And her fabled generosity had a curious dead end, for although, on a whim, she bought Jack Gee a five-thousand-dollar Cadillac and paid cash on the spot for it, she consistently underpaid the performers who worked for her. Moreover, her temper, as the Van Vechten incident suggests, was not only mean, it was titanic: she felled women and men with indiscriminate ease. But Albertson's portrait of Bessie Smith is not all sombre. He points out, for example, that one of the reasons she preferred Philadelphia to New York was that she could, when necessary, shuffle down to the corner store in her slippers and bathrobe without so much as a head's turning.

Albertson has set right the confused circumstances of her death, and he makes it clear that because of sheer stupidity and needlessness it was a far more melancholy event than we had long believed. Bessie Smith did not die of her injuries in her automobile accident because she was refused admittance to a white hospital. She was quickly taken to a black hospital, and there she died, because there was almost nothing the doctors could do. She had lost a great deal of blood, she was in severe shock, an arm had been amputated, and she had irremediable internal injuries. Albertson has found the white doctor who happened on the accident — Bessie Smith's car piled into the back of a slowly moving truck on a dark, narrow Mississippi road — and it is his opinion that even under today's care she might not have survived.

It had looked at last as if she had everything going for her again. Lionel Hampton and John Hammond and even Benny Goodman wanted to record her; there was substantial talk of her making another movie (she was an expert dancer and something of a comedian, and she could probably act); and her last appearances in New York had been widely and favorably reviewed. She had worked almost unbearably hard throughout her life, but she had an iron constitution and was far from worn out. She had been doubly damned — by the white world and by the rigid stratification within her own black world — and she had survived. She was the best-known, best-paid black entertainer of her world and generation, and had she lived, she, too, would have moved onward with the ease of a Sammy Davis, Jr., or a Louis Armstrong or a Mahalia Jackson.

Albertson fails us on only one count. (Never mind the writing in the book, which is come-as-you-are; faulty prose has yet to slow Bessie Smith.) We know no more about the origins of her great gifts than we knew before. But then Bessie Smith had no idea herself. (Ma Rainey's influence on her is debatable, Albertson feels.) Like all transcendent primitive artists, she simply and miraculously was.

*

MARCH 21ST: BY THE TIME the label "avant-garde" is applied to a pioneer movement, its work is mainly done. All that remains is consolidation, embellishment, and dissemination. This last calls forth imitators, students, and other admirers, who absorb much of the luster of their model. In time, a new avant-garde appears, and the preceding movement, which helped feed it, becomes respected and part of the mainstream, its middle-aged paunch keeping it afloat and in the eye of history. The present avant-garde in jazz is almost ready for the mainstream. It appeared fifteen or sixteen years ago, with the emergence of Cecil Taylor, who was soon followed by Ornette Coleman, Elvin Jones, John Coltrane, and that hybrid called third-stream music. All contributed bits and pieces to it. Jones moved away from the regular four-four beat and experimented with complex polyrhythms. Coleman and Coltrane abandoned chordal improvisation, replacing it with an improvisation based on motifs, on clusters of notes, on certain tones, or on a particular *feeling*. The conventional chorus and the measure were discarded. Taylor's approach was similar, but it was heavily infused with twentieth-century "classical" harmonies. The third stream was a compositional attempt to blend these rhythmic and improvisational departures with classical forms and instrumentations. A second *vague* of musicians and composers came along in the early sixties. It included Paul and Carla Bley, Pharoah Sanders, Roswell Rudd, Eric Dolphy, Mike Mantler, Milford Graves, Don Cherry, Albert Ayler, John Tchicai, and Archie Shepp. (Sun Ra, who was much older and had been banging his own avant-garde pots for a long time, also became a part of it.) In 1964, a nucleus of this group of musicians formed the Jazz Composer's Guild and the Jazz Composer's Guild Orchestra. The orchestra gave a series of ground-swell concerts in Judson Hall late that year, and even poked its strange head into the sunlight at the 1965 Newport Festival, which wasn't ready yet.

But the Guild, suffering from the internal scrimmaging that is one of the customary diversions of visionaries, fell apart, and on its ruins Carla Bley and Mantler built the Jazz Composer's Orchestra Association and *its* attendant orchestra. It is still going strong. Indeed, it has become a glistening little nonprofit institution that has its own record label, JCOA, and one of J. P. Marquand's sons, Timothy, as its president. Two or three times a year it gives a series of free in-the-round concerts in New York, at which works in progress by various composers are played, and it has released two big, ambitious boxed albums — "The Jazz Composer's Orchestra" and "Escalator Over the Hill: A Chronotransduction by Carla Bley and Paul Haines." (The Association does things with style. Both albums are handsome and glossy and have well-designed booklets full of futuristic poetry and good photographs. Even the press releases are written studiously.) The JCOA had nothing to do with producing a third album, "Charlie Haden: Liberation Music Orchestra," which has been released by another label (Impulse), but many of the orchestra's members appear in it.

They have a good time in disguise. The reeds include Perry Robinson, Gato Barbieri, and Dewey Redman, the brasses Cherry, Mantler, Rudd, Bob Northern, and Howard Johnson, the rhythm section Carla Bley, Sam Brown, Haden, Paul Motian, and Andrew Cyrille. The album has political overtones, but they are only frosting on the music, which is made up of four songs from the Spanish Civil War, three Bley pieces, Ornette Coleman's "War Orphans," two compositions by Haden (one a "re-creation" of some of the oppressive shenanigans indulged in on the rostrum during the 1968 Democratic Convention, and the other a memorial to Che Guevara), and "We Shall Overcome." The Spanish Civil War songs are lumped into one long piece, which proceeds roughly like this: there is an oompah opening ensemble and brief solos by Cherry and Rudd; Brown plays a long flamencan guitar passage, and Haden follows with a stirring single-note solo, and then shifts into guitarlike flamencan chords; the brass section floats in over a two-note ground bass, and Rudd plays a mock-ponderous solo in half time; the ensemble enters and the whole piece slows down; Barbieri plays a romantic melody and gradually works himself into a squealing frenzy — one of the unfortunate hallmarks of JCOA reedmen — and the piece goes out. The rhythms change continually, and there are brief cacophonic ensemble bursts, patches of straight, warm melody, and an over-all feeling of fun and games. The second side is notable for Haden's marvelous flamencan thrumming in "Song for Che," for Carla Bley's quiet, lyrical piano in Coleman's piece, and for the grinding collective passages in Haden's salute to the Democratic Convention. Best of all, though, is the one-chorus version of "We Shall Overcome." The orchestra dips the melody in heavy, thick harmonies while Rudd improvises above, throwing in an utterly rending bent note halfway through. The version recalls the wonderful single-chorus ensemble rendition of "Abide with Me" that Thelonious Monk recorded in the late fifties with Coleman Hawkins and John Coltrane.

The first JCOA album comprises five compositions by Mantler — four "Communications" (Nos. 8 through 11) and "Preview." They are concertos that are built around the soloists — Cherry and Barbieri, Larry Coryell, Rudd, Sanders, and Taylor. The orchestra, twenty-odd strong throughout, includes many of the musicians in the "Liberation Music" album, together with such luminaries as Jimmy Knepper, Randy Brecker, Lloyd Michels, Steve Marcus, and Lew Tabackin. There are five bassists for each number, among them Steve Swallow, Eddie Gomez, Ron Carter, and Richard Davis. Mantler's compositions have an oppressive monochromatic density, but in general they set the soloists off adequately. As always, there are no fixed rhythms, and the forms seem aimless, for the pieces simply swell and subside, swell and subside, until they are done. (One wishes that the JCO composers would occasionally resort to a regular sounded beat and that they would even use some of the older soloists around. The effect would be like coming on a "gee whizz" in a George Higgins novel.) Taylor pounds, slides, spins, skates, and scrambles his way all over the keyboard for the thirty-three minutes of "Communications No. 11," but Rudd is more impressive in "Communications No. 10," which is less than half as long. He is far and away the most inventive of the new trombonists, and he is a highly knowledgeable revolutionary, who came up through conservative musical ranks (Eli's Chosen Six and Eddie Condon). A decade ago, his style was apoplectic, and made up of elephant shrieks, roars, blats, and thousand-note runs. But always visible were his origins, in particular the playing of Dickie Wells and J. C. Higginbotham. They are in even stronger evidence now, for Rudd seems to have discarded the more frenzied aspects of his style. In "Communications No. 10" he plays a couple of passages that are fine tributes to the great, undersung Higginbotham, and the rest of the way he never goes much over the boiling point.

"Escalator Over the Hill" is a very different kettle. It is a sort of opera, in that there is instrumental music, a libretto, singing, recitative, narration, and choruses. (I don't know what to make of Carla Bley's Greco-Latin subtitle — "A Chronotransduction." "Chrono," of course, has to do with time, and "transduction," according to the infallible American Heritage Dictionary, is "the transfer of genetic material from one bacterial cell to another by a bacteriophage." That last word is defined as "a submicroscopic, usually viral, organism that destroys bacteria." Wouldn't something like "I've Got You Under My Skin" have been easier?) But here the resemblance to opera ends, for there is no story beyond the fact that the first part of "Escalator" is set in an old hotel somewhere in

the Western world and the second in a desert in India. Paul
Haines' libretto is in Dada verse that goes like this:

> GINGER: Nurses dyeing their hair
> Don't care
> If the horse is locked
> The house still there.
> It doesn't seem
> To matter to them
> The traces
> Of horses
> And pineapple
> And cheese
> So many ingredients
> In the soup
> HIS FRIENDS
> (*on their sides*):
> No room for a spoon.

There are also marginalia in the libretto that do not appear in
the performance, and these are often in the form of inside-out
epigrams:

> Two skins better than one
> No skin better than none.

The singing is largely by Carla Bley, Jeanne Lee, Linda
Ronstadt, and Jack Bruce, the last of whom was once with
Cream. The narration is by Viva and others, the recitative by a
host of people, and the intermittent music by a small rock
group and elements from the JCOA. There are good solos here
and there by Cherry, Rudd, and Barbieri. The tone of the
album is satiric, for there are takeoffs of a society band and of
a Broadway musical, and there are patches of funny electronic
music. But the most impressive things in "Escalator" are
Carla Bley's melodies, which are often quite beautiful. She has
demonstrated this lyric talent before, and it's too bad that she
has to bury it under such brouhaha.

APRIL 10TH: THE RAGTIME REVIVAL continues apace, and at its head, willy-nilly, is the astonishing Eubie Blake. Indeed, we are being inundated with Blakeiana. The flood began four years ago when Columbia released "The Eighty-six Years of Eubie Blake," a collection of thirty rags, marches, and blues, most of them by Blake. Although he had been in semi-retirement for more than thirty years, his playing on the record is rumbustious and attractive. Then he was at festivals, on television, in solo concerts, in night clubs, and in recording studios. And now three new albums — "Eubie Blake, Featuring Ivan Harold Browning," "Eubie Blake: Rags to Classics," and "Eubie Blake and His Friends Edith Wilson and Ivan Harold Browning" (Eubie Blake Music) — have been issued. In the first, he plays six loosely structured rags, five of them his own, and then, in eight numbers, accompanies Ivan Browning, a member of the Four Harmony Kings, who appeared in Blake and Noble Sissle's celebrated all-black 1921 Broadway show, "Shuffle Along." Browning is eighty-two, but his singing, which is affectingly of its period, remains clear and steady. Blake plays thirteen remarkably varied numbers on the second record. He wrote eight of them, and these include a new waltz (his first published tune, "Charleston Rag," was written in 1899); rags, one of them also new; a fine ballad, "You're Lucky to Me"; and several études, one of which, written in 1923 and called "Rain Drops," suggests Debussy's short piano pieces. The third record has five more Blake-accompanied Browning efforts and three by Edith Wilson, a jazz-oriented singer of the twenties who worked with Blake in one of the later editions of "Shuffle Along." Again, there are more Blake piano solos, among them "Memphis Blues," his new "Eubie Dubie," written with the pianist Johnny Guarnieri, and his ballad "I Can't Get You Out of My Mind," done for a 1937 W.P.A. show called "Swing It." But Blake has also been supervising Blake reissues. "Eubie Blake: Blues and Rags"

and "Eubie Blake: 1921" (Biograph) contain twenty-two transcriptions of the thirty known piano rolls that he set down
between 1917 and 1921. These are largely pop tunes, but the
playing is vigorous and even audacious, particularly on the
rolls that were not fancied up by their publishers before they
were issued. The last of the reissues, "Sissle and Blake: Early
Rare Recordings" (Eubie Blake Music), contains fourteen
records that Sissle and Blake, who were known in vaudeville
as the Dixie Duo, made between 1920 and 1927. They are
charming, peppy, and innocent. Then, on the crest of this
efflux, comes a cheerful book, *Reminiscing with Sissle and
Blake* (Viking), by Robert Kimball (who, with Brendan Gill,
compiled *Cole*) and the pianist-composer William Bolcom. It
consists of sketches of Sissle and Blake's lives, along with
countless photographs and reproductions of sheet music,
newspaper reviews, ads, posters, programs, and the like.
Blake's earlier world now seems almost antediluvian. The only
child of former slaves (his father was secretly taught the
Spencerian hand by his owner's daughter), he grew up in
Baltimore and at fifteen was playing piano in a local bawdy
house — a way of life that sustained him until 1915, when he
teamed up with Noble Sissle, who was already a lyric writer
and singer. His theatrical career began with "Shuffle Along"
and lasted into the thirties, and by 1940 his first life was over.
The book, though, sidesteps several curious things about
Blake: that he should find himself the guidon of the ragtime
resurgence when he was neither a full-time ragtime performer
nor even a pure one (he generally took liberties with his
materials), that he had so little to do with the great black music
— jazz — that was marshalling its forces everywhere about
him when he was at his peak, and that the predominant feeling
in both his composing and his playing has always been more
white than black.

*

APRIL 12TH: WHAT RAGTIME WAS REALLY ABOUT is demonstrated in a new and beautiful recording, "Scott Joplin: The Red Back Book" (Angel). It was instigated by the Joplin scholar Vera Brodsky Lawrence and carried through by Gunther Schuller, the sometime critic, jazz historian, French-horn player, conductor, composer, and present head of the New England Conservatory. Eight of Joplin's marvelous rags are played by a twelve-piece ensemble made up of trumpet, trombone, clarinet, flute or piccolo, tuba, piano, drums, two violins, viola, cello, and bass. (Two of the rags are also done as solos by the ensemble's exceptional pianist, Myron Romanul.) The instrumentation and arrangements are taken from "Fifteen Standard High Class Rags," a collection of stock arrangements made for dancing, parades, band concerts, and the like by E. J. Stark, D. S. De Lisle, and various unknown hands in the early years of the century and generally known as "The Red Back Book." Schuller has conducted the group, which is made up of Conservatory students, and the impeccably played results are a unique and graceful chamber music. The group, blessed with a knowledge of jazz which its turn-of-the-century predecessors rarely had, swings irresistibly, and delights abound: the intricate, superbly orchestrated "The Rag Time Dance"; Romanul's feathery solo version of "The Entertainer," and the way he and the ensemble work in unison in the opening strain of "Rag Time Dance"; the crystalline, staccato Charles Lewis trumpet solos, with their alarming intervals, in "Easy Winners," "Sun Flower Slow Drag," and "Maple Leaf Rag"; the piccolo solo in the first strain of "The Entertainer," backed by billowing oompah piano figures; and the sedate, subtle, gliding "Maple Leaf Rag."

APRIL 18TH: CHURCHILL'S, at Third Avenue and Seventy-third Street, is a small bar-and-grill where, four nights of the week,

Brooks Kerr holds forth on a tiny bandstand, playing stride piano and Ellington tunes that no one else, including the Master himself, remembers, singing in a pleasant, impassioned manner, and accompanying the former Ellington cornettist, violinist, singer, and high-jinks specialist Ray Nance. Drummers sit in on a house snare, and tap-dancers frequently take to the floor. At least, all this happened tonight during the ten numbers I heard, among them a fine "I Can't Get Started," in which Nance sang and played two muted, yearning choruses; a cheerful "When You're Smiling," with excellent Nance and a couple of dashing Kerr choruses; an introvert "Shadow of Your Smile," played smokily by Nance on violin; and "Just a Lucky So-and-So," sung by Kerr, who also sang a forgotten 1932 Ellington tune called "Best Wishes." The music at Churchill's lasts from eleven until four, which must make it the last place in the city that still swings until curfew time.

APRIL 20TH: SEVERAL MONTHS AGO, the Royal Box, long an East Coast layover for Las Vegas behemoths, changed to a policy of small jazz bands and dancing. The band in residence at the moment (and which will be back in the fall) is led by Bobby Hackett, and it is the best one he has ever had. With him are Vic Dickenson, Hank Jones, the guitarist Remo Palmier (Palmieri when he came forward in the forties), the Yugoslavian bassist George Mraz, and the drummer Jackie Williams. The ensembles tend toward gracious, hat-doffing contrapuntal exercises or fleet unison riffs. In between, the soloists each take at least two choruses, and what beauties they left lying around the bandstand tonight! Hackett, who is nearing sixty, is unbelievable. Although his improvisations, with their intense swing, resilience, and flawless tone and execution, have long been beyond reproach, he continues to polish and refine his style. Thus, the face liftings he gave tonight to such old parties as "In a Mellotone," "East of the Sun," "Broadway," and "How Come You Do Me Like You Do." Dickenson is a consummate foil for Hackett, and, like him, has steadily furbished his playing. He minted endless triplets, smears, plunger-muted passages, growls, and floating legato asides. But Hank Jones, who has long been hidden away in the studios, stole the evening. Jones' solos consist largely of a delicate array of single-note lines that are lighted by occasional chords and that rarely move in the direction one expects. They turn suddenly, like shy lodgers, and are gone; they bowl through adventurous notes with grace and precision; they come up glistening from the deeps of the keyboard; they flicker and dart and flash like evening swallows. He was particularly nimble in "Hindustan" and "Blue Skies," and he even quickened "Muskrat Ramble."

MAY 1ST: JIM HALL AND RON CARTER have played as a guitar-and-bass duo for several years, and they work together like a team of pickpockets. They shadow each other's flights, echo them, celebrate them, and even anticipate them. But their first record, made late last summer at a brilliant concert given at the Playboy Club, has only just been brought out on Milestone as "Alone Together: Jim Hall-Ron Carter Duo." Of the eight numbers, five are standards and the rest are originals by Sonny Rollins, Carter, and Hall. The standards are in ad-lib or slow-to-medium tempos, and they are languorous and ingeniously arranged. "Softly as in a Morning Sunrise" consists mostly of a string of ad-lib, a-cappella eight-bar exchanges, with some Dick McDonough chords from Hall. In the title song, Carter states the melody, using quavering, mirage-like notes, makes way for a luminous Hall solo that starts several beats late with a gliding two-note phrase, and returns for a solo while Hall brushes in chords in the background. "I'll

Remember April" has a complex contrapuntal ensemble, a fine
medium-tempo Hall solo, and a long, walking Wilbur Ware
statement by Carter that is full of retards and sidestepping
notes. The originals are chancy and sometimes breathtaking.
Carter's "Receipt, Please" is a complex rising-and-falling
melodic line with several smart key modulations, and Hall's
"Whose Blues" is a fragile blues with strange fur-bearing
chords planted in the last four bars of its melody. This is
generous music. One can first study the rhythmic patterns in a
number, then its melodic surprises, then its harmonic weights,
then its textural shadings, then its wholeness and unity. And
then rewardingly go back and do them all over again.

MAY 11TH: BARNEY JOSEPHSON first brought Nellie Lutcher, the
helter-skelter singer, composer, and pianist, from the West
Coast to Café Society Downtown in the mid-forties, and she
became an immediate success. Now he has brought her East
again to the Cookery, after a long period of semi-obscurity, and
she may well be off again. It's easy to see why. She is a
genuine primitive performer who effortlessly works both sides
of the tracks. She is — with her striking, high-cheekboned
face and her long, scuttling, dancing, crablike fingers — a
funny and magnetic entertainer. But she is also, under all her
explosive nonsense, a fine pianist and jazz singer. She grew up
near Lake Charles, Louisiana, and when she was fifteen played
in a band that included Bunk Johnson. At the same time, she
listened to Earl Hines' radio broadcasts from the Grand
Terrace, in Chicago. These country-mouse-and-city-mouse
experiences remain side by side in her work and allow her, in a
number like "Lake Charles Boogie," to play in a jangling,
down-home, bedspring style, and, in a number like "The Lady's
in Love with You," to deliver expert Hines arpeggios and

rhythmic bursts. But Lord knows where her singing came from. She has a light, glancing voice which gives the impression of forever slipping off its notes, and she is a master of melismatics: a six-noted Lutcher syllable is commonplace. Her diction is as casual as Jack Teagarden's, and when she tires of making sense out of her words she slides into whole choruses of scat singing beflagged with falsetto hums, mumbles, and cries. She sang all her own old hits tonight — "Fine Brown Frame" (an apt and laconic description of Big Sid Catlett, with whom she stepped out in the forties), "Hurry On Down to My House," and "Real Gone Guy" — and they were funny and good. But the best things she did were the fillers, which included a blindingly fast "Perdido" (her accompanists, Skeeter Best on guitar and Morris Edwards on bass, floated out behind her like coattails); a medium-slow "St. Louis Blues," in which each beat had a Bessie Smith gravity and presence; a rocking, singsong "Bill Bailey, Won't You Please Come Home"; and a fast "Alexander's Ragtime Band," which rattled around the room like hail on a tin roof.

JUNE 9TH: THERE WAS A TIME IN JAZZ when a good many of its appreciators spent more time classifying, stratifying, and categorizing their idols than they did listening to them. The guidelines they set out were as rigid as two-by-fours. Thus, it was decreed, Zutty Singleton played only with the likes of James P. Johnson or Pee Wee Russell or Sidney Bechet, and when he popped up on an early Dizzy Gillespie-Charlie Parker record his admirers were incredulous. But economic needs and the grim reaper have done their work, and no one even blinks now at the sort of group that Marian McPartland has brought into the Royal Box. It includes a member of the Kansas City school (Buddy Tate), the Chicago school (Jimmy McPartland), and the New York school (Marian McPartland), as well as two young eclectics, the bassist Rusty Gilder and the drummer Jackie Williams. The range of their material tonight was equally generous. Among other things, they played "You Turned the Tables on Me," "The Girl From Ipanema," "What's New," " 'Round Midnight," and "St. Louis Blues," and they played them with aplomb. It was not Chicago music or Kansas City music or New York music but lyrical, first-rate jazz. (Needless to say, this non-classifiable music *has* been categorized, and is frequently referred to as "mainstream" music.) Jimmy McPartland, who has been having embouchure troubles of late, played well, and it was a pleasure to hear Bix Beiderbecke's ghost rise up behind every solo. Marian McPartland, long accustomed to the format of a trio, was tight and sharp; she said what she had to say in a chorus or two, and there was none of the cloud-gazing she sometimes engages in. Tate played his customary tenor saxophone, but he also played alto, baritone, clarinet, and flute, lending each of them his lyricism and drive and drama.

JUNE 12TH: SOMEWHERE BETWEEN their inception and their completion, most jazz recordings curdle. The causes are myriad: a Simon Legree A. & R. man; a poorly chosen personnel; a musician with a bad cold or a gully-low hangover; an inept choice of materials or tempos; insufficient takes or too many takes; a chilling recording-studio atmosphere. But the greatest hurdle facing the makers of jazz recordings — both the producers and performers of them as well as the new breed of producer-performers — is how to judge on the instant what is good, what is right. Judging a performance of written music involves certain objective criteria, but judging improvised music is largely subjective. One listens in a solo for the mystical balance of technique and inspiration, of relaxation and tension, for the coupling of timing and energy that is swinging. Beyond that, it is a question of mood, digestion, and the fit of one's shoes — all of which explains why music that sounds glorious in a recording studio can mysteriously sound gelid on the record, and why a seemingly humdrum session can ultimately produce a superlative record. Yet a surprising number of musicians record easily and well throughout their careers. One, it has long seemed, was Art Tatum, who appeared equally brilliant and assured whether he recorded in a studio or on the concert stage. Now a new and extraordinary recording — "Art Tatum: God Is in the House" (Onyx) — proves that this wasn't so; that, indeed, as legend has had it, there were two Tatums. One was the virtuoso who moved with consummate ease through a world owned and run by whites, and the other was the secret genius who went uptown after his regular hours and played unbelievable music for his own pleasure in small black clubs for black audiences. (Not enough has been made of the fact that there is a great difference in the way many black musicians perform before white audiences and before black ones.) Musicians who heard Tatum in such circumstances have repeatedly touted this aspect of his playing, but it was impossible to believe them. How *could* there have been another and even better Tatum? Well, there was, and he is on every track of the Onyx record. The recording was done in acetate on a portable recording machine in 1940 and 1941 by a Columbia student named Jerry Newman. Three of the sides were made in his apartment and the remaining ten in Harlem after-hours clubs — the Gee-Haw Stables, Reuben's, and Clark Monroe's Uptown House. They make it clear that Newman, who is now dead, was a master reporter; he was steadfastly self-effacing and he invariably seemed to be in the right place at the right time. (Some of his Harlem field recordings of Charlie Christian were issued over twenty years ago, but nothing else had appeared until now. The liner notes of the Onyx album do not tell us where

Newman's trove has been all these years, why it has unexpectedly become available, or how much more exists.) The numbers recorded in Newman's flat open the album, and, though rather short, they forecast the wonders to come. The longest, "Georgia on My Mind," is dazzling and perhaps even definitive. It is taken at a strong medium tempo and has two shattering passages — an abrupt arhythmic one and a long, racing double-time line. The Tatum who played for whites often confined himself, in a strange combination of the put-on and simply showing off, to breathtaking but empty semi-symphonic displays, but the Tatum of "Georgia on My Mind" is altogether different. He is a driving, aggressive jazz pianist whose flights of virtuosity are completely in proportion to the whole piece. The same is true of "Sweet Lorraine," "Fine and Dandy," and "Begin the Beguine," all of them done at Reuben's and all of them packed with ferocity and inventiveness. Reuben Harris, the proprietor, accompanies Tatum using whiskbrooms on a piece of newspaper, and there is a steady flow of idle, delighted audience chatter. And the piano Tatum plays is classically out of tune, but he surmounts this obstacle with such ease that the instrument sounds, in the flashier passages, like a Steinway grand. (The quality of the recording throughout the album is remarkably good.) The next five sides were made at the Gee-Haw Stables. There is a bravura, funny "Mighty Lak a Rose"; a gorgeous, rococo "Body and Soul"; a rampaging "There'll Be Some Changes Made," with a vocal by Ollie Potter, whose off-key singing only serves to spur Tatum on; and a couple of slow blues, in which Tatum sings. The album rises to its climax in two long final tracks, done at Clark Monroe's Uptown House with Frankie Newton and Ebenezer Paul (bass) sitting in. Newton, with his legato, barefoot approach, is a perfect foil for Tatum, and the tunes — "Lady Be Good" and "Sweet Georgia Brown" — are marvelous contrapuntal displays. ("Sweet Georgia Brown" is fascinating

for another reason. Tatum's first solo choruses, with their
weird notes and displaced rhythms, are an obvious parody of
the adventurous melodic lines that Charlie Parker and Dizzy
Gillespie were beginning to evolve. Pioneer beboppers often
jammed at Monroe's, and perhaps some of them were in the
house that night.) Newton plays a riff while Tatum slips into
an engulfing left-hand tremolo; Newton looses a tricky descending figure, which Tatum immediately parodies; Newton
starts to float along far behind the beat and Tatum races into a
double-time arpeggio; Newton fashions a high, annunciatory
figure and Tatum rumbles around in the lowest registers.

What a record!

JUNE 29TH: THE 1973 NEWPORT JAZZ FESTIVAL-NEW YORK
began in a tureen of mist and rain and puddles in the Wollman
Rink at seven minutes to noon, which may be the first time in
the history of jazz that an event has started early. It also
started with class. Gerry Mulligan pushed an eighteen-piece
pickup band through six of his recent compositions, and it
hummed and rolled and swung. The best soloists were Bob
Brookmeyer, Jimmy Owens, Tom Scott (a wild West Coast
saxophonist), and Mulligan himself, who was particularly
moving in a slow version of "Waltzing Matilda." The Newport
Ensemble, with George Wein (piano), Roland Prince (guitar),
James Spaulding (flute and alto saxophone), Larry Ridley
(bass), and Al Harewood (drums), was a puzzling outgrowth of
Wein's various Newport Festival All-Stars, which were given
to pleasant middle-of-the-road musings. It played two Mingus-
like numbers that included startling, impressionistic Wein
solos. Long embedded in the Fats Waller-Teddy Wilson
school, Wein sounded as if he had spent his off moments
during the winter boning up with Lennie Tristano. The
afternoon closed with two small groups led by the tenor
saxophonists Charles Lloyd and Gato Barbieri.

A sea of bald pates, bifocals, and paunches flowed into Carnegie Hall early this evening to hear the Benny Goodman Quintet (Teddy Wilson, Lionel Hampton, Gene Krupa, and Slam Stewart). The music itself was mediocre (one exception: Teddy Wilson's solo in "Body and Soul"), but it was full of ghosts. Phrases first carved by Jimmie Noone, and even Pee Wee Russell, kept surfacing in Goodman's solos; and in Krupa's brief statements one heard the straight-ahead, marching rimshots-and-rolls that Zutty Singleton perfected in the twenties. Earl Hines stood dimly behind Wilson, and even Hampton, and Stewart's bowing summoned up Jimmy Blanton. Between numbers, Goodman himself seemed to be listening to these voices, for, seated on a stool, he would hook one foot on a rung, rest his clarinet on his knee, and gaze for long moments into space before finally turning to his musicians and telling them where to go next. A new group, composed of Ruby Braff (cornet), George Barnes (guitar), Wayne Wright (rhythm guitar), and John Giuffrida (bass), opened the concert, and in a lyrical fashion it, too, summoned up the past, by sounding remarkably like some of the small-band records that Django Reinhardt made with American musicians in Paris in 1937.

On to Philharmonic Hall at ten o'clock to hear a reprise of a blues concert first given at six. The concert, by and large, was a bibulous shambles. But Muddy Waters, with his great, sad, broad face and his slow, heavy, summer-mind voice, sang four mighty blues, and so did Big Mama Willie Mae Thornton. She has lost considerable weight since her last appearance in New York six years ago and, with her stringy gray thatch, her immense hands, and her wandering, beanpole legs, she looked like a huge shorebird. But she hasn't lost her booming voice, and she shivered the timbers when she exploded in her first number with "*Earlyonemorning*, my baby left me in my back door cryin'." B. B. King acted as the m.c., and when his turn came to play he launched a monologue about Big Mama and how fine it was to be in this fine hall with so many fine blues singers, and he went on so long there was no time left for him to sing.

JUNE 30TH: I HAD AN UNCLE who lived in a Victorian house where the rooms seemed to follow one another aimlessly around, and he used to say that the only way to improve the house would be to tear it down and start again. The same could be said of Philharmonic Hall. Despite the endless acoustical tinkering that has gone on since it was built, its sounds remain inexact and confusing. High notes screech, pianos sound as if they had false teeth, and low tones breathe heavily. And the confusion is compounded by amplified instruments turned to peak volume. Such aural indecencies plagued the seven-thirty concert this evening, and perhaps even influenced the players themselves. Sonny Rollins, stunning in a white suit and clearly immersed in his image, did little until his sensational cadenza in his final number, "There Is No Greater Love." Mary Lou Williams did not fare much better, and neither did Gil Evans, who, leading a fifteen-piece band, played four long numbers decorated with gongs, chimes, rattles, and taped wind sounds, and with interminable solos by Billy Harper (tenor saxophone) and Howard Johnson (tuba). Keith Jarrett ended the evening with an unaccompanied piano solo. It had spacious tremolos; Tatum runs; snatches of gospel, Charles Ives, and George Gershwin; rubato and double-time passages; and so forth — all based on the still-fashionable notion in jazz that if a soloist goes on long enough the flower will inevitably bloom. It didn't.

Holding jam sessions at midnight in Radio City Music Hall was good P. T. Barnum last year, but jam sessions belong in small, intense, attentive places where the walls vanish and even nuances ring. Very little happened tonight at the first of the two affairs to be given this week at the Music Hall. There were good musicians — Gerry Mulligan, Jimmy Owens, Elvin Jones, Tom Scott, and Roland Hanna, to name a few — and there were creditable solos, but one was never moved beyond the awareness of being in Radio City Music Hall at a midnight "jam session."

The second Wollman concert seized the day. It was taken up by guitarists, who, famous for their melodic garrulity, must have plucked a million notes. But an impressive number were well considered. George Barnes went through three fine numbers, the best of them a tough, medium-tempo blues that was unfortunately marred by a blown-out amplifier. Chuck Wayne and Joe Puma fashioned three unaccompanied duets, notable for their closing contrapuntal ensemble in "There Will Never Be Another You," in which the two kept passing and repassing one another, and for Wayne's fleetness and Puma's grave deliberation in "L'il Darlin'." George Benson, backed by a rhythm section, showed just where the thin line between invention and virtuosity lies. Much of his first number flashed and sang, and then he stepped over the line, and his remaining solos, though mercurial, were locked in and mechanical. Following was a brilliant performance by Jim Hall and Tal Farlow, accompanied on Fender bass by the exceptional Jay Leonhart. Farlow has not played much in recent years, and he creaked a little, but this unintentionally set off Hall, who, with his legato authority, his beautiful choice of notes, his silences, and his invariable rightness, gives the impression of cease-lessly surveying his melodic domain before picking his next note. His solo in "Prelude to a Kiss" was of the highest order, and after a single-note passage in "Summertime" he slipped into a succession of soft, blurred chords that seemed to have their faces pressed against the melody. There were two other rewards: Leonhart's quiet, radarlike accompaniment throughout, and his brief, remarkable solo in "St. Thomas," in which, using carefully spaced notes, he turned the melody over and over, each time infinitesimally altering it by adding a beat or dropping a note a tone or two. The rest of the concert included Pat Martino, Larry Coryell, and Roy Buchanan, who slid loudly into electronic swamp.

JULY 1ST: THERE WERE THREE FERRYBOAT RIDES up the Hudson to the George Washington Bridge today, each staffed with the same two appropriate groups — the Preservation Hall Band, led by the trumpeter Percy Humphrey, and a quartet that included the drummer Buzzy Drootin and his brother Al, who plays clarinet and tenor saxophone. I took the one-o'clock, and, like all boat rides on rivers, it had a loose, dreaming quality that allowed one the rare chance, after the music had been sampled, to slip back to those unanswerable space-time-motion questions that fretted our childhoods: Is the boat or the riverbank moving? Why does the sun move along with us? And why does the water move fastest of all?

At six o'clock in Carnegie Hall, Ray Charles and James Baldwin gave the first of two run-throughs of their musical-dramatic collaboration "The Hallelujah Chorus — The Life and Times of Ray Charles." It didn't work, and for good reasons. Both men were born poor, black, and gifted, but beyond that they have little in common. Charles remains a canny, tough, pinewoods primitive, and Baldwin is a delicate urban vision-ary; trying to weld their alien souls didn't make sense. What there was of the production went like this: Charles and his big band played a couple of slow numbers, one of them graced with two choruses of Charles' piano, and then Baldwin, at a lectern on the side of the stage, gave a brief "testimony service" about the tribulations of black people in this country. Baldwin moved to a stool set in the curve of Charles' piano and asked him simplistic questions (one fine, unrehearsed Charles response: "I came to earth with my music like any other necessary organ"), and after each one, Charles played. A couple of meaningless dramatic interludes involving Cicely Tyson, David Baldwin, and David Moses followed (one was taken from James Baldwin's short story "Sonny's Blues"), and Baldwin and Charles resumed their interchange. But by then a strange and moving thing had begun to happen. Apparently, Baldwin had suggested to Charles that he abandon his regular show, with its pop tunes, gospel numbers, and country-and-Western songs, and concentrate on his old blues. Charles did, and the results, in blues after blues, were superb.

The Duke Ellington concert at ten in Philharmonic Hall was a mishmash of bad taste (the trumpeter Money Johnson parroting Louis Armstrong in "Basin Street Blues" and "Hello, Dolly!"), beauty (the tonal elegance of the clarinet trio, piano, and muted trumpet in "Creole Love Call," and Harry Carney's mother-earth statement in "La Plus Belle Africaine"), and virtuosity (five vocals by the winsome and extraordinary Swedish soprano Alice Babs). During the intermission, a colleague passed on a broadsheet announcing the publication by Rutgers University of a new semiannual jazz magazine, *Journal of Jazz Studies*, in which such aesthetic delights as these will appear: "Authenticity and Originality in Jazz: Toward a Paradigm in the Sociology of Music," "It Ain't the Blues: Billie Holiday, Sidney J. Furie, and Kitsch," and "Institution Participation, Social Stratification, and Psychological Boundaries of Montreal Jazzmen." The last should make news in Montreal.

JULY 2ND: THIS AFTERNOON Professor Longhair, a semi-legendary singer and barrelhouse pianist from New Orleans, started the Wollman concert with eight numbers, and it was good to hear the antediluvian turns of Jimmy Yancey and Pinetop Smith and Champion Jack Dupree in his playing. He is one of the last repositories of this sort of rolling, heavy-weave piano, and it will be a sad day when it is finally gone. Baby Laurence brought on his troupe of tap-dancers (John T. McPhee, Buster Brown, L. D. Jackson, and Chuck Green), and they were accompanied by Jo Jones and Milt Buckner (on organ). Laurence gave a breathtaking performance, full of galloping offbeats and lightning sweeps across the stage, but it was too bad he and Jones didn't exchange breaks. There is nothing more exhilarating than drummers and tap-dancers attempting to outwit each other, and Jones has a genius for such badinage. Mechanical performances by Charlie Mingus' new quintet of three of his best numbers — "Goodbye Pork Pie Hat," "Fables of Faubus," and "Pithecanthropus Erectus" — proved again that his melodies, so original and lyrical and stark, shouldn't be entrusted to the weak in spirit. The afternoon went out with Don Cherry, who sat cross-legged on the stage and, surrounded by women and children and a small galaxy of musicians, played occasional pleasant melodic bursts on his pocket trumpet that were interlarded with sleigh bells, a screeching saxophone, and a conch.

JULY 3RD: AN INVALUABLE, IF ERRATIC, CONCERT was given early this evening at Philharmonic Hall. It was a celebration of American songwriting loosely based on Alec Wilder's marvelous study *American Popular Song*, and nine or so soloists, groups, and singers offered about forty songs by Irving Berlin, Fats Waller, Eubie Blake, Cole Porter, Duke Ellington, Harold Arlen, George Gershwin, Jimmy Van Heusen, Richard Rodgers, and Alec Wilder. Berlin was treated well by a group consisting of Jimmy McPartland, Herbie Hall, Vic Dickenson, Art Hodes, Al Hall, and Al Harewood. Indeed, one of their numbers was a lilting, exact reading by Herbie Hall of "A Pretty Girl Is Like a Melody." Few jazz musicians pay such gentle, intelligent homage to those who provide most of their fuel. Earl Hines shot through four Waller tunes, the best of them a rampaging "Honeysuckle Rose." Teddi King and Ellis Larkins handled Cole Porter well, but Rahsaan Roland Kirk, accompanied by Marian McPartland, Larry Ridley, and Harewood, did an odd thing to Ellington and Billy Strayhorn: He made luminous songs like "Mood Indigo," "Black Butterfly," and "Satin Doll" sound brooding and savage. Barbara Carroll struggled somewhat with the complexities of "Blues in the Night," which has a steplike, fifty-eight-measure chorus, but she surfaced neatly in "Come Rain or Come Shine," and then went on to accompany Sylvia Syms, who did wonders with Arlen's difficult "Out of This World." For some reason, the four numbers from "Porgy and Bess" done by the Modern Jazz Quartet caused them to frieze. But the two final composers got choice treatment. Mabel Mercer, a little harried in voice and manner, sang Rodgers and Hart's "My Romance," "It Never Entered My Mind," "He Was Too Good to Me," and "I Wish I Were in Love Again." She was joined by Stan Getz, who provided support, and then soloed in a hymnlike manner he hasn't shown in years. Gerry Mulligan rounded out the evening with praise for Alec Wilder's "It's So Peaceful in the Country," "While We're Young," and "I'll Be Around." He played the melody of each tune first, not touching a hair on its head, improvised a couple of choruses, and returned briefly to the melody. Even Wilder, who was in the audience and is given to intemperate language when performers change or miss his notes, was pleased. ("Not one of his notes was an enemy," he said.)

All Marian McPartland's banners were rippling at the beginning of this afternoon's Wollman concert, and she set down six exuberant numbers from her current repertory. The Modern

Jazz Quartet stayed largely within the confines of the blues in its six selections, and there were joyous moments from John Lewis ("Monterey Mist") and Milt Jackson (his surprising accents in "True Blues" and the fast, glistening curve of notes with which he started his solo in "Bag's Groove").

JULY 4TH: SCORES OF MUSICIANS went out to the Singer Bowl, in Flushing Meadow, this afternoon to help change its name to the Louis Armstrong Stadium, and they did it with dispatch. Every motion, every sound was telescoped, and when a musician paused long enough to lay some eloquence on the audience, it was startling. This happened in an etched, perfect Ellis Larkins version of Benny Carter's "Blues in My Heart," and in four crisp, kingly eight-bar Gene Krupa breaks in "Stompin' at the Savoy." When I left, after three hours, the parade onstage was barely half over, but the platoon of m.c.s had already made three references to how much Louis — it was his birthday — must be digging the proceedings from up yonder.

A counter-festival, the New York Musicians Five Borough Jazz Festival, is going on all over the city this week, and it is being played, in the main, by little-known musicians and by aging avant-garde or hard-bop players. George Wein has incorporated a good number of its musicians into the Newport Festival this year at six concerts at Alice Tully Hall. I went early this evening, and it was a dampening experience. Three groups — led by the tenor-saxophonist Paul Jeffrey, the pianist Walter Bishop, Jr., and the trumpeter Tommy Turrentine — played endlessly in an area somewhere between hard bop and early avant-garde, and the only rewarding music was some smart drumming by Thelonious Monk, Jr.

It is not really clear why anyone wants to re-create jazz that was improvised and fresh fifty and more years ago; the results

are no different from an expert Vermeer copy. But much of the
ten-o'clock Philharmonic Hall concert was taken up with such
resurrections. Turk Murphy brought his King Oliver-Jelly Roll
Morton band from the West Coast and managed, as always, to
sound the way jazz might have if it had existed in mid-
Victorian times. Wally Rose played five rags, demonstrating
poor time and weak phrasing. Bob Greene played two eerily
perfect Jelly Roll Morton piano solos, and was joined for five
Morton instrumentals by the likes of Danny Barker and
Tommy Benford (both played with Morton) and Herbie Hall,
who again stole the honors. The Preservation Hall Band closed
the evening. Its re-creations are deceptive, for they are
attempts to recapture what its players never had in the first
place.

JULY 5TH: THE STAGE AT THE WOLLMAN RINK at one o'clock this
afternoon was filled with percussion instruments — massive
gongs, small gongs, chimes, bells of every size and description,
drums and more drums, xylophone-type instruments, and
vibraphones. Here and there were thick golden stands of
saxophones, ranging from a tiny soprano to a massive bass.
Five musicians, two with painted faces and one in a red
hardhat and dirty coveralls, threaded their way onstage, a
gong was struck, and the Art Ensemble of Chicago began its
première New York performance. Its only number, which was
entertaining for a third of the forty-five minutes it lasted,
consisted of a sounding stream, single- and multi-layered, that
flowed up and down through crescendos and diminuendos,
some of which had a hocus-pocus majesty. In one, a bass
clarinet played a tattered melody while assorted gongs were
struck, the bass saxophonist made Queen Mary sounds, and a
muted trumpet played. It took twenty minutes to clear the
stage after the Art Ensemble had finished, and the steady

shuffling, scraping, clicking, and bonging were, to all intents and purposes, the group's second number. The Art Ensemble never stopped calling attention to how its music was made, so it kept one on the outside looking in. The next group had the reverse effect. Made up of Sam Rivers (tenor saxophone, flute, and piano), Richard Davis (bass), and Norman Connors (drums), it created a cantankerous vortex that in time enfolded one almost completely. Indeed, when its one long excursion was over, the immediate feeling was of having just eased out of a pair of tight shoes. The next group, an expert nine-piece Latin band led by Ray Barretto, afforded comic relief, and then Archie Shepp appeared with a couple of trombones, a reed-man, a poetry reader, and a rhythm section, and we were back in the vortex.

There were accompanists for Ella Fitzgerald all over Carnegie Hall early this evening, and they included a re-creation of the Chick Webb band (six members were alumni); Ellis Larkins, whose tapestried backgrounds almost smoothed some surprisingly unsteady Fitzgerald singing (she overstepped phrases and even got blown about by her vibrato); and a small group (Roy Eldridge, Eddie Lockjaw Davis, Al Grey, Tommy Flanagan, Joe Pass, Keeter Betts, and Freddie Waits) that was first allowed to jam seven ballads and up-tempo standards. Eldridge was the winner. He is sixty-two but in "Stardust" he put it together again: the steam-whistle effects, the red-banner flights, the stepping middle-register passages, and the coursing melodic lines.

I was late for the ten-o'clock concert at Philharmonic Hall, and when I arrived the first of the three winners of a talent search conducted by the Tea Council of the United States was already onstage. It was from Houston and was called the Lightmen Plus One, and it resembled a Horace Silver group. Petrus, from Rochester, played circular music. And Electric Black, out of Denver, was largely Motown. Chuck Mangione played three numbers on electric piano and flugelhorn, and revealed that he is the Harry James of the seventies. Then the spectral John Blair, who affects a shaved head, a black cape, and black boots, plucked and sawed an electric violin for a long time. He should make a pilgrimage to the Fount of Venuti.

JULY 6TH: GEORGE WEIN has become Broadway-minded. We have had the American popular-song production, the Ray Charles-James Baldwin production, and the Ella Fitzgerald production. And tonight at Carnegie Hall we were offered one called Jazz Cabaret. Tables with checked cloths had been set up onstage, and their occupants were served drinks throughout the concert, which began with yet another re-creation — the Cab Calloway band of the late thirties and early forties. But it was more than a re-creation, for better than half its members — among them Dizzy Gillespie, Doc Cheatham, Tyree Glenn, Quentin Jackson, Walter (Foots) Thomas, Danny Barker, Milt Hinton, and Cozy Cole — were alumni. We were about to hear the Cab Calloway band in the flesh again! But it never really happened. The band started with that old splendid coasting Charlie Christian riff, "A Smo-o-oth One," and suddenly Honi Coles and the Copasetics, a troupe of five good tap-dancers, flew onstage for three numbers. Nellie Lutcher sang five of her jangling, hooting tunes, and gave way to Louis Jordan, the funny, adept alto saxophonist and singer. He rolled through three songs, accompanied by a quartet from the band, and in one of them, a blues, he gave Doc Cheatham three choruses, which were exquisite. Ah, the band again and a number featuring Dizzy Gillespie! But then Esther Phillips, a raucous soul singer, towed an organist and drummer onstage and sang five interminable numbers, while the band sat soundless behind her. Now Calloway himself appeared, and there was hope: This fine assemblage would at last play its heart out. But I'd forgotten how much space Calloway used to hog on his records, and he did it again tonight. When his last vocal was over, the lights went up, and there the band sat, all warmed up and no place to go.

The second jam session at the Music Hall was no more a jam session than the one earlier in the week or the two given there last year. There were, in effect, six night-club sets: a group that included, among others, Red Rodney, Art Farmer, and Bill Watrous; a quartet with Bill Evans, Gary Burton, Eddie Gomez, and Marty Morrell; a trio with Jeremy Steig, Gomez, and Morrell; a big group involving Dizzy Gillespie, Jon Faddis, Stan Getz, Art Blakey, and Cecil Payne; Anita O'Day, accompanied by Jimmy Rowles, Larry Ridley, and Oliver Jackson; and another large group, which included Jackson, Milt Hinton, Larry Coryell, Earl Hines, Louis Jordan, and Sonny Stitt. Inevitably, there were moments. Rowles got off an exemplary chorus in "I Can't Get Started." Gary Burton was Corbusier. Faddis ran down some of Gillespie's well-tested circumlocutions. And Hines provided some largesse accompaniment. But why not put a first-rate group onstage and just let them go, as in the old Kansas City jam sessions? When the pianist tires, replace him. When the drummer weakens, bring on another. Such an organic affair might also make one forget the surroundings, which again blocked the suspension of disbelief.

A jazz festival should be a catalyst that brings musicians together who ordinarily and necessarily pass in the night. That ideal was certainly realized this afternoon in Alice Tully Hall at a youth concert organized by Marian McPartland and the music-educator and former drummer Clem De Rosa. The first three groups were coached by the trumpeter Joe Newman, the bassist Paul West, and the composer Eddie Bonnemere. Then De Rosa's local seventeen-piece All City High School Jazz Orchestra appeared, and wonders began. After its warmup number, the band went into Dee Barton's ingenious and extremely difficult arrangement of "Here's That Rainy Day." The first chorus is scored for four trombones, in unison and harmony, and they wafted through it. And so did the whole band in the rest of the arrangement, which is full of introverted harmonies and tricky voicings. Sonny Stitt, who had been invited to sit in, dived into the old riff blues "Jumping with Symphony Sid." The band, with De Rosa's remarkable seventeen-year-old son on drums, immediately settled in behind him, playing riffs and old Basie-band hums, and Stitt took off. He played a dozen choruses (on tenor saxophone), and they were intricate and soaring. Then he picked up his alto saxophone and played a slow "Lover Man" that was a masterpiece, and, still smoking, he returned to his tenor and played another masterpiece — a version of "I Got Rhythm" in three tempos, the first of them slow and swaying.

JULY 7TH: THE FINAL CONCERT in the Wollman Rink was devoted largely to drummers. We heard, in various settings, Max Roach, Freddie Waits, Art Blakey, Roy Haynes, Elvin Jones, Mel Lewis, Tony Williams, and Jo Jones. The last, using only his high-hat cymbals and playing less than two minutes, accomplished more stylistically and rhythmically than all his present "children." At the outset of the concert, Jones gave Gene Krupa a plaque apparently signed by almost every drummer in the world. Krupa's acceptance speech: "Drummers are the most beautiful people in the world."

Wein's final production, given early this evening at Carnegie Hall, was mysteriously called "So-Lo Piano," and was dedicated to Art Tatum, despite the fact that half of the ten pianists (all of them unaccompanied) either antedated Tatum (Eubie Blake, Earl Hines) or had little or nothing to do with him (Art Hodes, Brooks Kerr, Bill Evans). The evening belonged to

Jimmy Rowles, who gave excellent readings of "Jitterbug Waltz" and "My Buddy," and to Ellis Larkins, whose version of "I Want a Little Girl," with its delicate, sliding rhythms and intricate shelves of sound, was beautiful. Art Hodes and Bill Evans were affecting, and so was George Shearing's single-note watercolor of "Greensleeves." Shearing, a wag, also played "Happy Days Are Here Again," but as a dirge.

AUGUST 10TH: IT TOOK A LONG TIME for Artie Shaw to subside. He became a Presence on the American landscape in 1938 when his first Victor release — Jerry Grey's arrangement of Cole Porter's "Begin the Beguine" — sold a million copies. Nothing could have been more surprising. Shaw, who was twenty-eight, was just another big-band leader; the tune, a Porter oddity with a hundred-and-eight-bar chorus, had not gone much of anywhere in its three-year existence, and Victor, which had been against recording it in the first place, pushed the "A" side of the record, a bouncy version of "Indian Love Call." (Alec Wilder writes of "Begin the Beguine" in *American Popular Song*: It is a "maverick, an unprecedented experiment, and one which, to this day, after hearing it hundreds of times, I cannot sing or whistle or play from start to finish without the printed music. . . . I suppose it conjures up for the listener all sorts of romantic memories embodying the ultimate tropical evening and the most dramatic dance floors ever imagined. . . . [But] along about the sixtieth measure I find myself muttering another title, 'End the Beguine.' " Yet the song was unquenchable. In 1944, when Eddie Heywood recorded his elegant, stylized piano version, it became the only hit, barring Billie Holiday's "Strange Fruit," that Commodore Records ever had, and a decade after that it was still a high-school glee-club staple.)

The public began gobbling up practically everything Shaw

recorded ("Back Bay Shuffle," "Nightmare," "Deep Purple," "Traffic Jam"), and Shaw, who had been scuffling since he was fifteen, found himself hilariously netting as much as thirty thousand dollars a week. Then, late in 1939, he pulled the first and most celebrated of his disappearing acts by walking off the bandstand of the old Pennsylvania Hotel's Café Rouge in midevening and going to Mexico. It was unprecedented, astonishing, and seemingly suicidal. But less than three months later, Shaw had put together a new band, combining an oboe, a flute, a bass clarinet, a French horn, and a fifteen-man string section, and *its* first recording, a Mexican ditty called "Frenesi," became another sizzling success, or $ucce$$," as Shaw spells it in his autobiography, *The Trouble with Cinderella.* "Frenesi" was joined by "Temptation," "Stardust," "Concerto for Clarinet," "Dancing in the Dark," and "Moonglow," and the land was swimming in Shaw's music. He also made News in 1940 by marrying Lana Turner (who was followed in the next six years by Jerome Kern's daughter, Ava Gardner, and Kathleen Winsor), and in 1941 he made more by hiring a black musician, the rough-and-ready trumpeter Hot Lips Page. (It was the fashion for white leaders to hire black trumpeters. Benny Goodman had his Cootie Williams and Gene Krupa his Roy Eldridge. Shaw, though, had long been a racial pioneer. In 1937, he hired Billie Holiday and kept her with the band, through a lot of heavy weather, for a year and a half. Shaw appears in her autobiography as one of her few knights: "There aren't many people who fought harder than Artie against the vicious people in the music business or the crummy side of second-class citizenship which eats the guts of so many musicians. He didn't win. But he didn't lose either. . . . And people still talk about him as if he were nuts because there were things more important to him than a million damn bucks a year.") In 1942, Shaw put together what was widely regarded as the best of the service bands, and after the war he hired Roy Eldridge and assembled his last good big band. The great days of big bands were over, though, and Shaw knew it. He began ducking in and out of music, and in 1952, as if to ring the curtain down, he published his autobiography. It was well received as a piece of scorching confessional writing. Purged, Shaw Quit Music Forever in 1954, and moved to Spain, where he remained until 1960, when he settled, sumptuously, in Connecticut. There is little resemblance between the handsome, wavy-haired Lothario of the thirties and forties and the present Shaw, who balances his near-baldness with a huge mustache and ferocious eyebrows. Little resemblance visually, that is; he can still talk your ear off.

Shaw belittles the musical side of his $ucce$$ in his book, but he did have the best of the big white bands. What, after all, were the others like? Glenn Miller's band, with its bosomy reed voicings and high-heeled rhythm section, had a feminine air, as did Harry James' band, which was dominated by his divalike trumpet. Jimmy Dorsey's band was bland and buttery, while his brother's veered back and forth between *Walpurgisnacht* and moonsville. Bob Crosby's Dixieland band was enmeshed in the spidery wood-blocks-and-cowbells drumming of Ray Bauduc, and Charlie Spivak's suggested angel food. Jan Savitt and Glen Gray operated well-oiled pumps, and so did Benny Goodman, except for that brief, green time in the summer of 1941 when he had Cootie Williams and Mel Powell and Charlie Christian and Sid Catlett. Claude Thornhill's band, though, was a beautiful loner; he used French horns and the damask arrangements of Gil Evans, who achieved textures and voicings that were as choice as Duke Ellington's.

Each of Shaw's bands had a different face. The "Begin the Beguine" outfit was tight and springy; it was a snappy Ford coupé. The "Frenesi" band, with its bouffant strings and walk-along tempos, was gentle and subtle, but it had an unmistakable jazz persuasion. It was also a peerless *dance* band. The 1945 band, with Roy Eldridge, was the closest Shaw came to an out-and-out jazz group. It was a disciplined, swinging, straight-ahead band. Yet it was Shaw's clarinet playing, always admired more widely by musicians than Goodman's, that gave his bands their final stamp. He had an innocent, delicate, impeccably tailored style. His tone was not robust. In the low register, he was soft and convincing, but he lacked the velvet spaces of Goodman and Edmond Hall and Pee Wee Russell, and when he went into the top register, which he often did, he sounded thin and synthetic. His solos, whether embellishments of the melody or full-tilt improvisations, were faultlessly structured. He had a way of playing the melody that invariably suggested that *this* is the way it should sound. And he was right. If the melody had any excess weight he eliminated a note here, a note there. If it was on the skinny side he added flourishes or moved down to the chalameau register, which tends to make every note sound treasured. He impressed his melodic approach so thoroughly on certain tunes that when they surface anew one automatically hears Shaw's rendition. *Vide* "Moonglow" and "Stardust" and "Dancing in the Dark." Shaw's improvising was canny and agile, and, I suppose, resembled his way of talking. He used a great many notes, complex little runs that were almost asides, an on-the-beat attack, almost no vibrato, and soaring ascensions into the upper register. And he demonstrated considerable emotion on an instrument that resists it. The intensity and honesty of what he felt simply shone through.

Several editions of Shaw's band are on three reissues — "Free for All: Artie Shaw and His Orchestra" (Epic), "This is Artie Shaw" (Victor), and "Artie Shaw Featuring Roy Eldridge" (Victor). The first album has sixteen numbers, set down in 1937 by Shaw's second band (the first, garlanded with strings, had been formed the year before, but the public wasn't ready for such heresy). It was an eager group that is summed up pretty well in the five-and-a-half-minute "Blues March," which — Shaw excepted — is a funny and rather touching instance of white boys trying to play those low-down Negro blues. The second album has twenty sides, made between 1938 and 1941, and it covers Shaw's banner years. It starts with "Begin the Beguine," goes through "Back Bay Shuffle," "Deep Purple," "Frenesi," "Temptation," "Stardust," and "Moon-glow," and ends with an odd date that Shaw did for Lena Horne, who is also backed by Henry Allen, Benny Carter, and J. C. Higginbotham. There are three sides by Shaw's first Gramercy Five, whose harpsichord caused a lot of deep thinking among the faithful. The LP also has the only vocal — and it is a marvelous one — that Billie Holiday recorded with the band; at least, it is the only one ever released. The side is again singular in that it was recorded at the session which produced "Begin the Beguine." (There were always several Shaws operating simultaneously.) The album with Roy El-dridge was done in 1944 and 1945, and the arrangements are fresh and modern. There are nine big-band sides and seven by the second edition of the Gramercy Five, and all but one (a vocal by Eldridge) are graced by the trumpeter. He had an electric effect on a big band. He was unmistakably *there* in the ensemble passages, and his solos, even if they were only eight bars long, had a lyricism and drive that caused lights to go on all over. Shaw's musical life, to all intents and purposes, ended with this band, and perhaps it's just as well. He always had good timing.

SEPTEMBER 21ST: WORD HAS COME, in the benighted form of a notice buried at the foot of the *Times'* obituary page, that Ben Webster has died in Copenhagen at the age of sixty-four. But this passing reference is not altogether surprising, for Webster spent most of his mature years in semi-obscurity or in the shadow of his two great colleagues, Coleman Hawkins and Lester Young. (Weary of racism, the lack of steady work, and his second-banana status, he emigrated to Europe in the mid-sixties and never returned.) It had become increasingly clear by the late fifties, though, that Webster was at last pulling even with Young and Hawkins, whose styles had come loose in their final years. There were even heretical whispers to the effect that the two colossi of the tenor saxophone were not Young and Hawkins but Young and Webster. Young's easy majesty was unassailable, these dissidents claimed, but Hawkins' was not, for although his enormous authority never waned he eventually became the prisoner of the very innovations that had shaped every saxophonist — barring Young and Bud Freeman — of his generation. He began to seem locked into his endless chord progressions, his unbroken flow of notes, and his almost tyrannical rhythms. Webster, in contrast, had become a huge-toned, airborne marvel. His early style, assembled in the bands of Bennie Moten, Andy Kirk, Fletcher Henderson, and Cab Calloway, stemmed directly from Hawkins, but it went through a subtle reshaping during the three years he spent with Duke Ellington in the early forties. He fell under the lyrical sway of Johnny Hodges, and this released a poetic outpouring that continued the rest of his life. But it was an intensely disciplined poetry. Unlike most jazz musicians, Webster had an elastic and governing sense of dynamics. He generally started a solo softly, sliding under his first notes and continuing throughout the chorus in a glancing, flickering fashion. A silken tension immediately took hold. He gradually raised his volume in his second chorus, and, depending on his mood (he was a man of temper, one of whose nicknames was the Brute), turned on an abrasive growl or moved through proclamatory phrases that carried into his final chorus and then gave way to the musings he had begun with.

He was most celebrated for his slow ballads, and rightly; they were profound melodic embellishments. Using an enormous tone, a breathy, enveloping vibrato, and terrific glissandos, he constructed castles of sound that were romantic but never sentimental, luxuriant but tasteful, yearning but free of self-pity.

Webster, with his parrot nose, hooded eyes, and prowlike front, was a formidable-looking man. (His hats, though, were a tipoff to his astringent humor. They were too small, and he wore them brims up, on the back of his head. There is a looming photograph of him by Fred Seligo, taken low and from the front, in which he is in complete, featureless silhouette. But the massive shape, crowned with its ridiculous pillbox, is unmistakable.) One recalls Webster in many different weathers, and among the sunniest was his brief stay at the Three Deuces, on West Fifty-second Street, not long after he left Ellington. He was in a quartet led by Sidney Catlett and including John Simmons and Marlowe Morris. He would stand motionless beside the equally formidable Catlett, his back straight, his instrument slightly raised, and, his eyes closed, deliver one of his whisper-to-shout-to-whisper solos, turn expressionlessly to watch Morris and Simmons solo, and, facing front again, matter-of-factly exchange racing, four-bar breaks with Catlett, then softly restate the melody. The number done, he would open his eyes and peer deadpan over the assembled heads out front. The Brute, in his great eloquence, had spoken.

OCTOBER 4TH: AT THE RAINBOW GRILL, where Cleo Laine, the English singer, is causing a sensation. She is, in the best sense, a showoff. Her voice, which ranges from around C below middle C to F above high C, is consistent in its texture, and she can do anything with it: slow ballads that are dense mixtures

of Billy Eckstine, Sarah Vaughan, and the middle-period Billie
Holiday; rhythm tunes dressed in a variety of growls; unerring
two-octave intervals; rapid and precise scatting; and the
mimicry demanded by Noël Coward's "Mad About the Boy."
Tonight, she sang, among other things, Bessie Smith's "Gimme
a Pigfoot"; "I'd Like to Make It with You"; a fast "I'm Gonna
Sit Right Down and Write Myself a Letter" and a slow "Tea for
Two"; a punching "On a Clear Day," topped by an Alpine
climax; a declamatory "Bill"; a skipping, swinging "Please
Don't Talk About Me When I'm Gone"; and a weaving-and-
bobbing passage of scat singing done in unison with John
Dankworth's alto saxophone. Dankworth is her husband and
accompanist, and he is an impassioned admirer of Benny
Carter and Pete Brown and Johnny Hodges. Cleo Laine is a
reportedly accomplished West End actress (Ibsen, Shakespeare, Brecht-Weill, William Walton), and it showed. She
was poised and subtle, and every part of her was in the right
place at the right time. She is not, as she has been touted, a
great jazz singer. Her technique comes first and her content,
despite its variety, comes after; it is the other way around with
jazz singers.

OCTOBER 10TH: DICK WELLSTOOD, the forty-seven-year-old
pianist, has no verifiable style of his own, but he has filled this
lacuna with an extraordinary pianistic gallery. He can *be,* in
whole or in part, Scott Joplin, Jelly Roll Morton, James P.
Johnson, Zez Confrey, Fats Waller, Earl Hines, Joe Sullivan,
Jess Stacy, Art Tatum, Wesley Wallace, Pete Johnson, Art
Hodes, Hank Duncan, Luckey Roberts, Jimmy Yancey, and
even Bill Evans. But he is not just an eclectic; he is a pianistic
actor who slips inside other men's styles and brings them, with
the help of his own considerable improvisational energies,
startlingly to life. He did this tonight, time and again, at

Michael's Pub, where he is leading a trio with Kenny Davern on soprano saxophone and clarinet and Cliff Leeman on drums. He saluted Fats Waller with "Keepin' Out of Mischief Now," with the rarely heard "Viper's Drag," and with "Handful of Keys." He executed a brilliant reading of James P. Johnson's "Carolina Shout," which, with its contrary left-hand patterns, is the stride pianist's supreme test, and he offered an exact version of Johnson's lacy "Snowy Morning Blues." He did Morton's beautiful "Sweet Substitute," filling the closing chorus with tremolos. He made Joplin's "Maple Leaf Rag" and Hines' "Rosetta" swing. He fashioned a Joe Sullivan dirge out of "Brother, Can You Spare a Dime," and he put Pete Johnson in charge of a cycling "Memphis Blues." Davern has listened to Sidney Bechet and Pee Wee Russell, while Leeman constantly recalls Dave Tough. But Leeman does more than that, for he has a talent that has almost vanished from jazz drumming — the fashioning of explosive four-bar breaks. Their split-second dynamics, varied textures, and unexpected accents are those of Sid Catlett. A typical break rushes by like this: a quick silence, a ringing offbeat rim shot, another lightning silence, two eighth notes on the bass drum, a triplet on the sock cymbal, and a couple of concluding rim shots, preceded by an offbeat on a tom-tom. It is peerless, epigrammatic drumming.

OCTOBER 17TH: BEN WEBSTER and now, also at the age of sixty-four, Gene Krupa. Although he lived for a long time, his life had a fleeting quality. Between 1936 and 1942, he was, as a sideman with Benny Goodman and as the leader of his own big band, a famous man. Indeed, he was the first jazz musician to become a matinée idol. A small, good-looking man who played drums melodramatically — hunched over and gum-chewing, his black hair a wild flag — his image was in every eye and his

name in every household. It was front-page news when he
went to jail, briefly, on a drug-connected charge, and it was big
news when he left Goodman in 1938 to form his own group.
He became, particularly for those who grew up in the Depression, a phoenix rising. Then, in the next decade, everything
went awry. He was overtaken by his admirer Buddy Rich and
by the new complexities of bebop, and the big bands, which
had formed his backdrop, faded out. On top of that, jazz
students, peering through the tatters of his radiance, decided
that the true pioneers of jazz drumming during Krupa's
halcyon days had been Jo Jones and Chick Webb and Sid
Catlett. Krupa's reputation never fully recovered from these
reverses, but his contributions as a consolidating pioneer were
genuine and invaluable. He absorbed in Chicago in the
twenties those two founts of drumming — Baby Dodds and
Zutty Singleton; he listened to Cuba Austin and Chick Webb in
New York in the thirties, and he put together a streamlined
composite of their styles. By simply playing with enormous
dash and style, he brought jazz drumming up from the cellar it
had been in since New Orleans days. He was, as well, the first
drummer to solo at any length, and he has been indirectly
blamed for the sins of other and lesser drum soloists ever
since. (There have been, to be sure, very few good drum
soloists. Among the best have been Rich, Jo Jones, Elvin
Jones, Max Roach, Joe Morello, Krupa, Webb, and Catlett, the
last of whom was the fairest of them all. Those who decry
drum soloists should remember that there have been only a
handful of great improvisers on any instrument.) Such adven-
turers as Catlett and Jo Jones certainly listened to Krupa in his
ongoing days, and learned from him, and the reverse was true,
too. Drummers, a high-flying breed, are as pleased to plunder
as they are to be plundered. Krupa, who at his best rocked as
hard as any of his peers, was no exception.

*

NOVEMBER 20TH: THE SMITHSONIAN has established a Division of Performing Arts, and within it a Jazz Program, which is headed up by Martin Williams. Williams is the American counterpart of the French jazz *philosophe* André Hodeir. During the twenty-odd years he has been writing about jazz, he has produced a number of books, among them two critical anthologies (one of them taken from the defunct monthly *Jazz Review,* which he helped found and edit), a primer on the music, a biographical-critical look at New Orleans jazz, a collection of his incidental essays, a collection of short, summing-it-all-up essays on the great jazz figures, and monographs on King Oliver and Jelly Roll Morton. Along the way, he has developed an uncluttered vision of jazz which has been notable for its lack of faddism, its firmness with the second-rate, and its sound, semi-musicological approach. One does not always agree with his enthusiasms and assessments, nor does one always admire his prose; the rustle of the academician's card file is always audible in it. Now, in his role at the Smithsonian, he has produced a brand-new history in six LPs called "The Smithsonian Collection of Classic Jazz." It consists of eighty-four recordings (some are excerpts) taken from the vaults of seventeen companies (a feat, considering the possessiveness of most recording outfits) and stretching from a 1916 Scott Joplin piano roll to a 1966 Cecil Taylor. There is also a pleasantly designed forty-eight-page booklet by Williams which contains a history of the music, technical explanations of rhythm, form, and improvisation, a capsule guide to each record, and such thoughtful addenda as a jazz bibliography and a list of the principal jazz-record shops here and abroad. The collection fills a void. There have been similar endeavors before, but they have been pirated and abortive or else assembled by recording companies from their own necessarily incomplete catalogues. Williams has made it possible for the first time to survey in one sweep the main pinnacles of the music, and what a panorama it is! Here are some of the principal beauties: Robert Johnson's spooky, deep-night blues, "Hellhound on My Trail," which starts "I got to keep movin', blues fallin' down like hail/I can't keep no money with a hellhound on my trail"; Bessie Smith's majestic "St. Louis Blues"; three of Jelly Roll Morton's 1926 Red Hot Peppers sides, which mark the high point of New Orleans jazz; Sidney Bechet's mourning five-minute clarinet blues, "Blue Horizon," set down in 1944; the extraordinary Louis Armstrong-Earl Hines 1928 duet, "Weather Bird"; Armstrong's "West End Blues," and his two seminal solos, one muted and the other open-horn, in his 1930 "Sweethearts on Parade"; Red Allen's marvelous avant-garde statement on Fletcher Henderson's "Wrappin' It Up"; a graceful 1927 Fats Waller piano solo, "I Ain't Got Nobody" (listen, in particular, to the last couple of measures, when, in the highest register, he drifts into a slow-motion passage that gives the impression he is leaning on air); Meade Lux Lewis' choice "Honky Tonk Train"; Teddy Wilson's lovely solo in the Benny Goodman Trio version of "Body and Soul"; two superb Coleman Hawkins selections — the 1939 "Body and Soul" and the multi-layered 1943 "The Man I Love," made with Eddie Heywood, Oscar Pettiford, and Shelly Manne; two Billie Holidays, from 1937 and 1941, and two Art Tatum solos, from 1949 and 1956; Roy Eldridge's great "Rockin' Chair," recorded with Gene Krupa's band in 1941; three Count Basie numbers from his classic late-thirties days; and two Benny Goodman sextets, with extensive Charlie Christian solos. There are, as well, eight Duke Ellington numbers, the best made in 1940 and 1941 ("Harlem Air Shaft," "Concerto for Cootie," "In a Mellotone," "Ko-Ko," and "Blue Serge"); a stunning duet, recorded at a New York concert in 1945 by Don Byas and Slam Stewart; eight numbers by Dizzy Gillespie and/or Charlie Parker, the finest being Parker's great slow blues ("Parker's Mood") and his two unbelievable 1947 versions of "Embraceable You"; six Thelonious Monks from the forties and fifties, of which his sly piano solo, "I Should Care," and the nine choruses of medium blues excerpted from Miles Davis' "Bag's Groove" are the cream; Miles Davis' brooding paraphrase of "Summertime," posed against one of Gil Evans' richest draperies; Sonny Rollins' ten or so choruses of blues on his 1956 "Blue 7"; a resplendent 1960 version of John Lewis' "Django," by the Modern Jazz Quartet; and an excerpt from Ornette Coleman's thirty-six minutes of free improvisation for double quartets made up of trumpet, reed, bass, and drums.

But these beauties are occasionally flecked with dross. Why bother with Fletcher Henderson's stodgy 1926 "The Stampede," even if it *is* an example of nonswinging jazz? And why include a middling Ella Fitzgerald and *two* of Sarah Vaughan's parabolas, and omit Mildred Bailey and Ivie Anderson altogether? Again, when there are so many exciting Lionel Hampton small-band sides ("Ring Dem Bells," "Haven't Named It Yet," "Hollywood Shuffle"), why include the so-so "When Lights Are Low"? Puzzling, too, is the presence of one of Ellington's pioneer extended pieces, "Creole Rhapsody"; it remains static and dull. Equally puzzling is Erroll Garner's "Fantasy on 'Frankie and Johnny,'" done in 1947, when he hadn't got himself together. Finally, are *eight* Ellingtons and *six* Thelonious Monks and *three* Ornette Colemans necessary in a limited survey of this kind?

At the outset of Williams' booklet, he carefully points out that the collection is by no means comprehensive, that much good material has been omitted, etc. But this hedging doesn't excuse the token inclusion of such masters as Sid Catlett, Ben Webster, Dickie Wells, and Charlie Mingus (the Mingus included is one of his least impressive rabble-rousers) and the complete absence of, among others, the Original Dixieland Jazz Band, any of the Metronome All-Star bands (what good

illustrative catchalls they are!), Jack Teagarden, Pee Wee
Russell, Bobby Hackett, Dave Tough, J. C. Higginbotham,
Frankie Newton, Bill Coleman, Edmond Hall, Joe Turner, and
Ray Charles, the last two of whom are surely, in their own
ways, nonpareil. And this is to say nothing of the big bands of
Benny Goodman, Woody Herman, Benny Carter (his 1933
one), and Andy Kirk. Secondary figures are sometimes more
instructive than their big brothers.

DECEMBER 1ST: A REMARKABLE if not widely celebrated musical
movement took place in Detroit and its environs during the
forties. Set off by the spectacular doings in New York of
Charlie Parker and Dizzy Gillespie and supported by a congen-
ial social fabric, it produced an outpouring of jazz musicians
that rivaled the earlier musical massings in Kansas City and
Chicago. Among its graduates are Milt Jackson, the Jones
brothers (Hank, Thad, and Elvin), Billy Mitchell, Julius Watkins, Donald Byrd, Lucky Thompson, Paul Chambers, Doug
Watkins, Yusef Lateef, Barry Harris, Tommy Flanagan, Kenny
Burrell, Roland Hanna, Art Mardigan, Curtis Fuller, Pepper
Adams, and Frank Rosolino. One of the most gifted of these
musicians is the elusive Tommy Flanagan, who has spent
much of his career as a sideman or as an accompanist of
singers. Flanagan, a forty-three-year-old pianist, grew up in
the shade of Art Tatum (he was dappled, too, by Teddy Wilson,
Billy Kyle, and Bud Powell), and, like such compeers as Hank
Jones, Dave McKenna, Jimmy Rowles, and Ellis Larkins, he
values touch, delicacy, and subtlety. His solos generally
consist of signpost chords, often played offbeat, which punctu-
ate single-note lines that come at you like whitecaps and slide
away into brief silences, followed by more directional chords.
They have a purling sound, and yet there is always a tough,
rhythmic undertow. Flanagan was in fine form tonight at

Bradley's, where, accompanied by the eloquent bassist Wilbur Little, he is making one of his rare solo appearances. He is a short, shy, bespectacled man who seems to delve into the keyboard when he plays, and the trophies he came up with included a medium-tempo version of Billy Strayhorn's "Chelsea Bridge," in which he let loose a wicked double-time Tatum run; intent readings of Rodgers and Hart's "Glad to Be Unhappy" and "I Didn't Know What Time It Was"; and a medium blues with a lilting ballad quality. "Willow Weep for Me" was a different matter; it tended to play Flanagan. But this happens to almost every jazz musician who attempts the tune, for it is one of a small number of first-rate American popular songs — "Stormy Weather," "Blues in the Night," "In My Solitude," and "Sophisticated Lady" are a few of the others — that by virtue of their definitive melodic outlines, their leakproof structures, and their ample lyricism seem to resist improvisation; melodic embellishment is as far as the wise improviser should go.

DECEMBER 12TH: THERE IS A REVAMPED ZOOT SIMS afloat — elegantly tailored, punctual, and clear of mien — and he has joined the guitarist Bucky Pizzarelli for an unlimited engagement (minus occasional side gigs) at Soerabaja. Such duos are proliferating. They have recently been made up of two guitars, guitar and bass, piano and bass, trumpet and piano, and trombone and piano. These duos are an admirable idea, for their spareness prevents padding and loafing and calls forth an intense cross-pollination impossible in larger groups. Pizzarelli is a discreet, highly melodic player who has a cushioned tone, and he sets off Sims perfectly. Sims, who began in the forties as an acolyte of Lester Young, has lately brought more of Ben Webster's ornamentations into his style, and so one can hear side by side Young's lean meditations and Webster's looming rhapsodies. These antithetical approaches are governed by Sims' own inventions — his boyish sound, his underpinning melodic planks, his thrifty runs-within-runs, and his way of pushing his notes a little out of shape, as if he were trying to make them encase you. There were singing renditions of "The Man I Love," "Sweet Lorraine," "Memories of You," a blues, and "Indiana," the last done by Sims on soprano saxophone, which he plays not like a soprano saxophonist but like a tenor saxophonist playing the soprano. He has taken to offering the sort of short, Napoleonic set that Coleman Hawkins favored in his palmy days on Fifty-second Street. He also leaves enough time between sets for everyone not only to savor and digest the walking, compact lyricism he broadcasts in every number but to bake bread or take a nap.

DECEMBER 20TH: EDDIE CONDON (1905–73) was an idea in human form. The idea was simple and revolutionary: that jazz music is a complete way of life, encompassing both the prankish and the celestial, the Georg Brunises and the Louis Armstrongs. The human form was equally unadorned: A short, smooth, tightly packed man who, with his flat hair combed precisely just off center, his small, symmetrical face, and his flawless bow ties, had an unremittingly pumiced appearance. (In his later years, alcohol and its attendant miseries made him baggy and ghostly.) But Condon was more than just his own idea. He steadfastly celebrated it with his tongue, which, moving faster than thought, was sharp, witty, and original. He seemed driven by propellers of persiflage.

On the French jazz critic Hugues Panassié, who came to America in 1938 to supervise some recordings by American musicians:

> I don't see why we need a Frenchman to come over here and tell us how to play American music. I wouldn't think of going to France and telling him how to jump on a grape.

On Stan Kenton:

> Every Kenton record sounds to me as though Stan signed on three hundred men for the date and they were all on time. Music of his school ought to be played close to elephants and listened to by clowns.

To a modish lady at a party:

> Madam, is that a hat or a threat you're wearing?

His introductory remarks to the sparse audience at his first Town Hall concert, in 1942:

> Lady and gentleman.

Throughout most of the forties Condon seemed to be all over jazz. He organized record dates, some of which have taken on a classic stamp. With the help of his energetic admirer Ernie Anderson, he instituted his long series of Saturday-afternoon Town Hall concerts, which were broadcast as well. He officiated at public jam sessions. He put together an autobiography, *We Called It Music*, with Thomas Sugrue. He opened his own jazz club in the Village. He ran pioneering jazz television programs. And for a time he and Richard Gehman did a record-review column for the *Journal-American* that was pure Condon froth. All the while, he battered away at the color bar by enlivening his own floating school of musicians (Max Kaminsky, Brad Gowans, Joe Bushkin, Joe Sullivan, George Wettling, Dave Tough, Pee Wee Russell, Georg Brunis, Bud Freeman, Wild Bill Davison) with such great black figures as Fats Waller, Red Allen, James P. Johnson, Sid Catlett, Rex Stewart, Sidney Bechet, Benny Morton, Vic Dickenson, Edmond Hall, Hot Lips Page, and Louis Armstrong. But there was a worm in the rose, and by the early fifties the music Condon had touted so long — a basically white and self-

limiting version of the black music its practitioners had heard
when they were kids in Chicago in the twenties — was just
about worked out. The inventions of Charlie Parker and Dizzy
Gillespie had become outgoing and unbridled, while Condon's
music had begun to feed on itself.

Condon's tenure as the mouthpiece of jazz was a mammoth
houseparty. There were no yesterdays, todays, or tomorrows.
There was only tonight. From nine in the evening until five or
six in the morning, one drank, played, listened, gabbed,
laughed, and kicked the gong around. Very few of the children
who grew up at this marathon knew their fathers. A good deal
of the mad esprit that shaped those years has now been caught
in *Eddie Condon's Scrapbook of Jazz* (St. Martin's), and in two
albums of reissues — "Eddie Condon & Bud Freeman" (Atlantic) and "Eddie Condon's World of Jazz" (Columbia). The
book, assembled by Condon and Hank O'Neal not long before
Condon's death, contains hundreds of photographs, inter-
spersed with letters, record labels, concert programs, drawings
(the marvelous one done by Will Cotton in 1945 for the Profile
of Condon written for *The New Yorker* by Rogers Whitaker),
newspaper and magazine clippings, posters, ads, sheet music,
and swatches of text by Condon, his wife, Phyllis, George
Avakian, and others. The photographs are often invaluable.
Among the best are Condon, a shining sixteen, with Hollis
Peavey and his Jazz Bandits; Pee Wee Russell and Bobby
Hackett at Nick's, both of them looking dewy and newborn; a
Sunday-afternoon jam session at the old Jimmy Ryan's, in
which Condon, Zutty Singleton, Joe Sullivan, Sidney Bechet,
Hot Lips Page, Sandy Williams, Max Kaminsky, Russell, and
several unidentifiable musicians are roaring through the invariable Ryan's finale, "Bugle Call Rag"; Sidney Bechet, leaning
against a piano, and Sid Catlett, enthroned at a snare drum,
jamming backstage; Artie Shaw, Duke Ellington, and an
unbelievably tiny Chick Webb playing at a party; that fine,

short-lived 1944 band of Davison, Rod Cless, Williams, James
P., and Kaiser Marshall; and Condon the impresario, hobnob-
bing with Yul Brynner, Johnny Mercer, Bing Crosby, Dimitri
Mitropoulos, Joseph Szigeti, and Rita Hayworth. One wonders, though, why many of the pictures of Condon in his last
years were included; they reveal that the party was indeed
over.

The Columbia album, designed as a companion to the book,
contains twenty-seven numbers recorded between 1927 and
1954. They are meant to illuminate the musical world that
Condon moved through, and many do. Among these are Louis
Armstrong's regal 1931 "Just a Gigolo," with its subtle opening muted solo; two of the wild-eyed Rhythmaker sides done in
1932 by Red Allen, Russell, and Singleton ("Shine on Your
Shoes" and "Yellow Dog Blues"); a good 1936 Bunny Berigan
("That Foolish Feeling"); a number from Condon's first record-
ing date ("Sugar"), made in 1927, with Jimmy McPartland,
Frank Teschemacher, Bud Freeman, Joe Sullivan, and Gene
Krupa, that is notable for the closing ensemble, which, with its
accidental mélange of keys, may be the first atonal passage in
jazz; a previously unissued take of Freeman's excited 1933
"The Eel"; and one of the extended numbers ("Blues My
Naughty Sweetie Gives to Me") recorded in 1954 for George
Avakian by two driving Condon bands working in tandem.
Some of the nonsense on the rest of the record is pretty funny
— in particular, vocals by Condon ("Indiana"), Johnny Mercer,
Bing Crosby, and one Danny Stewart, who sings "Marie" in
Hawaiian. Condon, a good rhythm guitarist, is on just nine
sides.

The Atlantic album consists of twenty-four sides made for
Commodore in 1938 and 1939. The first twelve are by three
Condon bands. There are Pee Wee Russell's long, languorous,
breaking-ground solo in "Love Is Just Around the Corner" (his
rhythmic and melodic departures here are still singular);

Hackett's already immaculate work in a slow "Jada"; Russell, Hackett, Jack Teagarden, and Jess Stacy in "Embraceable You," "Diane," and the pell-mell "Meet Me Tonight in Dreamland"; the great, kicking drumming of Dave Tough in the opening choruses of "Tappin' the Commodore Till" (one of the few times Tough comes through clearly on records); and Russell's shaded, falling-away solo in "Sunday." The remainder of the album is given over almost wholly to a Bud Freeman trio that involves Stacy and George Wettling. Stacy is a marvel, notably in "You Took Advantage of Me," "Three's No Crowd," "Blue Room," and "I Don't Believe It." He manages to slide under Wettling's heavy, footling drumming, and his ingenious accompanying makes Freeman's jouncing solos sound inspired.

1974

JANUARY 4TH: HARD ON THE HEELS of Martin Williams' "The Smithsonian Collection of Classic Jazz" has come Columbia's huge survey of the music. It consists of no fewer than thirty-one albums (the Smithsonian's has six), which contain almost four hundred and fifty numbers (the Smithsonian's has eighty-six), ranging from kindergarten efforts in the early twenties by Louis Armstrong and Duke Ellington and Sidney Bechet to the work in the sixties of Armstrong and Miles Davis and George Benson. This omnibus goes under the strange title of "Aimez-Vous le Jazz," or "Do You Like Jazz," for it was apparently prepared in France by Henri Renaud. It is a highly uneven, non-comprehensive collection, and the packaging is minimal. The album covers are heavy glossed paper and the sporadic liner notes are inconclusive. And the sound is come-as-you-are (several of the rarer numbers have been transferred directly from scratched, cracked 78s). The discographical aspects are a maze. Some of the material had gone out of print. Some that had been reissued had again vanished. Some had never been reissued. And some had never been brought out at all. (This refers only to American releases, and does not take into account the frenzied pirating now going on here.) Among the more familiar efforts are Art Tatum's superlative 1949 California concert (Volume 2); sixteen Charlie Christian-Benny Goodman numbers, one of which ("The Sheik of Araby") has never been reissued (Volume 3); the guitarist George Benson's first Columbia record (Volume 19); seven of King Oliver's 1923 sides (Volume 21); two Miles Davis albums from the fifties and sixties (Volumes 1 and 17); and two volumes of live Benny Goodman trio and quartet numbers (Volumes 7 and 15). Far less familiar are four selections done by Sidney Bechet in 1938 with the baritone saxophonist Ernie Caceres, who provides a rooting alter-voice to Bechet's soaring (Volume 4); Duke Ellington's "Liberian Suite" and "A Tone Parallel to Harlem" (Volume 6); eleven of Teddy Wilson's earliest piano solos, done between 1935 and 1937 and never reissued before (Volume 8); sixteen 1939–41 Cab Calloway big-band numbers, also never reissued, that are resplendent for some early I-*think*-I-know-where-I'm-going Dizzy Gillespie solos, Chu Berry's runneth-over tenor saxophone, and Cozy Cole's schoolmarm drumming (Volume 10); the historic numbers Armstrong and Bechet made in 1924 and 1925 (Volume 14), a collaboration that, unfortunately, was tried only once more, in 1940; a spirited Fats Waller stew from 1922, 1929, and 1931–32 and including four more of the above-mentioned Red Allen-Pee Wee Russell Rhythmaker sides, several bumptious numbers by a Ted Lewis band that included Muggsy Spanier, Benny Goodman, and Bud Freeman, and three rolling selections with Jack Teagarden (Volume 18); sixteen Duke Ellington big- and small-band sides from 1947 and 1951, among them "Three Cent Stomp" (winner of the Pun of the Year Award in '47) and a rocking blues, "Hy'a Sue" (Volume 20); fourteen 1929 and 1930 numbers by the Luis Russell band, which had Red Allen and J. C. Higginbotham and possibly the first genuinely swinging rhythm section in jazz (Volume 22); three brilliant early Gil Evans arrangements, done in the late forties for Claude Thornhill's unique big band (Volume 27); thirty-two Ellington tunes from the middle to the late twenties, among them both takes of the affecting, mysterious "Black and Tan Fantasy," in which the avant-garde Jabbo Smith replaced Bubber Miley (Volume 29); and no fewer than four LPs (Volumes 23, 25, 26, and 28) of Louis Armstrong in the twenties, accompanying such singers as Maggie Jones, Nolan Welsh, Clara Smith, Sippie Wallace, Hociel Thomas, Bertha Chippie Hill, Blanche Calloway, Victoria Spivey, and Lillie Delk Christian, the last of whom not even Armstrong, who is herculean throughout, can heft.

Some of the most precious material in the Columbia collection has been assembled in three LPs. The first offers four tantalizing glimpses of Django Reinhardt, jamming in Paris in 1945 with such Americans as Joe Shulman, Ray McKinley, and Mel Powell (Volume 12). The second, given over to Coleman Hawkins, includes all the Chocolate Dandies sides made in 1930 with Jimmy Harrison, Benny Carter, and Bobby Stark, the ten graceful numbers Hawkins and Red Allen recorded in 1933, and the two fine, winging ones Hawkins did in 1941 with Count Basie's big band (Volume 31). The third LP is fascinating. On it are alternate takes of three Basie small-band classics — the 1936 "Shoe Shine Boy" and the 1939 "Dickie's Dream" and "Lester Leaps In." They are easily as rewarding as the takes first released. Also on this LP are six of the oddest records ever made. Lee Castle is on trumpet, Lester Young on tenor saxophone and clarinet, Glenn Hardman on organ, Freddie Greene on guitar, and Jo Jones on drums. Hardman is a two-ton cocktail-lounge organist, but his colleagues envelop him like a school of fish, allowing us to concentrate on their glistening beauties. Young is extraordinary on both his instruments, and his two choruses on tenor in the slow blues match anything he recorded (Volume 24).

*

JANUARY 6TH: BROOKS KERR has gradually been assembling a band at Churchill's, and it is all but complete. It has strange bedfellows. Paul Quinichette (ex-Basie) is on tenor saxophone, Matthew Gee (ex-Basie and ex-Ellington) on trombone, Franc Williams (ex-Ellington) on flugelhorn, and Sam Woodyard (idem) on drums. Quinichette (pronounced "Quinishay") has long held a day job, and it is a pleasure to hear him again. Because of his speaking similarity to Lester Young, he was nicknamed Vice-Pres when he appeared, in the fifties. But Quinichette grew up in the territory bands of the Southwest, and the special quality that infuses the playing of so many Southwestern musicians presses steadily to the fore. The skin is Young but the stuffing is Herschel Evans and Buddy Tate. That was noticeable this afternoon at Churchill's when Quinichette delivered Evans' anthem, "Blue and Sentimental." His tone was somber, and there were blue notes, low-register booms, and abrupt high exclamations. It was the sort of naked lyrical performance that Young could never have lowered his cool for. It was equally fine to hear Woodyard, who has been out West for a long time. He is a deceptive drummer. When he was with Ellington, his gangling looseness gave the impression that he might fall off his drum stool or commit some musical atrocity. But his insouciance hides a subtle drive and precision. His foot-pedal work is sparing and clean, as are his fills on the snare drum, and his cymbal work pushes. He listens, and he has immaculate time. Williams was also a surprise. He is not known for his solo work, but he has a pure tone and a gentle, quiet, Shorty Baker attack, which was especially impressive in "Solitude." Gee is a good if somewhat congested trombonist who recalls Bennie Green, and he had an excellent turn in "Sophisticated Lady," played in honor of Harry Carney, who dropped by to check on everyone's deportment. Brooks Kerr kept everything together — the son leading his spiritual fathers.

FEBRUARY 2ND: MARY LOU WILLIAMS has been filling in at the
Café Carlyle for Bobby Short, and seeing her in such genteel
surroundings is like being served steak at a garden party. She
has been playing with great strength and invention in the past
couple of years, and she was again tonight. She was also, I
suspect, bowing to her surroundings, for she chose straight-
away tunes she does not ordinarily play — "The Man I love,"
"My Funny Valentine," "Temptation," "Love for Sale," and
"The Surrey With the Fringe on Top." But after obeisance to
the melody, each of them took on a driving, blues quality, and
it was business as usual.

FEBRUARY 15TH: NO MATTER HOW DILUTED or coarsened or
aged some of the music may be, one can still hear in the flesh
almost every style of jazz — ragtime (not jazz, but an
inseparable progenitor), stride piano, boogie-woogie, blues
shouting, New Orleans jazz, Kansas City jazz, Chicago jazz,
Dixieland, big- and small-band swing, bebop, hard bop, and the
various Babelean experiments of the last fifteen years. But
recently there has been a distinct and subtle change in the
provenance of jazz: It is no longer, except for the music of its
rapidly diminishing originators, a folk art. Its underground,
wayward, untutored, father-to-son customs have almost vanished. The music is now courted by academics, by govern-
ments, and by institutions, and it, in turn, is courting them.
Jazz musicians play comfortably in concert halls and museums
and palaces. They apply successfully for grants, get degrees in
jazz, and hold down chairs of music in colleges. The Smithsonian Institution has assembled the first intelligent and comprehensive recorded history of jazz. Most of the nominations for
the brand-new hall of fame established by the National Acad-
emy of Recording Arts and Sciences are jazz records. Duke
Ellington is a member of the National Institute of Arts and

Letters, and he and other jazz musicians have begun amassing honorary degrees. The first number of the *Journal of Jazz Studies*, published by the Rutgers Institute of Jazz Studies, and designed to meet "the need for a multi-disciplinary and inter-disciplinary publication for scholarly articles about jazz and related musics," is out. A large, if quirky, selection of jazzmen is listed in the latest *Who's Who in America*. (Some who are in: Count Basie, Bob Brookmeyer, Ornette Coleman, Jim Hall, Freddie Hubbard, Percy Humphrey, Elvin Jones, John Lewis, and John Tchicai. Some who are not: Jo Jones, Milt Hinton, Hank and Thad Jones, and Zutty Singleton.) But the most recent episode in this headlong rush of jazz and the Establishment toward one another is the appearance this winter of no fewer than two jazz repertory companies — the National Jazz Ensemble, founded and directed by the bassist Chuck Israels, and the New York Jazz Repertory Company, founded and headed up by George Wein. They make it official: Jazz has a Past.

Repertory companies, devoted until now to formal music, drama, and dancing, have long been considered ongoing and beneficial. They provide paid, on-the-job training, they delight audiences by giving them delusions of critical grandeur, and they keep worthy works alive. But such companies are by nature interpretive, whereas jazz is largely an improvisatory music — which raises all sorts of troublesome questions: How should a jazz repertory company re-create, say, Jelly Roll Morton's 1926 "Grandpa's Spells"? Transcribe the entire recording, thus precluding any improvising? Transcribe the ensembles and allow new solos? Or simply let loose musicians still conversant with Morton's style? Should the company play Ellington when Ellington can still play himself supremely well? How should it treat great recorded solos? Transcribe them or improvise on them? Should it fool with material that is readily available in night clubs or on records? Should it commission fresh works? And here is a genuine puzzle — how should it bring to life one of the great recorded performances by Frankie Newton, Sidney Bechet, J. C. Higginbotham, and Sidney Catlett, when most of its beauties flowed from the musicians' unique, inimitable timbres and attacks? To date, the two companies have each given two concerts, and they have raised as many questions as they have answered.

The National Jazz Ensemble, based in Alice Tully Hall, is the Little Brother of the two. It has a single, sixteen-piece orchestra, limited funds, and a schedule of four concerts this season. The New York Jazz Repertory Company, based in Carnegie Hall, is a behemoth in comparison. Its many orchestras are drawn from almost a hundred musicians of every persuasion, it is amply funded, and it will give fifteen concerts this season. But Little Brother, by opening its series on November 21, got off the mark first. The concert, by turns, was charming, ingenious, dull, exciting, and esoteric. Its twelve pieces were by Louis Armstrong, Ellington, Charlie Christian, Charlie Parker, John Carisi, Thelonious Monk, Israels, Bill Evans, and Miles Davis. The band included, to name a few, Randy Brecker and Lew Soloff on trumpet, Garnett Brown on trombone, Jim Buffington on French horn, George Barrow and Sal Nistico on tenor saxophone, Benny Aronov on piano, Pat Martino on guitar, Herb Bushler on bass, and Bill Goodwin on drums. Israels conducted and occasionally played. The first number, which lasted less than a minute, very nearly topped everything that came after. It was a transcription of the thirty-two-bar solo Louis Armstrong took in his 1927 Hot Five recording of "Struttin' with Some Barbecue." The few rough spots in the solo had been ironed out, and the band, playing the solo in unison, soared. One of Armstrong's most adventurous early solos became a new, lyrical, almost avant-garde statement that had a sculptured, larger-than-life quality. And this became even clearer when the number was repeated at the close of the evening. The next selection was a mistake. It was a thinly voiced, somewhat stiff reading of Ellington's complex, sashaying "Rockin' in Rhythm." Since every Ellington composition comes in three interlocking parts — the melody, its orchestration, and the band's rendition — any other version is necessarily incomplete. (Relish this triple phenomenon now; it is irreplaceable.) Moreover, "Rockin' in Rhythm" is very much a part of Ellington's current repertory. In the next number, Charlie Christian's "Seven Come Eleven," the band caught a good deal of the flow of Christian's melodic lines, as well as the smooth bicycling of the Goodman sextet, but Martino's solo — he gets a jangling, five-and-ten sound — was obtrusive. Then came an apt study, carried forward by a trumpet and an alto saxophone, of the ensemble figure that Charlie Parker wrote in his "Confirmation." Israels made it plain that not enough has been done about Parker's ensemble lines, which, in their complexity, daring, and originality, sometimes exceeded the solos they enclosed. (It should be pointed out, though, that the original recordings of "Seven Come Eleven" and "Confirmation" are available.) Israels' notions of what a jazz repertory orchestra should do took unmistakable shape in John Carisi's "Israel." The tune was first recorded by the Miles Davis Nonet in 1949. Israels, however, used the arrangement Carisi devised in the fifties for Gerry Mulligan's big band and interpolated a transcription, played by his trumpet section, of Davis' solo in the Nonet version. It worked, even though the long solos that were added tended to weaken the over-all design of the piece. The big-band arrangement written by the late Hall Overton in 1959 of Monk's "Little Rootie Tootie" followed, and it included a transcription of Monk's solo from his early trio recording of the tune. The first half of the concert was closed by Israels' own three-part variation on "Stella by Starlight." This had written and improvised solos, and sections that recalled the "Rhapsody in Blue" and "L'Histoire du Soldat."

Bill Evans sat in for the second part of the evening and reaffirmed the curious fact that he is far more relaxed as a sideman than as a leader. His unflaggingly brilliant solos were full of leap-frogging Bud Powell runs, short, intense phrases clustered around one or two sharply struck notes, and rich chordal fillings. When he is in such superb shape, he is the premier pianist of his generation. Israels' boxes-within-boxes devices were also in full view. "Nardis Variations" was an orchestration of a 1963 Evans trio recording, and on it Evans erected a whole new solo. And in the densest effort of the evening, Miles Davis' "All Blues," Israels, according to the program, "transcribed the melody as Davis played it on the record, and then orchestrated Evans' accompaniment to Davis' improvised solo, fleshing it out so that Evans [could] use it as a springboard for a new piano solo." Henry James would have relished such intricate footwork.

The National Jazz Ensemble's second concert, given late in January, was largely an extension of the first. "Lester Leaps In" incorporated an ensemble transcription of Lester Young's original 1939 solo. Horace Silver's "Moonray," written in 1958, was a salute to Silver's trumpet-and-tenor-saxophone ensemble, which was padded out here and there by the whole band and broken up by Randy Brecker and Sal Nistico solos. Miles Davis' "Solar" was a variation, both improvised and written, on Davis' original recorded solo. Ornette Coleman's "Tears Inside" was given similar treatment, but it failed to pin down the singular texture and timbres of the Coleman-Don Cherry version. The rest of the evening included, among other things, a new Herb Pomeroy piece, "Jolly Chocolate, " which was an Ellington stew salted with Charlie Mingus poly-rhythms; Charlie Parker's "Bloomdido," in which sections of a transcription of Parker's solo were dropped in between new solos; and "Dolphin Dance" and "Maiden Voyage," by Herbie Hancock, which served as miniature concertos for their composer, who sat in.

So Israels' approach to a jazz repertory orchestra appears set. His tastes are catholic ("Struttin' with Some Barbecue" was played again that night), but he specially favors the music he grew up with (he is thirty-seven, and his idols include Parker, Clifford Brown, Davis, Bill Evans, with whom he worked for five years, and John Coltrane). He rejoices in improvisation, and he celebrates it intelligently with his transcriptions and adept orchestrations. And he enjoys intellectual catch-me-if-you-can musical games. His band for the most part serves him well. It is primarily an ensemble group, whose soloists, though sometimes long-winded, are largely icing on the cake. The band does not always swing, but some of the mazes Israels takes it through discourage such refinements.

Four days earlier, Big Brother puffed into Carnegie Hall for its first concert, breathed heavily for three hours, and brought forth a mouse. The concert was in three lengthy parts. In the first, a seventeen-piece band, which included such as Zoot Sims, Budd Johnson, Eddie Bert, Joe Newman, Jon Faddis, Jimmy Lyon, George Barnes, and Panama Francis, played eleven of Sy Oliver's arrangements for the old Jimmie Lunceford band. (Oliver is one of the musical directors of the New York Jazz Repertory Company. The others are Billy Taylor, Gil Evans, and Stanley Cowell.) The Lunceford band, with its predilection for two-beat rhythms, short solos, vocal trios, and showmanship, had a strong Mickey Mouse streak, and this trait was emphasized on the occasion as we bounced through "Ain't She Sweet," "By the River Sainte Marie," "Margie," "My Blue Heaven," "Cheatin' on Me," "Annie Laurie," "Organ Grinder's Swing," and " 'Tain't What You Do." But the Lunceford band had a serious, driving side, too, and such redoubtable numbers as "Yard Dog Mazurka," "Battle Axe," "Chocolate," "Impromptu," and "Uptown Blues" should have been aired. (These last are not Oliver arrangements, but limiting the program to his work suggests the sort of ego-tripping that has no place in a repertory company.) How fine it would have been to hear the slow, stark "Uptown Blues," and to have had its solos by Willie Smith and Snookie Young scored, respectively, for the reed and trumpet sections! But this N.Y.J.R.C. orchestra, which, ironically, played Oliver's arrangements better than Lunceford did, was doubly wasted. It ignored Lunceford's better half and it played material that Oliver's own band has used all over town for the past several years.

There was more waste in the second section of the evening, which was devoted to material that Gil Evans has been parading in night clubs. A curious thing has happened to Evans in the past couple of years. His best work is still ahead of its time, yet he has been trying to keep up with what he has already passed. That is, he has loaded down his sumptuous orchestrations with a synthesizer, rock rhythms, amplifiers, interminable solos, and a congested percussion section. The results suggest Jacob Marley's famous trip up Scrooge's stairs. The last section of the concert centered on a five-part piece, "Collection Suite," that was written, arranged, and conducted by the trumpeter Charles Tolliver and played by a thirty-piece group — a big band plus a four-man percussion group, a tuba, and eight strings. The music, tossed back and forth between the strings and the horns, and interlarded here and there with suffering solos, had severe Kentonitis.

The next N.Y.J.R.C. concert was as inscrutable as the first. Dizzy Gillespie brought a seventeen-piece band onstage for an announced program of his big-band pieces from the forties, and one looked forward to such eminences as "Ow!," "Two Bass Hit," "Things to Come," "Ool-Ya-Koo," and "Woody 'n You." Instead, the band played his lovely but later "Con Alma," and then settled into a grim, twenty-minute Gillespie composition, "The Burning Spear," which was arranged by Chico O'Farrill and is full of busily changing tempos, ostinato figures, and a discordant "free" ensemble passage.

A twenty-two-piece band conducted by Billy Taylor completed the evening with two Oliver Nelson compositions, "Soundpiece for Jazz Orchestra" (1964) and "Jazzhattan Suite" (1967). Both are reminiscent of the "modern" soundtrack music that Neal Hefti, Henry Mancini, André Previn, Lalo Schifrin, and others have been turning out for Hollywood — a blues-tinged, brassy, baritone-bound, rhythmically bombastic music. These men have swept away the Dimitri Tiomkins, but, in their own way, they have become as insistent and as static. But there was a saving moment, and it came in "Jazzhattan Suite." Jimmy Knepper, using a plunger mute, took several blues choruses, which offered an abundance of his curiously revolving phrases, his surprisingly placed notes, and his dense, unique tone. The sound throughout the evening was unsettling. Microphones were used only for the soloists (but not for pianists and guitarists), while the various sections, sounding as if they were in the next county, were left to blow themselves purple.

So Israels is already on his special, intelligent way, but Big Brother needs retooling. In the meantime, here are some suggestions for music to be studied, re-created, or distilled by the two companies: the 1940–41 Cab Calloway band, a surprising number of whose alumni are still playing; a big-band program of Benny Carter tunes and/or arrangements; a John Carisi retrospective; the Miles Davis Nonet; the Gerry Mulligan sextet; the John Kirby band; and transcriptions of such great solos as Louis Armstrong's in "Basin Street Blues" (1933), Bix Beiderbecke's in "I'm Coming Virginia," Charlie Parker's in his first "Embraceable You," and Don Byas' in Count Basie's 1942 small-band version of "St. Louis Blues."

MARCH 15TH: COUNT BASIE himself does not know exactly where his style came from. Asked about its origins a while ago, he sent up a cloud of defensive, deep-voiced "um"s and "ah"s, and then said, "Honest truth, I don't know. If my playing is different, I didn't try for it or anything like that. I stumbled on it. I do know that in the earlier years I always loved Fats Waller's playing, and that Fats and the other guys had such fast right hands there was no use for me to try and compete with them. Another thing that helped was my rhythm section with Jo Jones and Walter Page and Freddie Greene. They gave me so much freedom. I could run in between what Page and Freddie were doing. I didn't think a lot of execution on my part meant anything with them there. It would have just cluttered it up. My greatest kick was having fun with the rhythm section and setting things up for the band. Of course, I've always listened to the pianists who play a whole lot of notes. Like Tatum, who was impossible. If he'd stayed up nine years playing, I'd have stayed up nine years to listen to him. Oscar Peterson is kind of ridiculous, too, and so is Phineas Newborn. But for me, simplicity has always seemed right."

This simplicity evolved between the late twenties, when Basie was still a Waller pianist, and the mid-thirties, when his unique telegraphic style began to appear on recordings. And he has refined it and refined it until he can now play an eloquent chorus of the blues with just three or four notes sounded a dozen times. But his piano is remarkable for another reason. Most improvisers feed chords and melody and rhythm into their creative hopper, where, instantaneously and astonishingly, these musical ingredients are transformed into brand-new melodic lines that are simultaneously flashed to the musician's fingers and lips. Basie, though, goes through one more step. Before his melodic lines reach his fingers, they are exactingly edited, so we hear only what he considers the ultimate parts of his original invention. Thus we get four notes of what might have been a twenty-note run, a single note from a triad, silence where a connective passage might have been, and a trill instead of a flatted ninth. But Basie's original melodic lines are always implied, and one can hear them running along in the distance — a train behind low hills. Basie, who edits not only his notes but the length of his solos, will go at several choruses of a slow blues like this: He will start with an ascending four-note figure in the right hand, pause, drop in an offbeat single note, pause again (this time for a couple of measures), play a two-note octave phrase, pause, and finish the first chorus with a fragment of melody sounded in the highest register. More silence eases by, and then it is suddenly broken by three or four heavy descending chords in the left hand, these capped by a simple right-hand chord, which he holds for over a measure. He pauses again, then starts a riff, breaks it off after he has played it twice, and inserts several offbeat notes, which are echoed by left-hand oompahs, and we go into the third chorus. Four or five single notes, spaced a beat apart, walk down through the middle register, and then there is a long pause, which ends in a rich, right-hand chord that is repeated as Basie goes into a stride bass, raises his volume, and — bang! — brings in the band. The rhythm section, of course, has been flowing steadily along — a quiet stream easily supporting Basie's boat.

When the solo is over, one realizes its perfections and relishes again the fact that Basie has probably not ever played a wrong note, a wrong accent, or a cliché. One also realizes that the offhandedness of the solo, delivered as if he were leaning against a post and idly kicking at the dust, accomplishes the opposite effect: It has swung hard, for he is a master of concealing tension with relaxation, of making climaxes seem like releases. And one realizes how eloquent the solo has been, how the precise, inspired placing of a single minor note accomplishes everything that a horn player's slur or bent note does. The solo, too, has been full of Basie's humor, which, learned so well from Waller, never fails him. It is the humor of surprise, of picking singular notes and chords and placing them where no one else would dare. Basie also learned the organ from Waller, and it is a pity he does not play it more often. He goes at it the way he goes at the piano, but with even more care, for he constantly amends the *instrument*. He suppresses its bombastic characteristics by making it whisper and sigh and flutter, by making it muse. His organ accompaniment is particularly attractive. It sounds like wind blowing through a window screen, and it provides a cushion that makes average soloists seem better than they are and first-rate soloists seem perfect.

Basie is a short, slow, shy man who really feels that his playing is not all that much, and as a result he has recorded only about a dozen solo (with rhythm) numbers in his forty-five-year career. But he has recorded a fairly large number of revealing small-band sides, and there are eleven of them in "Count Basie: Super Chief" (Columbia), which has, in all, twenty-eight numbers made by Basie or Basie-affiliated musicians between 1936 and 1942. Ten of the numbers, among them both air checks and studio sessions, have not been issued before, and an almost equal number are being re-issued for the first time. There are wonders in addition to Basie all through the album — Jess Stacy's short, way-out solo in "Life Goes to a Party," which is under Harry James' name and involves a group made up, with the exception of the leader and Stacy, of Basie personnel; the dancing, staccato muted solo Harry Edison plays near the end of the entire band's "Miss Thing"; Jack Washington's fine pre-Gerry Mulligan noodling behind Edison, once more muted, in "Somebody Stole My Gal"; and the Don Byas solo in "St. Louis Blues," which proves again one of the most astonishing things about a first-rate recorded solo: It is surprising no matter how many times you hear it. The rest of the cake is Basie's. Listen to the way he plays plain old Waller stride piano in "Shoe Shine Boy," and then to the almost avant-garde accompaniment, full of strange notes and accents, he gives Jimmy Rushing in "Evenin'," Helen Humes in "Where Shall I Go," and Edison in "Miss Thing."

Basie is nonpareil not only as accompanist but as band pianist. He *leads* his band with the piano — he rarely gives any visual signal aside from a nod or a look — and he does it with extraordinary variety. In slow tunes, he noodles along behind his soloists, making cryptic musical comments and jokes about what they are playing, and he decorates ensemble passages with approving garlands of notes. In fast numbers, he moves down into the lowest registers and issues rocking, invincible chords that have literally made his audiences and even his musicians shout. Listen to him all the way through the four wonderful small-band sides made in Chicago in 1939 and never before brought out because of the poor quality of their recording. They include "I Ain't Got Nobody," an unusually fast "Love Me or Leave Me," which has a full and extremely busy Basie chorus, "Going to Chicago Blues," and "Live and Love Tonight" — the last two played on organ in his best wind-in-the-willows way. And listen to the only solo track in the album, "Café Society Blues," in which he is accompanied by Greene, Page, and Jones. It denies completely Basie's assumption that he should not make solo records. His playing is robust and cheerful, and he beefs up his telegraphy here and there with fat chords, passages of stride piano, and rolling boogie-woogie. He plays more notes than is his wont, and he sounds relieved at doing it. All aphorists babble occasionally.

APRIL 6TH: A GREAT DRUMMER dances sitting down. A great tap-dancer drums standing up. But the only instrument a tap-dancer has is himself, so he is a special — and fragile — breed. Such was Baby Laurence, who died earlier this week in New York, at the age of fifty-three. Laurence was born (in Baltimore, as Laurence Donald Jackson) twenty years too late.

Tap-dancing, which evolved in this country over the course of a hundred years from the ring shout, jigs and clogs, the soft-shoe, and the buck-and-wing, reached its apogee in the twenties and thirties, and went out of fashion when vaudeville was overrun by the movies. Laurence nonetheless patched together a career. He started at twelve, as a singer, when such child stars as Buddy Rich and Jackie Coogan were international darlings, but by his late teens he had turned formidably to dancing. He came to the fore on Fifty-second Street, around 1940, with a singing-and-dancing act that sang Jimmy Lunceford arrangements in six-part harmony, and then he went out as a single, hoofing mainly in the Midwest. In the forties and fifties, he danced with Duke Ellington, Count Basie, and Woody Herman, and occasionally surfaced at small clubs in Harlem. After a long illness, he materialized again, at the Showplace, on West Fourth Street, in the winter of 1960. He danced at the small Max Roach-Charlie Mingus rump festival in Newport that summer, and in 1962 he graced an abortive jazz festival sponsored by the government in Washington. A few months later, he appeared with sensational effect at the Newport Jazz Festival, along with such dancers as Pete Nugent, Honi Coles, and Bunny Briggs. (The first time Briggs watched Laurence dance, in the thirties, he paid him the tap-dancer's highest compliment: "I saw a fellow dance," he told his mother, "and his feet never touched the floor.") Then he drifted into an oblivion that finally ended in 1969, when word came that he was back in Baltimore, had a day job, and was dancing weekends in a restaurant in a shopping center in Gaithersburg, Maryland. It was a sad gig. Laurence, backed by an excellent trio led by the drummer Eddie Phyfe, who was also, willy-nilly, Laurence's guardian-manager-employer, danced a couple of times a night on a swaying plywood platform set up in the center of a big, dark room. He was in raw shape, and his steps were heavy and uncertain. The stolid

Maryland burghers, sawing at their New York Cut sirloins, paid him little heed. But Laurence finished strong: Early in 1973 he suddenly reappeared in New York, and during the year he headed up those successful Sunday-afternoon tap-dancing sessions at the Jazz Museum, took in students, danced at the Palace with Josephine Baker, did some television, and gave his triumphant performance at the Newport-New York Jazz Festival.

He was a strange little man. His arms and legs were pipes, his face was scarred, and he had hooded eyes. In the wrong light, he looked sinister, and, indeed, orphaned at thirteen and later hemmed in by drugs and alcohol and financial troubles, he tended to be devious and self-pitying. Yet his dancing belied all that. In many ways, he was more a drummer than a dancer. He did little with the top half of his torso; holding his head upright, he either let his arms flap at his sides or crooked them. But his legs and feet were speed and thunder and surprise. Unlike many tap-dancers, who rely on certain changeless patterns, Laurence constantly improvised. His sound was not the serene clickety-tick-tick of Bill Robinson or Chuck Green; it was a succession of explosions, machine-gun rattles, and jarring thumps. There were no frills to his dancing. He would start a thirty-two-bar chorus with light heel-and-toe figures, drop in a heavy, off-beat heel accent with one foot and echo it with the other, go up on his toes, and then release a double-time splatter of heel beats, resume the heel-and-toe steps, breaking them frequently with ominous flat-footed offbeats, spin completely around, and start crossing and recrossing his feet, letting off sprays of rapid toe beats each time his feet touched wood. Laurence tended to work in a small area. (Briggs often skitters thirty or forty feet across a stage, like a stone skipping over water), but next he might move in a large circle, each toe stuttering alternately on the floor as he moved, and, the circle complete, abruptly begin violent knee-pumping, followed by toe-to-heel explosions that might last ten seconds before giving way to a terrific double-time burst, a leap into the air, and a deep bow.

APRIL 29TH: THE JAZZ REPERTORY MILLS are going again, and their subject, not surprisingly, has been Duke Ellington, who is seventy-five today. The first attempt to bottle the Master's music for posterity was made early last week in Washington, at a Smithsonian Jazz Heritage concert given by Gunther Schuller and the New England Conservatory Orchestra, and the second was made a few days ago in Carnegie Hall, by the New York Jazz Repertory Company. Schuller is an Ellington scholar, and he took the puristic approach. The orchestra, made up of sixteen Conservatory kids, played note-for-note transcriptions (solos included) of fourteen Ellington records, some of them well known ("Cottontail," "Jack the Bear," "Koko," "Reminiscing in Tempo"), some less well known ("C Jam Blues," "Moon Mist"), and some of all but forgotten ("Azure," "Subtle Lament," "Blue Light"), and by and large it played them well — particularly the ensemble passages. The lapses were predictable: Most of the transcribed solos (Ben Webster's in "Cottontail" excepted) sounded awkward and chunky, and there were persistent rhythmic problems that were accented by drab drumming. The best thing about the group was the way it illumined various aspects of Ellington's ingenuity — his weird, atonal, futuristic piano solo in "Clothed Woman"; his fine hide-and-seek scoring, especially in "Koko," "Dusk," "Subtle Lament" (a lovely clarinet-alto-saxophone-soprano-saxophone voicing), "Carnegie Blues" (the trombone trio and the baritone saxophone calling back and forth); the grace and deceptive simplicity of almost every piece; and the revelation, in "Reminiscing in Tempo," that he had been listening to George Gershwin. Schuller firmly believes that his

is the best way to preserve Ellington (the note-for-note transcriptions were the result of a dismaying discovery on his part:
much of the early printed Ellingtonia has disappeared or been
destroyed), but, as has been pointed out before, the Ellington
œuvre contains his melodies, his scoring of them, his piano
playing, and his band, and when anyone else plays his music it
invariably sounds Xeroxed. All the Ellington notes were there
in Washington, but only a few of them had the right flavor.
After Ellington and the scores of musicians who have worked
for him are gone, the chief evidence we will have of how he
played his music, how he brought it to its unique completion,
will be his available recordings, which at best are as fallible as
photographs.

The New York Jazz Repertory Company's Ellington celebration was a big, feasting, we-love-ya-Duke show, which went
like this: the Billy Taylor trio wandered around through five
Ellington numbers; Brooks Kerr resurrected "Bird of Paradise"
(1924) and "Soda Fountain Rag" (1913), and was joined by
such Ellington graduates as Sonny Greer, Russell Procope,
Joya Sherrill, and Ozzie Bailey; Bob Wilber led an eight-piece
band that included Pepper Adams, Taft Jordan, and Quentin
Jackson through such small-band pieces as "Subtle Slough,"
"Echoes of Harlem," "Love in My Heart," and "Junior Hop,"
and the group summoned up the timbres and accents of Cootie
Williams, Johnny Hodges, and Tricky Sam Nanton; the Ruby
Braff-George Barnes quartet ruminated eloquently in "Just
Squeeze Me" (the final version of "Subtle Slough") and "It
Don't Mean a Thing If It Ain't Got That Swing"; and a big
band, led by Sy Oliver, played nine Ellington numbers, among
them "Birmingham Breakdown," "Boy Meets Horn," "Ring
Dem Bells," and the insuperable "Main Stem." Some of it was
Schuller-pure Ellington and some of it — particularly rhythmi-
cally — was Sy Oliver-Jimmy Lunceford Ellington.

*

APRIL 30TH: BUDDY RICH, wearing his Superman costume, has come to town. He has dumped his big band, opened a club, Buddy's Place, at Second Avenue and Sixty-fourth Street, decorated it with pictures of himself, and stocked it with a seven-piece group made up of Sonny Fortune and Sal Nistico on reeds, Kenny Barron on piano, Jack Wilkins on guitar, a Fender bassist, a conga drummer, and himself. The band is sleek, musicianly, driving, and, apparently at Rich's behest, very loud. It is a pile driver, a rock-crusher, a blithering explosion. Four or five numbers tonight put one in mind of some angelic minutes that took place during a concert Rich gave seven or eight years ago on Riker's Island; feeling that he wasn't reaching his audience, he picked up his wire brushes and did a funny, delicate, dancing duet in "Green Dolphin Street" with his pianist, John Bunch. That whispering, joyous performance brought the house down.

MAY 2ND: THERE IS AN OBSESSIVE QUALITY in much of the experimental jazz of the sixties and seventies. This hectoring strain is new in jazz. Before the sixties, most good jazz had a pleasant, show-off quality, a casual, look-no-hands lyricism. Its practitioners enjoyed doing sensational things — Louis Armstrong's 1933 flights and Coleman Hawkins' "Body and Soul" and Charlie Parker's "Embraceable You" — and they didn't care whether the listener understood it all, as long as he listened. But free jazz, whether out of the unsureness that dogs experimentation or out of deep racial bitterness (free jazz is the blackest jazz there is) or sheer messianic drive, tends to bully the listener. At least, that is what the pianist McCoy Tyner, now thirty-five, has been up to in the past several years. Tyner spent five years as a sideman baking in John Coltrane's oven, and by the time he left Coltrane most of the ingredients in his work — in particular in his newest album, "McCoy

Tyner: Enlightenment" (Milestone) — had risen: the continually shifting modal patterns, the racing, almost glissando arpeggios, and the hammering chords. The album, recorded by Tyner at last year's Montreux Jazz Festival in company with the tenor and soprano saxophonist Azar Lawrence, the bassist Joony Booth, and the drummer Alphonse Mouzon, contains two LPs, on which there are just four numbers — the three-part "Enlightenment Suite" (twenty-six minutes), "Presence" (ten and a half minutes), "Nebula" (eight and a half minutes), and "Walk Spirit, Talk Spirit" (twenty-five minutes). Despite its fervor and density, the music is fairly conventional in form. The melodies are simple (part of "Enlightenment" has a strong "Summertime" flavor), there are opening and closing ensembles, and the rhythmic patterns are clean and clear. Lawrence resembles Gato Barbieri: He holds the few notes he uses a long time and he has a sumptuous vibrato. Mouzon is a busy drummer in the current mode, and the equally fashionable Booth favors notes that whine along just below pitch. One hears Art Tatum and Bud Powell and the less cluttered side of Cecil Taylor in Tyner's playing, but the exact center of his style goes ceaselessly in and out of focus: keys shift like light on whirring spokes, his rhythms move ecstatically from set time to double time to triple time, his arpeggios and single-note lines seem vertical rather than horizontal, and he constantly returns to his stockpile of massive, loud-pedal chords. His playing is agitated, absolutely sure, and quite new. It is hard to turn away from his brilliant baths of sound.

MAY 10TH: WHEN JIMMY ROWLES at last began his brave invasion of New York City, a little over a year ago, perhaps a hundred people took note. But this was hardly surprising. Rowles' previous visits to the city, in the forties and fifties, had been brief and in the semi-visible guises of accompanist for Evelyn Knight and Peggy Lee and of big-band pianist for Benny Goodman and Woody Herman. Moreover, the rest of his career had been spent around Los Angeles, in a variety of equally subaqueous roles that included studio work, fleeting night-club appearances, countless recordings for other people, and coaching singers and non-singers, one of whom was Marilyn Monroe. "The studio sent me over to this sumptuous office on the lot where she was supposed to be," he said recently, "and when I got there the blinds were drawn and the place looked empty. Then I saw this form asleep on the sofa. I didn't know what to do, so I sat down in a chair and lit a cigarette and dug it all. 'Here I am,' I thought, 'sitting alone in the dark with the most beautiful woman in the world.' Then I got nervous. So I cleared my throat several times and she woke up." In January of last year, Johnny Mercer brought Rowles with him as his accompanist for his Town Hall concert, and five months later, Rowles took a two-week gig at Michael's Pub and concurrently appeared in the Newport Jazz Festival- New York. Perhaps a hundred more people took note, and one of them was Barney Josephson who has brought Rowles into his Cookery for a seven-week engagement that sets one Rowles record and nearly breaks another: It is the longest solo stint he has had outside Los Angeles, and the second-longest he has had anywhere.

I went down to the Cookery tonight to listen to Rowles and talk to him. It was half an hour before his first set. Rowles was sitting by himself at a table near the piano. He does not stand out in crowds. Compact and medium-sized, he is gray-haired and bespectacled and clerkly looking. His face is chipped and worn, and he has a low, gravelly voice. His mod California clothes, instead of accenting him, almost extinguish him. I asked him how everything was going. "It was a little strange in here at first," he said. "I felt like I was playing in a

cafeteria, what with all the dish sounds and steady talking.
And I don't think I ever played in a club without a bandstand,
with the piano right down on the floor in the middle of the
tables. A bandstand gives you a little defense, a little privilege.
But I'm getting used to it, and Buster Williams, the bass player
who'll be with me until Tommy Bryant takes over, is a big help.
A lot of the tunes I play he doesn't know, but he's got awful
ears. He grabs the structure and chords of a new tune after the
first chorus, and he doesn't forget it if I play it a couple of
nights later. But *my* ears have been giving me trouble.
They've been stuffed up ever since I got off the plane, like as if
I caught a little cold out there and carried it East with me. I've
been thinking more and more lately that it's time for me to be
doing something like this. I'm fifty-five years old, and it won't
be that much longer before I get away, like all my friends seem
to be doing. This past year, Ben Webster, Don Fagerquist, and
Frank Beach all passed. And a couple of weeks ago it was
Bobby Timmons, who was only in his thirties. So I figure it's
time to play the way I want to play, time to see if I can make a
go of it outside the studios and accompanying people." Rowles
paused, and waved to a waitress. "Honey, get me a vodkatonic, please. My wife, Dorothy, was all for the move, and that
means everything to me, because she's smart musically and
every other way. Lord! The other night, I found myself staring
at the back of some woman's legs because they looked exactly
like Dorothy's. That's how much I miss her already. We met
in '36. She was going to a high school on one side of Spokane,
where we were both born, and I was going to one on the other
side, and we met at a dance I was playing at her school. When
I went down to L.A. the first time, in 1940, I asked her to wait a
year, and if it worked out I'd send for her and we'd get married.
It did and we did, and it's been thirty-two years. She's been my
life's blood. Of course, it wouldn't be right if we didn't fight at
least once a week. She's thrown me out of the house as much

as two weeks at a time. Once, when I came back, she was gone, and there was a note: 'Try and straighten up. And feed the animals.' She stayed away two weeks, and I didn't find out until later that she was just around the corner.

"We've got three kids, and they're *all* musical. Several years ago, my older daughter — her name is Stacy — saw a trumpet up in the attic which Frank Beach had given me. Chuck Peterson, the high-note man with Tommy Dorsey, had taught me a little trumpet when we were in Skinnay Ennis' band in the Army. Stacy said 'How do you play it?' and I showed her the scales. And last year, when she was eighteen, she won first prize at a big-band contest, and then she played at the Monterey Festival, and was hugged and kissed by Dizzy Gillespie and Clark Terry. And my younger daughter, Stephanie, who we call Zip, is into the flute. So I asked Arthur Gleghorn, a great English flute player who works in the studios out there, would he come by and play for us. We laid in plenty of vodka, and his old lady brought him over and he sat by our pool and played for hours — Ravel and Debussy — and it was fantastic. My son, Gary, plays organ and guitar. He's thirty-one. He began to break away from me when he was fourteen. I couldn't tell him where the sun rose, he knew so much. But he came around in his early twenties. He's a car genius, and he stops by and gives my arm a squeeze and works on my car, and everything is fine.

"Uh-oh. It's five after eight. Time to work." Rowles took a small blue box out of his pocket. It had the words "Tacky-Finger" on the lid. With careful, ritualistic movements, he dipped the ends of his fingers into the waxlike substance in the box and then massaged them. "There. I saw a teller in a bank put this stuff on before she counted a pile of bills, and now I can't live without it. It keeps my fingers from slipping off the keys into my lap. Before, I used to rub them under any old table to get them tacky, and later I'd have to wash the keyboard." Rowles went to the piano, picked up the bench, and put it behind the cash register, near the front door. He replaced it with a Cookery chair. In one motion, he sat down, leaned over, poised his fingers a second over the keyboard, and sank into a very slow "Mood Indigo." He moved in a gentle, circular fashion, as if he were leafing through a stamp album, and he punctuated his felicitous phrases by pointing his right toe at the ceiling. It lasted close to ten minutes, and was followed by an equally long and introverted version of "Prelude to a Kiss." Rowles' engine steadied, and the tempo went up in "I Can't Get Started." A light seemed to go on within the tune, and one could see the outline of its pleasant bones. A ruminative "Skylark" came next, and Rowles closed the set with a candent version of Fats Waller's "Jitterbug Waltz."

He remained at the piano half a minute, and, letting his hands hang loose, vibrated them vigorously, like a swimmer loosening his muscles. He got up and stopped by the table. "I've got to go downstairs and chant with Buster," he said. "I'll be back in ten minutes." Jazz musicians, like poets, are prone to inscrutable remarks, and I remembered what Rowles had told a friend about Thelonious Monk. "I went into this restaurant in Tokyo six or seven years ago, when I was on a tour," he had said, "and there was Monk standing at the bar. He was wearing one of his funny hats, and the whole time he revolved slowly, his hands raised and fluttering like moths around his head. When he came face to face with the bar, he'd stop, take a drink, then start spinning again. I'd seen him before, of course, but I'd never talked to him, so I introduced myself. I made a couple of attempts at conversation. Silence. Then he said, 'You got any kids?' I told him I had a son who was twenty-four, and I was about to mention Stacy and Zip when he said, 'He's too old. Get rid of him.' And he never said another word." While Rowles was chanting, I pondered his style. His playing is extraordinarily intense, and it demands exactly as much as it offers. Every tune is multi-layered, and, except for those rare times when he tires and repeats certain phrases, it has no soft spots. His singular harmonic sense governs his attack. He uses strange, flatted chords that seem to leave his phrases suspended and unresolved. They are questioning chords. His delicate runs have the same upturned, searching air. They begin in odd places, and while a run is moving buoyantly up the keyboard it suddenly breaks off, there is a pause, and the run resumes, descending through the very notes just played, as if Rowles were trying to knit the two parts. The melody slopes along in the middle distance, and his immaculate time is a further stabilizer. His touch is almost Tatum-light, and even his rushes of hard, no-nonsense single notes in fast numbers have no clamor or urgency. His chords and broken, winding runs suggest a hesitant, puzzled attitude, a continual where-do-I-go-from-here approach. But this is only a delightful illusion, a polite way of not overwhelming the listener.

Rowles reappeared and ordered another vodkatonic. "I chant with Buster a lot," he said. "He's into the Buddhist thing, and chanting keeps him cool. 'Nam Myoho Renge Kyo' we go, over and over, in unison. I don't know what it means, but it makes you feel like you're doing your rosary. It makes you less conscious of yourself, and I always get in my own way during the first set every night. My playing is a matter of concentration, a matter of intensity. A jumble of things flash constantly through my mind, like people's faces and what I'm going to play in the channel, and all the while the melody is with me subconsciously. I have that, and I have the chords. They're the carpet, and my playing is like dancing on that carpet. I learned how to accompany singers and horn players by listening to the backgrounds that arrangers like Sy Oliver and Duke Ellington and Mary Lou Williams wrote for their soloists. Particularly Mary Lou when she was with Andy Kirk.

In fact, I want to meet her while I'm here. It's unbelievable
how much I owe that woman. It's unbelievable how much I
owe a lot of people. Like Donald Brown, a Blackfoot Indian
from Montana, who got me going in the right direction when I
was a kid. He played tenor. When I first knew him, I was deep
into Guy Lombardo. He was my favorite band, and I loved his
piano player Freddy Kreitzer. Brown heard me doing some
Lombardo tune at the piano in the gym at Gonzaga University,
where I went for a year and a half, and he said, 'Ace, what are
you doin' that for? You should be listening to the Benny
Goodman Trio.' He took me downtown to a record store, and
when I heard Teddy Wilson in the Trio, that was it. It changed
my whole life. Brown had absolute pitch and radar ears. If I
played a Wilson or Tatum record and asked him about certain
chords, he'd tell me to slow the turntable down, which you
could do on those old windup Victrolas, and he'd spell out
every note. Another person I'll always owe is Ben Webster. I
met him late in 1939, in Seattle, where I was studying law — or
at least my family thought I was — at the University of
Washington. My real father, whose name was Hunter, passed
when I was three months old, and I was raised by my mother
and a stepfather, who adopted me and gave me his name. My
mother had studied guitar, and she played the piano real well
by ear, but he was in the rug business and wasn't musical at
all, except when he'd come home with some cronies at two in
the morning and get me up to play the piano while they sang
gems like 'Ace in the Hole.' Anyway, Ben had just joined Duke
Ellington, and I knew Ben was *the* man. He introduced me
around to all the musicians, and when I was twenty-one and
legally free, I dumped the law thing for good and took off for
L.A. I played with Slim and Slam. Slim was into his crazy
vooterini talk then, and he played the piano with the backs of
his hands as well as the regular way. Then I played intermission piano for Art Tatum. Man, I was smothered I was so

scared. I couldn't believe his hands. They were stubby, but they stretched like cobras when he wanted to reach a tenth or more. And the way they moved, he didn't look like he was playing at all. I'd ask him how he did such-and-such, and he'd show me. But if I mentioned his fantastic touch, all he'd say was 'Oh, I don't know' and start talking about Westerns or baseball. Once, I hung out with him for three days and three nights, and sometimes he'd play seven or eight hours at a stretch. Dorothy and I were married by then, and when I got home she was so mad she Art-Tatumed me right out of the house for a week. I never travel without Art; I have six cassettes of him over in my hotel room. I worked with the Spirits of Rhythm, too. Teddy Bunn was in the group and so was Leo Watson. And I worked with Lee and Lester Young. Lester was the coolest man I ever met. He wasn't Pres to us but Bubba, after some nephews who called him Uncle Bubba. He had his own language. He'd turn to me on the bandstand and say, 'Startled doe. Two o'clock,' which meant if you looked into the audience at where two o'clock was you'd see this pretty chick with big eyes. 'Bob Crosby's in the house' meant a cop had just come in, and 'Bing and Bob' meant the fuzz were all over the place. When I first knew him, he said, 'There's a gray boy at the bar who is looking for you.' 'What's a gray boy?' I said. 'Man, *you're* a gray boy,' he said, smiling with those green teeth he had then, 'and I'm an Oxford gray.'

"And everything that was good was 'bulging.' It was a telescoping of a phrase that had started out 'I've got eyes for that,' which meant 'I like that,' and became 'I've got great big eyes for that,' and then 'I've got bulging eyes for that.' But if he didn't like something or somebody, all he did was puff out his cheeks — no words at all, just balloon cheeks.''

It was nine-thirty, and Rowles applied more Tacky-Finger, then went back to the piano. He began an intense study of "Willow Weep for Me," an immovable song that ultimately bowed to his relentlessly polite exploration. He seemed to tunnel right through "The Man I Love," circumventing its singsong, steplike melody. "My Buddy," its melody decked out with embellishments, and properly played as a waltz, followed. It gave way to "Miss Brown to You," which he sang in a pleasant, husky voice. Freddie Hubbard's "Down Under," Billy Strayhorn's "Lush Life," and an ancient tune called "In the Middle of a Kiss" came next, and he closed with a rocking, medium-tempo rendition of Duke Ellington's "Cottontail" which included a witty paraphrase of Ben Webster's famous solo.

Rowles put a fat, leather-bound loose-leaf book on the table, and went to get a fresh vodkatonic. "I call that *My Book*," he said when he returned. "It has all the tunes in it I play — maybe a thousand or so." The neatly typed titles were arranged by letter and by category. There were no fewer than seventy waltzes, among them "My Mom," "Dancing with Tears," "Millicent," "Charade," and "Many Happy Returns." The letter "I" began: "It's Like Reaching for the Moon," "I Was Doing All Right," "It Don't Mean a Thing," "It All Depends on You," "I'll See You in My Dreams," "I'll Never Be the Same," and "I'll Remember April." And the letter "S" started out: "Suppertime," "Some Saturday," "Solitaire," "Something," and "Skylark." "I've written some of my own songs and lyrics in the last couple of years. Just off-the-wall stuff. There's one about tennis, a game I love and think of as physical chess. And there's one about Monk, and one about Fred Astaire, and a thing about missionaries called 'Behind the Faith.' " He started to sing softly, "I loved the Matto Grosso/ All the wild Indians in it/ Shooting food with spears/ And shrinking heads." And he went on, "Just imagine their reaction/ When a missionary shows up/ And tries to tell them how to live/ As if they didn't know already."

I told Rowles I had enjoyed the Ben Webster he had put in

"Cottontail." "Ben and I used to play a lot of golf in the fifties, when he lived on the Coast," he said. "We'd tee up, and all these fancy types would be waiting their turn, mumbling under their breath about that big black guy who was holding them up. Ben would have one of his little hats on the back of his head, and he'd stand there before the ball, his big front sticking out, and talk to himself: 'Now, Ben, do it just like when you were in the Masters. Keep your head down, Ben, and not too many Wheaties.' And he'd take a terrific swing — pouf! — and the ball would dribble ten feet up the fairway. We only saw each other on the tees and greens, but we laughed our way around the whole course. Then last summer I got a feeling, a notion. I hadn't seen him for years, and something told me it was time to get over to Copenhagen, where he was living. After I worked the Newport Festival here, I went to Europe with Carmen McRae. She gave me a week off, and I got up to Copenhagen and stayed on Ben's couch. He wasn't in good shape. He was drinking a lot and his legs hurt him, and he was enormous. He never wore anything the whole time but his shorts, and he'd sit in a little swivel chair and talk about 'the Judge,' which is what he called Milt Hinton. Ben was a Jekyll-and-Hyde. He was a sensitive cat, and when he wasn't drinking he was soft-spoken and polite and as gentle as cream. But after two drinks, forget it. Benny Carter was the only man he'd listen to when he was like that. If Ben was roaring around and Carter happened to be there, he'd say, 'Cut it out, Ben. Go sit down and behave yourself,' and Ben would. Ben used to say of Carter, 'There's a man who can bake a cake as light as a feather and whip any man.' One night in Copenhagen, we put Ben to bed — there were always people flowing in and out — and went out to see the sights. I got back late, and there was Ben stretched out on the marble floor like a gingerbread man. I still don't know how I got him into bed again. When I had to leave to meet Carmen, Ben hung out the window, still in his

shorts, his huge shoulders and chest bare, and waved and
waved and kept saying, 'Come back, S.H.,' which is what we
called each other. 'Come back and see me soon.' Ten days
later, the cable came saying that he had got off."

MAY 12TH: GEORGE GERSHWIN — celebrated during his life,
hurrahed in countless books since, and cheered widely last
year on the seventy-fifth anniversary of his birth — has long
been regarded as the premier American musical whiz kid of
the twenties and early thirties. Even that ivied rococo snob Sir
Osbert Sitwell was impressed:

> In these years, too, William [Walton] became friends with
> George Gershwin, the Jazz Phoenix. Though Gershwin was
> not an intimate friend of mine, I knew him and liked him, and
> he would usually come to have luncheon with us when he
> visited London. He possessed a fine racial appearance:
> nobody could have mistaken him for anyone but a Jew. Tall
> and vigorous, his clearly cut face with its handsome ram's
> head, the features prominent, but, as it were, streamlined,
> indicated will power, character, and talent. I have always
> understood that he was the son of immigrants from Russia or
> Germany, and was brought up in the poorest quarter of New
> York: but his manners were notably excellent, his voice was
> pleasant, and though the force of his personality was plain in
> his whole air, he was modest in bearing, and I never noticed
> in him a trace of the arrogance with which he has been
> credited.

But the sands have been shifting, and it is now clear that
Gershwin was but one of four unique American musicians at
that time, the rest being Louis Armstrong, Duke Ellington, and
Bix Beiderbecke. Of the four, Beiderbecke has been the least
understood, and for good reasons. Gershwin, Armstrong, and
Ellington each realized the American dream, but Beiderbecke

died a penniless alcoholic, at the age of twenty-eight, in 1931. He was, save among musicians, who revered him, virtually unknown during his life, having been praised just twice in print. He rebelled against his German-American heritage, and was felt by his sanctimonious family to have betrayed them. And despite his recordings, few of which accurately capture his playing, his fragile beauties vanished with him.

Two new books should at last put him in perspective. The first, *Remembering Bix* (Harper & Row), is a remarkable, unashamedly idolatrous memoir by the painter and writer Ralph Berton, and the second, *Bix: Man and Legend* (Arlington House), by Richard M. Sudhalter and Philip R. Evans, which has been in preparation for seventeen years, is a huge, slow-beating, almost daily record of Beiderbecke's life. Berton's book, like all zealous works, is highly uneven. The prose sometimes comes unglued:

> Soon [the new society] would level the enchanted tower in which [Beiderbecke] still remained stuck like a fly in amber, becalmed in the void of his middle-class mudflat.

The first hundred pages are a plodding and largely superfluous account of his life and times. And Berton's argument that Beiderbecke, who was awe-struck by Stravinsky and Ravel and Debussy, was single-handedly struggling toward a new and unimagined American music seems silly. Beiderbecke, like George Gershwin, who was heading in the same compositional direction from the opposite side of the tracks (listen to the similarities between Beiderbecke's piano pieces and Gershwin's Piano Preludes), was simply ahead of his time; there are countless musicians now who play both jazz and formal music. But the rest of the book is acute and affecting. It is, in the main, a reconstruction of the months in 1924 when Berton, a precocious thirteen-year-old, was hanging around Beiderbecke, whom he had met through his brother, the drummer Vic Berton. Beiderbecke emerges as a classic American bucolic (he was from Davenport, Iowa) who happened to be possessed by music. He rarely bathed or changed his clothes; he was absent-minded; he was a fine natural athlete; he had, like many other diffident people, a laconic sense of humor; he had little will power, and already drank an alarming amount; he loved the possibly unique American pastime of horsing around; and he was wowed by learning and sophistication. But there was no foolishness in the musician. His ear was sharp and retentive, his tone summoned up bells and harvest moons, his improvisations were daring and unique, he was unfailingly inventive, and he was a brutal self-critic. The Sudhalter-Evans book fills out Beiderbecke's misshapen life by chronicling almost every day of his highly productive stay with Paul Whiteman in the late twenties (long thought by the mythmakers to have been a frustrating period for Beiderbecke); his nervous relations with his family (he discovered late in his life that all the recordings he had made with Whiteman and others and mailed proudly home had been stored unopened on a closet shelf); his unfailing kindness to lesser musicians; his restless relations with women; his admiration for Louis Armstrong; and his miserable, needless death. Neither book explains why such a frail vessel contained so much lyricism and originality. But some questions have no answer.

MAY 14TH: BEIDERBECKE would have been seventy-one this year, which is the age, give or take a few years, of the master violinist Joe Venuti, who opened tonight at Michael's Pub with Chuck Folds on piano, Milt Hinton on bass, and Joe Corsello on drums. Indeed, Venuti, a great, squat, square, bustling haystack of a man with a trombone voice and a huge Roman head, appeared in the last ten or so numbers Beiderbecke recorded. (Venuti was ubiquitous in the twenties. He was also in the Whiteman band that gave the première performance of Gershwin's "Rhapsody in Blue," at Aeolian Hall, fifty years ago.) For all that, he is an ageless man, who continues to play with a swing and freshness that few jazz musicians of any age have matched. His style is plunging but assured. He fashions frequent and enormous intervals, wild bent notes, and roaring double stops. His tone can be sweet and gypsylike or rough and hurrying, and his sense of dynamics is a marvel. He loves to double the tempo and play at hat-losing speeds. He is in constant motion onstage, tucking his tiny violin under his massive chin, gazing paternally around the room, tapping his accompanists on the shoulder to tell them when to solo, and rocking from side to side when he gets off a beauty. And he seems to know every tune ever written. They don't make Venutis anymore.

MAY 26TH: DUKE ELLINGTON had no interest in posterity. Nor, except for his lifelong reverence for his mother, who died in the thirties, did he care about the past. (He played his old numbers, his "Mood Indigo"s and "Black and Tan Fantasy"s, only because he was grateful for having admirers to request them.) He was obsessed by the moment, and he sank visibly into whatever he was doing: composing at his piano in his West End Avenue apartment at 4 A.M. (he was rarely there more than a month or two a year); gravely answering silly questions at a midnight press conference after a concert at a small college when he had spent the previous night driving four hundred and fifty miles and would leave early that morning for another engagement; playing for the thousandth time the opening piano solo of "Rockin' in Rhythm," his face bemused and his seesawing right shoulder pumping fresh notes out; eating his customary steak in a small, dingy dressing room at the Rainbow Grill while his tired back was kneaded; calling his New York physician, the late Dr. Arthur C. Logan, from a roadside phone in the middle of Alabama just before dawn about his current ache or cramp (he was a full-time hypochondriac); carefully breaking several packets of sugar into his inevitable Coca-Cola (he gave up drinking, at which he declared himself an undefeated champion, in the forties); or telling a reporter, when he was asked in 1965 how he felt about being denied a special citation by the Pulitzer Prize advisory board, "Fate's being kind to me. Fate doesn't want me to be too famous too young." He considered his newest composition his best, his newest recording his best, his newest blue ruffled shirt his best.

During his fifty-year career, Ellington wrote and recorded thousands of compositions (some of the best watermarked by his brilliant alter ego, Billy Strayhorn), maintained and shepherded his consummate and inordinately expensive orchestra fifty-two weeks a year (it was his palette, his sounding board, his heart), and repeatedly took his music up and down the world. Like Jane Austen, he ignored wars, politics, fashion, and economics; music alone propelled him. He did not regard his music as jazz, nor did he like the word; perhaps he found it limiting, or perhaps, being a conservative man under his celebrated cool, he found it vulgar. Nonetheless, we yaw without handles. His music *was* based squarely on the rhythms and harmonies and structures of jazz. He simply put these familiar components together in a new way. He rebuilt the old harmonies. He scored conventional instruments in mysterious voicings. He hired better-than-average jazz musicians and encouraged them to perfect previously unknown timbres and tones and effects. (Although he made several stars, he tended to avoid hiring stars, for there is only one sun in every firmament.) He used standard devices, such as a soloist playing against a reed background, but he made the background urgent and lyrical. He used improvisation, but in a private, guarded way: His soloists' materials were already semi-improvisations composed by Ellington in their own styles. And he daringly translated into his music much of what he saw and heard — trains and airshafts and twilight and urban hustle and tap-dancers and splendid New York nights. He saw music everywhere, and he spent his life getting it into notes on paper and teaching his musicians to play them as he had first heard them, in his head.

The last ten years of his life were crowded and sometimes confusing. In his middle sixties, he suddenly became an Honored Person. The doctorates, medals, citations, keys to cities, and inductions into distinguished bodies had swelled into an avalanche by the time he died. This outpouring made it appear that he had been appreciated all his life. But he hadn't been. When he was at the height of his powers, between 1939 and 1942, during that magical, superb period when he wrote and recorded with the best band he ever had some forty imperishable concerti, among them "Main Stem," "Jack the Bear," "Ko-Ko," "Blue Serge," "Never No Lament," "What Am I Here For?," "Sepia Panorama," "Bojangles," "Harlem Air Shaft," "Portrait of Bert Williams," and "Jumpin' Punkins," practically no one, outside of musicians, was aware of his momentous doings. But an unavoidable amount of Ellingtonia eventually accumulated, and in the mid-fifties he at last settled into focus. In reaction, he redoubled his efforts, though his best work appeared to have largely been done. A final absorption — composing his "sacred music" and playing it in churches and temples — came to mean more to him (he had read and reread the Bible) than anything he had done earlier, and in at least one exuberant number, "David Danced Before the Lord with All His Might," in which Bunny Briggs danced while the drummer Louis Bellson soloed and several choirs and the band shouted behind, one could understand why.

Ellington himself was as myriad as his music. It is doubtful whether more than a handful of people knew him well, for he did not have the time or the patience to probe the human condition. Indeed, he had, to an almost immodest degree, all the means for graciously keeping the world at bay. These included a beautiful smile, a dapper, Technicolor way with clothes, a courtly manner that became eloquent when he laid on one of his eighteenth-century compliments, a deep, sonorous voice, a limpid and elegant control of language (spoken, that is; his written words sometimes had a purple quality strangely at odds with the rest of him), a handsome mien, and a Nabokovian mastery of parry and thrust. This comes through forcefully in the last chapter of his autobiography, *Music Is My Mistress*. The chapter is set in the form of questions and answers. Thus:

> Q. Can you keep from writing music? Do you write in spite of yourself?
> A. I don't know how strong the chains, cells, and bars are. I've never tried to escape.
> Q. You must get extraordinarily exhausted on your travels. How do you recharge or revitalize?
> A. One must always conserve the agreeable or positive. It is not expedient to try to like or enjoy the negative.
> Q. Is the blues a song of sorrow?
> A. No, it is a song of romantic failure.

But there was another, earthier Ellington behind this façade, an Ellington who had little tolerance for stupidity (it wasted time) and none at all for greed and avarice, particularly if they impinged on artistic matters. Once, when he was traveling in his car in deep night from one job to another with Harry Carney, his baritone saxophonist, friend, and driver of almost fifty years, he went into a monologue on the evils of the recording industry. His voice darkened and became guttural, epithets flashed by, and he handed down harsh and angry indictments. It was startling but immeasurably reassuring.

One Ellington irony is that most of what he gave us is gone.

The great, buoyant band is rudderless, and of his music we have only his surviving compositions and his recordings, the latter several removes from the real thing. And we have our flimsy recollections: Ellington eating at three in the morning at Jilly's and wondering whether the trombonist Vic Dickenson still had his "three tones"; Ellington sitting backstage after an appearance at the Monterey Jazz Festival and listening attentively to an audition by a female singer he had never seen before and probably would never see again (such audiences, when he granted them, had an unmistakably royal air); Ellington fielding one of Johnny Hodges' malicious onstage looks with a warm smile; Ellington effortlessly and unwittingly upstaging his host at his seventieth-birthday party at the White House, and turning what in retrospect seems a politically motivated event into a grand evening; and Ellington on the road with Harry Carney:

> ELLINGTON (*eating a chocolate bar*): After a while, you eat in self-defense. It gets so you hoard little pieces of food against the time when there isn't going to be any.
> CARNEY: I've still got that fried chicken I bought in Orangeburg yesterday in the back.
> ELLINGTON (*laughing*): That's going to taste real good tomorrow, Harry.

And, again, after he and Carney had arrived in a town for a concert five minutes before curtain time and left town five minutes after the last number:

> ELLINGTON: If I'm in any place too long, I start taking on the local accent.

Carney once reminisced: "In the early days, when we traveled through the South we'd go by train. We had two Pullmans — one for the band and one for our trunks and instruments. We generally slept on the train, but if for some

reason we couldn't, we went to a colored hotel or to somebody's house in the colored section — maybe a schoolteacher's
or a doctor's or a minister's — and we ate there, too. Of
course, all the places we played down there, they were happy
to hear the band. The drag was they'd be screaming and
applauding and afterward you'd have to go back across the
tracks. One jump I'll never forget. In 1933, we jumped from
Paris, France, to Dallas, Texas, for a six-week theater tour. In
Europe, we were royalty; in Texas, we were back in the colored
section. It was some adjustment, but we were young and
could take it." Ellington not only took it — he characteristi-
cally transfigured it.

Ellington's life was an unending attempt to get that next
musical brick in place. So, day by day, month by month, year
by year, he slowly built (he composed literally everywhere he
went) a unique, intensely American music in the form of
operas, shows (Broadway and television), suites, songs, concerti, fantasies, tone poems, and religious music. (He once
pointed out that, like all the musicians of his generation, he
was conditioned by the three-minute length of the old 78-r.p.m.
record, with the result that his more ambitious pieces often
gave the impression of being mosaics made up of short
sections.) But, no matter what form it took, it all bore his
unmistakable stamp. Ellington had a singular and lofty vision
of life, and his music steadily reflected it. The music was
compounded of joyousness, sly humor (there were a lot of
sotto-voce black jokes in it), an unquenchable love of beauty
(natural and human), an illuminating intelligence, deep
warmth, and a pioneer directness. Ellington was a supreme
melodist but not a songwriter in the way of Richard Rodgers or
Irving Berlin, and it was generally a surprise when one of his
compositions became popular. A well-known example was
"Concerto for Cootie," which turned into "Do Nothin' Till You
Hear from Me." His music became a complete, free-floating

organism, and when one heard Ellington music in Ellington arrangements played by the Ellington band, it was — good performance or bad — an unparalleled experience.

FRIDAY, JUNE 28TH: WHEN GEORGE WEIN brought his Newport Jazz Festival — long a four-day, seven-concert baby — to New York in 1972, he surveyed his new domain, with its Radio City Music Hall, its stadiums, its great concert halls, and his Napoleonic tendencies locked into place. The first Newport Jazz Festival-New York lasted nine days, involved forty-five events, and employed close to six hundred musicians. Emboldened by a tiny profit, he added one more day in 1973, a dozen events (two in Shea Stadium), and three or four hundred musicians. But then his cuff landed in the soup, and he lost a hundred and fifty thousand dollars. The result is that this year's festival, which opened this evening in Carnegie Hall, will be as long but will have just thirty-five events, played by five hundred or so musicians. The opening affair was also the next-to-last of the fifteen Wein-sponsored repertory concerts during the past six months. These were, with few exceptions, erratic and poorly thought out, and they failed to catch on, either because of their artistic wobbles or because of the public's unreadiness for such semi-scholarly jazz ventures. Tonight's concert attempted to recapture the sound and feeling of Charlie Parker, and it began with four Jay McShann 1941–42 big-band numbers played by a seventeen-piece New York Jazz Repertory orchestra. Three of Parker's most resilient students — Sonny Stitt, Phil Woods, and Charlie McPherson — took the solos. A duplicate of Earl Hines' big band of 1942–44, which had included Parker, Dizzy Gillespie, and Sarah Vaughan, was scheduled next, but Hines' plane was stacked up and the N.Y.J.R. orchestra went into a handful of re-creations of the mid-forties Billy Eckstine band. At one time

and another in his original group, Eckstine had Parker, Gillespie, Fats Navarro, Dexter Gordon, and Art Blakey, but instead
of instrumentals, which would have been invaluable, since the
band was inadequately recorded during its best days, we were
given Eckstine vocals. (His famous baritone voice and rococo
phrasing have wilted, but they still make it plain that he
influenced more singers than he is generally credited with.)
Parker's small-band days were celebrated by Dizzy Gillespie's
group (Earl May on bass, Al Gafa on guitar, Mickey Roker on
drums), with Sonny Stitt sitting in. There were high-flying
passages, mostly from Gillespie in "Be-Bop," "I Can't Get
Started," " 'Round About Midnight," and "Salt Peanuts." (The
original recording of "Salt Peanuts," made with Gillespie,
Parker, and Sid Catlett, will never be surpassed; Catlett, in
exhilarating form, nailed every note and nuance forever in
place.) Then Hines appeared, and, presumably suffering from
jet lag, played two of his pre-Parker big-band numbers and a
Burt Bacharach song. The evening ended with a reworking of
four of Parker's recordings with strings — "Just Friends,"
"Everything Happens to Me," "I'll Remember April," and "If I
Should Lose You." McPherson and Woods split the solos. The
lights went down, and suddenly Parker's great slow blues
record, "Parker's Mood," began. The effect was the reverse of
the one intended: It eclipsed almost everything we had just
heard.

June 29th: Three helpings of the avant-garde and one of
the midi-garde were handed out in Carnegie Hall this afternoon. The first avant-garde group was led by Michal Urbaniak, a Polish violinist and soprano saxophonist, who had been
inspired by listening to Willis Conover's "Voice of America"
programs. In company with his wife (a remarkable soprano
named Urszula Dudziak), an electric pianist, a Fender bassist,

and a drummer, Urbaniak droned through four or five free-jazz selections embellished with electronic echo effects, ostinato figures, and his own romantic solos. Some of the numbers sounded like music on a weak shortwave band. Dewey Redman, a tenor saxophonist and a staunch admirer of Ornette Coleman, played five Colemanlike numbers that had mourning melodic lines, lots of double-time episodes, and interminable solos. One of the numbers, though, began as a slow, old-fashioned blues, a preaching blues, and it was quite beautiful until the tempo doubled. The avant-garde section of the program was rounded out by Norman Connors' Dance of Magic, a sideshow made up of another soprano (Jean Carn), a trumpeter, a tenor saxophonist, several percussionists, and three African dancers. The lights went up and down, Connors, a drummer, swam steadily through his cymbals, the dancers made semaphore motions, Jean Carn pretended she was Sarah Vaughan, and there were John Coltrane tenor solos and the usual ostinato background figures. The midi-garde was represented by the New York Jazz Quartet (Frank Wess, Roland Hanna, Ron Carter, Ben Riley), which played Hanna's "Wistful Moments," Sonny Rollins' "Oleo," and Miles Davis' "All Blues."

Between 1938 and 1947, Barney Josephson ran Café Society Downtown and Café Society Uptown, and they were the best night clubs New York has ever known. They were also revolutionary, for it was Josephson's intent to present integrated entertainment to integrated audiences in the pleasantest possible surroundings. With the help of John Hammond, Josephson launched some famous people, among them Imogene Coca, Josh White, Zero Mostel, Jack Gilford, Nellie Lutcher, Sarah Vaughan, and Lena Horne, and he also furthered the careers of such luminaries as Art Tatum, Billie Holiday, Mildred Bailey, Mary Lou Williams, Teddy Wilson, Red Allen, Joe Turner, Jimmy Savo, and Pete Johnson. All of which brings us to this evening's unbelievable concert in Carnegie Hall. When George Wein was a stripling, he, too, went to the Café Societys, and he, too, has never forgotten. But his attempt tonight to repay Josephson with a "Salute to Café Society" decried almost everything Josephson accomplished. Tables had been set up on a platform along the back of the stage, and behind them was a screen painted with the outlines of a dozen musicians. This tableau had nothing to do with either club, nor did much of the show. Three of the attractions (the Dixie Hummingbirds, a gospel group; Dorothy Donegan, a somewhat overweight pianist who appeared in a see-through body stocking; and the singer Thelma Carpenter) never worked for Josephson at all, while two others (the boogie-woogie and blues pianist Sammy Price and the comedian Timmie Rogers) were incidental members of his original troupe. (Rogers was the m.c. of the evening, and he was crude and unfunny. In the old days, Josephson edited Rogers' materials, weeding out the tasteless jokes and Uncle Tom-isms.) Only Teddy Wilson, who appeared with a sextet that included Vic Dickenson and Doc Cheatham (both Downtown alumni and both in fine form) and Rose Murphy were solid reflections of what Josephson wrought. Josephson and his family were seated onstage throughout the evening. It was, he later reported with his customary politesse, an embarrassing experience.

The first of this year's two midnight jam sessions at Radio City Music Hall did little to dispel the miasmas of the Café Society concert. The session went by in slow motion: A rhythm section of Earl Hines, Larry Ridley, and Freddy Waits started Billy Strayhorn's "Take the A Train" in a medium tempo. They were joined by Budd Johnson on soprano saxophone. Art Farmer, long absent in Austria, played several exquisite choruses on flugelhorn. Teddy Wilson replaced Hines and soloed, as did Ridley. Vic Dickenson appeared, and suddenly one realized that something was wrong: Instead of remaining onstage to laugh and scratch and play inspirational riffs, the earlier horn players had vanished, leaving only soloists backed by rhythm. Richard Davis, a bamboo grove in a stiff breeze, replaced Ridley, and John Blair, the freak violinist, came out. Patti Bown took over from Wilson and soloed, and Dickenson and Budd Johnson reappeared and *did* play riffs, which were largely inaudible. Gary Burton soloed and Art Blakey supplanted Waits. Jimmy Owens took a couple of choruses, and he was followed by the virtuoso trombonist Bill Watrous. Jimmy Smith sat down at an organ at stage right, and John Blair, escaping from backstage, came on again. Smith played sharp, staccato single notes that sounded like pecans bouncing down a staircase. Then Stan Getz ambled into view and played three soft and impassioned choruses. He was joined by Gerry Mulligan, jammer *extraordinaire*. These two went into a rocking duet, and the place began to jump. Sonny Stitt appeared, and the number continued to ascend as Dizzy Gillespie soloed softly as in a morning sunrise, with Getz and Mulligan and Stitt behind him, but Art Blakey erupted, breaking the continuum. Many of the soloists reappeared, and there was an ensemble, an awkward pause, and the tune was carried jerkily forward again by Charlie McPherson, James Spaulding, and the gypsy violinist Elek Bacsik before it simply petered out. What ought to have been a noble hour and ten minutes had gone by.

JUNE 30TH: WE WERE OFFERED eleven pianists tonight in two Carnegie Hall concerts. One suspects that a good many people came to the first program to hear Jess Stacy, who has been in retirement on the Coast for fourteen years. It was an auspicious moment when he stepped onstage (after a witty Dick Wellstood performance and an unconscionably rambling Eddie

Heywood one), for it was the first time he had been back to the hall since that January night in 1938 when, as a part of the celebrated Benny Goodman concert, he took an unscheduled solo toward the end of "Sing, Sing, Sing" that, with its floating, ascending single notes and bell chords, remains one of the peaks of jazz. A little heavier, a little slower (he will be seventy later this summer), but with his handsome Irish face and sleek dark hair intact, he sat down at once and reeled off "How Long Has This Been Going On," "Lover Man," and "I Would Do Anything for You." Some of his fingering was uneven and his harmony went out of whack once (Stacy calls lapses of the kind "meatballs"), but the famous style was all there — the little tremolos, the light, upper-register chords, the inner runs, and the easy, enfolding rhythms. Johnny Guarnieri, another West Coast exile, performed two of his best stride-piano extravaganzas — an accelerando "Stealin' Apples" and a "Tiger Rag" that was faster than a hummingbird's wings. Marian McPartland, who acted as the m. c., offered a striking version of Duke Ellington's "Clothed Woman," with its odd mixture of ragtime and atonality, and Eubie Blake, declaring that he was "happy to be anywhere," played, among other things, a number that he wrote in 1907 called "Kitchen Tom."

The second concert involved Keith Jarrett, McCoy Tyner, and Herbie Hancock. Jarrett is a percussive melodist, but Tyner is a percussive rhapsodist. Hancock played his own "Maiden Voyage" and "Dolphin Dance," mostly on an electric piano surrounded by synthesizers and other gadgets, and he filled the hall with Tinker Bells and Peter Pans. All music — and jazz in particular — abhors cuteness.

JULY 1ST: VERY LITTLE TOOK PLACE at the festival this evening. There were six organists in Carnegie Hall, and from nine until

one Sy Oliver, Tito Puente, and Harry James played for a
pleasant dance at Roseland Ballroom. But from around midnight until 2 A.M. a stunning impromptu session took place at
Bradley's, in the Village. It was what George Wein wishes
would happen at his Radio City parades, and what used to
happen almost nightly on Fifty-second Street. Earlier in the
evening at Bradley's, Stan Getz had sat in with Jimmy Rowles,
who has moved there from the Cookery. Getz had packed up
and was about to leave when Zoot Sims arrived with Sidney,
his soprano saxophone. Getz and Sims are now the best and
almost the last of the crowd of white Lester Young admirers
who appeared in the forties, and a distinct if unspoken rivalry
has grown up between them. In two minutes, they were
unpacked and into a quiet, exploratory "That Old Feeling." A
curving "Gee, Baby Ain't I Good to You" followed, and it was
notable for Getz's high, soft lyricism, for Sims' stop-time
chorus, and for an alert, dodging closing ensemble. Rowles got
up and Horace Silver sat in. The group went into a medium-
fast version of "Tickle Toe," and the tension began to build.
Getz played hard, but Sims, driven by the very limitations of
his soprano saxophone, played just a little harder. The room
filled with thick, arching reed sounds — the creamed, light
tone of Getz and the smoking medium sound of Sims — and
the occasional piano and bass solos were oases. "Gone with
the Wind" went by, there was a rolling blues, a swaying
"All the Things You Are," and a final, crowning fast blues that
ended with Sims and Getz, who was now caroming around in
his highest register, exchanging long stop-time choruses that
were finally gathered into a blazing ensemble. And that was it.
Nobody present mentioned a cutting contest, as friendly
encounters of the sort are known, but Sims, with Sidney his
only weapon, had won.

*

JULY 2ND: IN THE LATE THIRTIES and early forties, Harry James was it. Everybody listened to his virtuoso exhibitions in "The Flight of the Bumble Bee" and "Trumpet Rhapsody," and everybody dug such jazz items as "Night Special" and "Feet Draggin' Blues" and "Back Beat Boogie." But then Dizzy Gillespie came along, Louis Armstrong revived, Roy Eldridge grew famous, a host of other sterling trumpeters bloomed, and everybody forgot Harry James. But there he was tonight at Carnegie Hall, leading a solid, creditable big band through such anthems as "Ciribiribin," "I'm Beginning to See the Light," "Tuxedo Junction," "Caravan," and "Don't Be That Way," and one wondered what all the fuss had been about. He looks much the same and he plays much the same, and he is what he always was — a trumpeter with a circus-band background, a good technique, leather chops, an admiration for Louis Armstrong, and a weakness for melodrama.

The second half of the concert was surprising. Lionel Hampton, Teddy Wilson, Milt Hinton, and Buddy Rich got together and played ten gentlemanly numbers, among them "Avalon," "Moonglow," "Flyin' Home," "The Man I Love," and "Indiana." Hampton didn't hog the solo space or do any of his high jinks; the sometimes somnolent Wilson played with a sharp, affecting authority; Rich did a lot of delicate, feathery things with his wire brushes; Hinton raced the tempo only once or twice. It was delightful music, and the group managed, as Hampton wryly pointed out, to "fill the house without Benny."

Sarah Vaughan has long been revered as a remarkable popular singer, and in many ways she is. She has a voice of operatic dimensions, and she uses it with a breathtaking fluency and control. But she has been dogged most of her career by a love of the rococo, by a tendency to cram ten notes into one syllable when one or two would do; she has an almost uncontrollable desire to dazzle. In this respect, she has much

in common with Art Tatum, and, like Tatum, she is difficult to
categorize; in another time and place Tatum might have
become a classical pianist and Sarah Vaughan a diva. It was
said tonight that the second half of her concert at Avery Fisher
Hall (which I unavoidably missed) was Sarah at her best. She
was controlled and lucid, her admirers contended, and she
sang her materials rather than herself. But she was at her
most florid during the first half of the evening. "I Remember
You" was all melismatics, and so was "I've Got a Crush on
You." There were phrases that took as long to get there as
some of Proust's sentences. "I Cried for You" was less
congested only because it was taken at a fast tempo, and
a closing medley of her old hits (among them "Moonlight
in Vermont," "Street of Dreams," and "My Reverie") was
largely in hand because she allowed herself just one chorus
for each number. She is one of the last grand masters of jazz
baroque.

JULY 3RD: ONE OF THE BEST CONCERTS during last year's festival
was devoted to American popular song, and tonight, at Avery
Fisher Hall, George Wein gave a second edition. A group
composed of Bobby Hackett, Vic Dickenson, Dave McKenna,
Larry Ridley, and Freddy Waits paid homage to four Irving
Berlin songs. They were followed by Jackie Cain and Roy
Kral, who sang four Alec Wilder numbers ("Mimosa and Me,"
"It's So Peaceful in the Country," "Walk Pretty," and "While
We're Young"). Together and separately, they extracted the
specific beauties in each tune, and the only lapse came in the
last tune when Kral went into a jazzy double-time passage that
wiped out the mood of high lyricism Jackie Cain had estab-
lished in her vocal. (She is, it is safe to say, one of the best
singers alive.) The Ruby Braff-George Barnes quartet (Wayne
Wright and Michael Moore round it out) saluted four Fred

Astaire-associated tunes ("I'm Putting All My Eggs in One Basket," "They Can't Take That Away from Me," "Isn't This a Lovely Day," and "Cheek to Cheek") with precision and wit. Since its first public appearance, at the festival last year, the group has become even more telling and streamlined, and it is a pity that it remains practically unknown in New York. Bobby Short, accompanied by Beverly Peer and Dick Sheridan, sang six Ellington or Strayhorn songs, two of which — "Love Like This Can't Last" and "I'm Satisfied" — have long been concealed somewhere in the massive Ellington oeuvre. He sounded nervous. Gerry Mulligan, accompanied by Hank Jones and Jack Six, drifted through Kurt Weill's "Lost in the Stars," "September Song," and "My Ship." He gave way to an unaccompanied Jimmy Rowles, who dropped without ado into a long, intense, inner-ear rendition of Jerome Kern's "Remind Me," topping it off with a short, flowing version of Kern's "Yesterdays." Then Johnny Mathis, a popular singer with a slight, slippered voice, sang six Richard Rodgers tunes, and brought on an unscheduled Mabel Mercer, who, in remarkably good voice, did half a dozen Bart Howard songs alone and with Mathis.

JULY 4TH: THE EARLY CONCERT TONIGHT at Avery Fisher Hall was presciently called "A Cool One." Gerry Mulligan played four workmanlike numbers with a sextet (Jones and Six were along again), and finally came fully to life in a slow, eloquent "Waltzing Matilda." Bill Evans, accompanied by Eddie Gomez and Marty Morell, fell into a reverie that lasted at least an hour. He played seven ballads, and he sounded as if he were wearing blinders. His hands, following each other ceaselessly around, never moved from the middle registers, his tempos never moved from the middle range, and his emotional speed never passed a walk. Then Stan Getz (Al Dailey on piano, Chin

Suzuki on bass, Billy Hart on drums) gave us six selections, including a blues, a bossa nova, "Lover Man," and a Chick Corea number. The Getz who had battled so mightily at Bradley's was nowhere in sight.

JULY 5TH: THE SPIRIT OF DUKE ELLINGTON has been invoked countless times this week, and tonight, in Carnegie Hall, Ben Webster and Eddie Condon were summoned up in an affair titled "Friends of Eddie Condon and Ben Webster." The two men would have been surprised for several reasons — at being lumped together, since their origins, styles, and musical peregrinations were totally dissimilar; at the general disorganization of the concert (Condon, at the very least, was a good musical batman); and at its frequent lassitude (Webster never took a lazy solo). Condon's Friends were divided into two small bands (Bobby Hackett, Wild Bill Davison, Yank Lawson, Bob Wilber, Barney Bigard, Joe Venuti, Vic Dickenson, and Jess Stacy), a duo (Stacy and Bud Freeman), and a vocalist (Maxine Sullivan). There were good moments — Davison's red-cheeked ensemble shouts, Hackett's egret sallies in "Baby Won't You Please Come Home," Dickenson's back-door approach to "Lady Be Good," and Maxine Sullivan's unfailing, tilted-chin ease. But the best came from Stacy, who, relaxed and all together, kept Bud Freeman's mind on his work (Freeman is wont, these days, to read aloud to anyone who will listen from his new autobiography, *You Don't Look Like a Musician*) and played an accompaniment to Bigard's "Mood Indigo" that was a beautiful solo in itself. Ben Webster's Friends came in three groups: a trio (Milt Buckner, Illinois Jacquet, Jo Jones) that was notable for Jones' incomparable brushwork, a flossy Clark Terry sextet, and a tenor-saxophone quartet (Zoot Sims, Buddy Tate, Budd Johnson, Lockjaw Davis) that got so entangled at one point that Davis and

Johnson were unknowingly playing each other's horns. Absent, though, was the one musician in town who perhaps knows and understands Webster's music better than anyone else — Jimmy Rowles.

The second concert of the evening, called "A Hot One," had a predictably hard-handed performance by Freddie Hubbard and three long, dispiriting numbers by McCoy Tyner's quintet. Tyner seemed to cover much the same ground in his solos that he did several days ago, but his work was overlaid by garrulous John Coltrane statements from the tenor saxophonist Azar Lawrence and by a zealous percussionist.

JULY 6TH: BIG-BAND TIME arrived today. The first half of a one-o'clock afternoon concert at Carnegie was played by a Detroit group called the New McKinney's Cotton Pickers, which was led by the alto saxophonist Dave Hutson, an estimable Charlie Parker disciple who used to be visible at sessions around New York nine or ten years ago. The original Cotton Pickers flourished mostly in the Midwest between 1928 and the early thirties, under the tutelage of Don Redman and Benny Carter, and its personnel numbered at various times Claude Jones, Joe Smith, Sidney de Paris, Cuba Austin, Coleman Hawkins, and Rex Stewart. It was a spirited, swinging band and an important early seed ground for Redman's and Carter's arrangements. The new group is made up of Detroit musicians, some of them young, and some old professionals, like the Jimmy Lunceford alumnus Ted Buckner, and Dave Wilborn, who sang and played banjo with the original band. The brass section had bite, the ticking after-beat rhythm section was just right, and the saxophones expertly maneuvered Redman's complicated melodic figures. One only wishes the group had stayed closer to the Cotton Pickers' materials instead of introducing numbers by Lunceford, Fletcher Henderson, and Bessie Smith. Then a New York Jazz Repertory orchestra, alternately led by Sy Oliver and the trombonist Warren Covington, and including such as Joe Newman, Norris Turney, Panama Francis, Eddie Bert, and Haywood Henry, re-created the Tommy Dorsey band of the late thirties and early forties, and held aloft again were Oliver's tweedy arrangements, the Pied Pipers, Dorsey's leaden rhythm section, and those peculiarly stolid solos (Dorsey's nonpareil melodic trombone excepted).

Maynard Ferguson and his former boss, Stan Kenton, shared the first evening concert in Carnegie. Ferguson, a high-note trumpeter, is primarily a showman, and he spent his six numbers shooting off stratospheric bursts and racing around and through his twelve-piece group (mostly brass). It was a spitfire spectacle, and the decibel level, even at the back of the hall, was shattering. Then old Kenton came on with one of his twenty-piece mastodons. He is in his sixties now and has been infirm for several years, and he spent a lot of time onstage sitting down or leaning like a tree against the piano. His music, too, displayed a weary majesty, particularly in a slow version of "Body and Soul," in which the reeds and trombones, both massed and separate, had a cathedral intensity. Such metaphors have always flocked to Kenton; one has long suspected that if the musical visions he has pursued all his life ever crystallized they would take the form of a dirigible or a Frank Lloyd Wright skyscraper.

It was too bad when Count Basie gave up his short-lived small band for another big band twenty-five years ago. He doesn't, as Ellington did, *need* a big band. How fine it would be to hear Basie again with a six- or seven-piece group in which he would have plenty of solo space and his ingenious, rumbling accompanying figures could shine through! But a nickel for such logic, for there he was tonight at the eleven-thirty

Carnegie Hall concert, getting off just ten solo choruses, and the rest of the time leading the band through no fewer than twenty-four numbers, nine of them vehicles for the singing of Joe Williams.

JULY 7TH: THE LAST DAY OF THE FESTIVAL was ethnic. There were three Hudson River ferryboat rides, heavily attended by middle-class whites and enlivened by a Preservation Hall band and The World's Greatest Jazz Band. There were two Carnegie Hall concerts of Latin music that drew stomping, hats-off Puerto Rican crowds. And there was a midnight "Jam Session for Diana" at Radio City Music Hall, in which Diana Ross, accompanied by a squad of jazz musicians, sang eight Billie Holiday numbers as well as some of her own materials for an audience made up largely of young middle-class blacks. She was preceded by three jam-session numbers played by Joe Newman, Urbie Green, Charlie Rouse, Milt Buckner, Charlie Byrd, and Lockjaw Davis, and by a drum battle between Art Blakey, Max Roach, Buddy Rich, and Elvin Jones. This consisted of ever-lengthening solos, which settled down to haymaker exchanges between Rich and Jones. Toward their end, Jones made an immense, kaleidoscopic statement. Then Rich plunged through his alphabet of crescendo-and-diminuendo rolls, bass-drum explosions, double-time multi-drum cascades, and congested, gobbling snare-drum figures. All four drummers played a massive mumbo-jumbo ensemble, and the fray was over. Jones picked Rich up and carried him around like a log, and when he put him on end Rich raised Jones' hand in the air, properly crowning him champion. Diana Ross sang as she did in "Lady Sings the Blues," but the audience was not there to hear her sing Billie Holiday; they were worshiping a symbol who had made it big even in her twenties. They flowed onto the stage during her finale, and when a new jam-session group, made up of Charles Mingus, Joe Farrell, Roland Hanna, and Howard McGhee, began "All the Things You Are," they flowed right out of the hall.

AUGUST 17TH: CHARLIE PARKER died at the age of thirty-four, in 1955, and he was one of the wonders of twentieth-century music. Like his all but interchangeable spiritual brother, Dylan Thomas, who died a year earlier, Parker was labyrinthine. He was a tragic figure who helplessly consumed himself, and at the same time he was a demon who presided gleefully over the skillful wreckage of his life. He was an original and fertile musician who had reached the edge of self-parody. He was an irresistibly attractive man who bit almost every hand that fed him. He lived outside the pale of his own times (he never voted and probably never paid an income tax), yet, though totally apolitical, he indirectly presaged, in his drives and fierce independence, the coming of Malcolm X and Eldridge Cleaver. And he was, albeit succored by a slavish cult, largely unknown during his life.

Parker was born in a Kansas City suburb to a knockabout vaudevillian, Charles Parker, and a local eighteen-year-old, Addie Boyley. When he was eight or nine, his parents moved to Kansas City proper, and when he was eleven his father, who had become a Pullman chef, disappeared from his life. Grammar school went well, but after he had spent three years in high school as a freshman he dropped out, and by the time he was sixteen his life had already begun to accelerate dangerously. He had got married and had a child, he had become a professional, self-taught alto saxophonist, he was a member of the musicians' union, he was a neophyte figure of the teeming Kansas City night world, and he had begun using drugs. When he was seventeen, he went to Chicago and then to New York, where he became a dishwasher in a Harlem restaurant and fell under the sway of its pianist, Art Tatum. He also played in a couple of taxi-dance-hall bands, and jammed tentatively around Harlem. In 1939, he joined Jay McShann's Kansas City band. John Lewis, then a student at the University of New Mexico, has noted the effect that McShann's radio broadcasts had on him: "The alto solos on those broadcasts opened up a whole new world of music for me. I'd known Jay McShann from the time he used to barnstorm in the Southwest . . . but the alto saxophone was new and years ahead of anybody in jazz. He was into a whole new system of sound and time. The emcee didn't announce his name [and] I didn't learn it was Charlie Parker until after the war." The effect of a McShann broadcast on the black members of Charlie Barnet's band was no less electric. Somebody played ten spectacular choruses of "Cherokee" during a McShann broadcast they heard back-stage at the Newark theater where they were working, and when their show was over they rushed to the Savoy, found out who the soloist was by asking McShann to play the tune again, and took Parker out to dinner. Parker quit McShann in 1942, and, after a period of rootlessness and semi-starvation in Harlem, joined Earl Hines' big band, a crazy, warring group made up almost equally of old-line musicians and young beboppers. He then passed briefly through the brilliant, short-lived avant-garde big band led by Billy Eckstine, and by 1945 had settled down with the many small bands he would lead and/or record with until his death.

He had also settled, irreversibly, into the role of Gargantua. He was divorced and remarried when he was twenty-two, and the new marriage was, as far as anyone knows, the last legal liaison of the four he had. He lived in hotels and boarding houses. He had become a baffling and extraordinary drug addict — one who, unlike most addicts, was also a glutton, an alcoholic, and a man of insatiable sexual needs. (He was ingenious, too, for he was never busted, although the police lifted his cabaret card, thus preventing him from working in New York in any place where liquor was served. This medieval form of repression has since been done away with.) He would eat twenty hamburgers in a row, drink sixteen double whiskeys in a couple of hours, and go to bed with two women at once. At times he went berserk, and would throw his saxophone out a hotel window or walk into the ocean in a brand-new suit. His sense of humor was equally askew. Early one morning he took a cab to the trumpeter Kenny Dorham's apartment (Parker spent a good part of his life in cabs, using them as his office, as rendevous, as places to sleep, as compact, mobile fortresses), got Dorham out of bed, asked for a light, and went on his way. In 1947, he collapsed, and spent six months in a state mental hospital in California. (He had gone to the coast the year before with the first bebop band to travel west of the Mississippi; it also included Dizzy Gillespie, Al Haig, Milt Jackson, and Ray Brown.) During his stay in the state hospital, where his astonishing recuperative powers soon became evident, Parker was cared for by a doctor who was also a fan. Ross Russell, Parker's first biographer, has set down the doctor's thoughts about him: "A man living from moment to moment. A man living for the pleasure principle, music, food, sex, drugs, kicks, his personality arrested at an infantile level. A man with almost no feeling of guilt and only the smallest, most atrophied nub of conscience. Except for his music, a potential member of the army of psychopaths supplying the populations of prisons and mental institutions. But with Charlie Parker it was the music factor that makes all the difference. That's really the only reason we're interested in him. The reason we're willing to stop our own lives and clean up his messes. People like Charlie require somebody like that."

Astonishingly, Parker's wild excesses never seemed — at least until the very end of his life — to interfere with his music. It is now agreed among jazz musicians that drugs dislocate and dilute their improvisations; it was just the other way with Parker. The only times he could not function were when he was strung out and needed a fix. His style had matured completely by the time he made his first small-band records, in 1945. (His only earlier recordings, done with McShann, provide brave if fleeting forecasts.) Parker's playing did not, as has often been claimed, spring magically from the virgin soil of the Southwest. Other musicians had a hand in its creation. When he was a teenager, Parker bathed night after night in the unique, rocking music of Kansas City. No matter where he went, he heard the blues — the heavy, sad, windblown blues of Lips Page, Pete Johnson, Joe Turner, Herschel Evans, and Buddy Tate, and the light, rolling, new-coin blues of Count Basie and Lester Young. Young became his idol, and when Parker first went on the road he took along all Young's records and committed his solos to memory. Parker also worked in Kansas City, with Buster Smith, a saxophonist whose style bears, on an album he made ten years ago for Atlantic, a speaking likeness to Parker's early playing. He picked up technical advice from a well-trained local bandleader, Tommy Douglas, and when he got to New York he studied Art Tatum, who unwittingly showed him how to play at lightning speeds, how to rip off sixty-fourth-note arpeggios, and how to devise wholly new harmonies. Some of these early wingings into the blue were disastrous. When he was fifteen or sixteen, he brazened his way onto the bandstand during one of the tough, endless Kansas City jam sessions, and, trying some fancy stuff in a roaring "I Got Rhythm," lost his way. The drummer, Jo Jones, stopped playing, grabbed a cymbal, and threw it on the floor at Parker's feet: He had been "gonged off" the stand. But it is from such embarrassing acorns that Parkers grow.

Parker had a unique tone; no other saxophonist has achieved as *human* a sound. It could be edgy, and even sharp. (He used the hardest and most technically difficult of the reeds.) It could be smooth and big and sombre. It could be soft and buzzing. Unlike most saxophonists of his time, who took their cue from Coleman Hawkins, he used almost no vibrato; when he did, it was only a flutter, a murmur. The blues lived in every room of his style, and he was one of the most striking and affecting blues improvisers we have had. His slow blues had a preaching, admonitory quality. He would begin a solo with a purposely stuttering four-or-five note announcement, pause for effect, repeat the phrase, bending its last note into silence, and then turn the phrase around backward and abruptly slip sidewise into double time, zigzag up the scale, circle around quickly at the top, and plummet down, the notes falling somewhere between silence and sound. (Parker was a master of dynamics and of the dramatic use of silence.) Another pause, and he would begin his second chorus with a dreaming, three-note figure, each of the notes running into the next but each held in prolonged, hymnlike fashion. Taken from an unexpected part of the chord, they would slip out in slow motion. He would shatter this brief spell by inserting two or three short arpeggios, disconnected and broken off, then he would float into a backpedaling half-time and shoot into another climbing-and-falling double-time run, in which he would dart in and out of nearby keys. He would pause, then close the chorus with an amen figure resembling his opening announcement.

But there was another, quite different Parker — the Parker who played extraordinary slow ballads, such as "Embraceable You" and "Don't Blame Me" and "White Christmas." Here he went several steps farther than he did with the blues. He literally dismantled a composer's song and put together a structure ten times as complex. New chords and harmonies appeared, along with new melodic lines that moved high above the unsounded original. (He would, though, always inject pieces of the melody as signposts for the listener.) He could do anything he liked with time, and in his ballads he would lag behind the beat, float easily along on it, or leap ahead of it; he would do things with time that no one had yet thought of and that no one has yet surpassed. His ballads were dense visions, glimpses into an unknown musical dimension. Although they were perfectly structured, they seemed to have no beginnings and no endings; each was simply another of the fragmentary visions that stirred and maddened his mind. Thus his 1948 version of "Embraceable You," which, so brief, so intense, so beautiful, remains one of the monuments of music. Parker's fast thirty-two-bar tunes were meteoric. He used multitudes of notes but never a superfluous one. His runs exploded like light spilling out of an opened doorway. His rhythms had a muscled, chattering density. He crackled and roared.

Parker turned the world of jazz around, and the effects are still felt. One hears him in the work of such saxophonists as Charlie McPherson and Phil Woods and Sonny Stitt and Sonny Criss, and less openly in the playing of Sonny Rollins and John Coltrane and Ornette Coleman. One hears him in almost every guitarist, pianist, trumpeter, bassist, drummer, and trombonist over forty, and he is still audible in the instrumentalists of the present generation, although most of them may not know it. But Parker's legion of admirers have, by and large, missed his main point. He widened the improvisational boundaries of time and harmony and melody, but he did not reject what had come before him, for at bottom he was a conservative, who found new ways of expressing the same things that King Oliver and Louis Armstrong and Sidney Bechet had said earlier. His admirers donned his form and ignored his content. Countless players appeared who used a thousand notes in every chorus, who had hard, smart tones, and who indulged in fancy rhythmic patterns. Yet they sidestepped the emotions that governed all that Parker played. The ironic results were the hard-boppers of the late fifties and the cul-de-sac avant-garde of the early sixties. Fortunately, most of this happened after he was dead, and so he did not suffer the horrors that Lester Young endured during the last decade of his life — the musical claustrophobia of hearing yourself reproduced again and again in the work of almost every young saxophonist and of knowing, at the same time, that your own powers have shrunk to the point where the new men are playing better than you are.

For a time after his release from the hospital in California, Parker cooled it. But the pace of his life quickened again, and by the early fifties it had got completely out of control. He collapsed on the street, he got into horrendous fights, he tried to commit suicide. He slept, when he slept at all, on floors or in bathtubs or in the beds of friends. He cadged drinks, and he panhandled. His horn was usually in hock, and he missed gigs. And at last his playing faltered; he began to imitate himself. One reason was physical; he no longer had the stamina to sustain his brilliant flights. The other was more subtle. Like Jackson Pollock, he felt that he had reached the end of his explorations. The blues and the thirty-two-bar song no longer were challenges. He had, he thought, discovered every chord change, every rhythmic turn, every adventurous harmony. He talked of big orchestral works, and he considered studying with the composers Stefan Wolpe and Edgard Varese. But there were exceptions, and one of them was a concert given in May of 1953 in Massey Music Hall, in Toronto. (A recording of the whole thing has been reissued by Prestige as "The Greatest Jazz Concert Ever.") On hand with Parker, who arrived without a horn and had to borrow one from a music store, were Dizzy Gillespie, Bud Powell, Charles Mingus, and Max Roach. Parker had long had ambivalent feelings about Gillespie. He admired him as a musician, but he resented Gillespie's fame — the story in *Life* about Gillespie and bebop, in which Parker was not even mentioned; the Profile of Gillespie written for *The New Yorker* by Richard O. Boyer. In addition to being a handy businessman, Gillespie is an accessible, kind, enormously funny man. He has long had life in sharp focus. Parker was the opposite — a closed, secret, stormy, misshapen figure who continually barricaded himself behind the put-on (using his deepest voice, he announces on the record that Gillespie's "Salt Peanuts" is by "my worthy constituent"). Gillespie was a challenge that night, and so was the rhythm section, which played with ferocity and precision. Parker responded, and in "Wee," "Hot House," and "Night in Tunisia" he soloed with a fire and a brilliance that match anything in his earlier work.

Parker's death was an inevitable mixture of camp, irony, and melodrama. He had been befriended by the Baroness Pannonica Koenigswarter, a wealthy, intelligent eccentric who lived in the Stanhope Hotel and drove herself to jazz clubs in a silver Rolls Royce. Her apartment had become a salon for musicians. In March of 1955, Parker secured a gig at George Wein's Storyville, in Boston, and on his way out of New York he stopped at the Stanhope to say hello. The Baroness offered Parker a drink. To her astonishment, he refused, and asked for ice water. His ulcer was acting up, and cold water would, he said, quench its fire. Suddenly he started vomiting blood. The Baroness' doctor examined him and said that he would have to go to a hospital at once. He refused, so he was put to bed and given antibiotics. Several days passed, and he seemed to improve. On a Saturday night, he was allowed to sit in the living room and watch Tommy Dorsey's television show. He was in good spirits. During a juggling act involving bricks, which he remembered having seen in Kansas City as a child, he started laughing, choked, and slumped in his chair. He died a minute or two later. At that instant, according to the Baroness, she heard a single huge clap of thunder. The official cause of death was lobar pneumonia, but Parker had simply worn out.

The tenor-saxophonist Buddy Tate had run into Parker not long before. "I first knew him in Kansas City in the thirties, when I was with Andy Kirk," he has said. "He hadn't gotten himself together yet, but he was admiring Buster Smith, who always played Kansas City style. When he first came to New York, we'd hang out together some. He didn't have any work, and nobody knew who he was yet, but he'd be up at Monroe Clark's Uptown House every night. I'd have him over to the house, and my wife would put on a pot, but he would never eat. I tried at the time to get him into Basie's band, but Basie wouldn't have him, and he never forgot that. But he was always nice and kind and soft around me. I never saw him mad at anybody.

"One morning a week before he died, I was walking down Forty-second Street toward Grand Central. It was about ten o'clock, and I'd been on some sort of big-band record date, just playing clarinet. I saw this man way down the sidewalk, and it was Bird. He was hard to miss, with those out-of-style suits that didn't fit, and those big, old, wide granddaddy suspenders he always wore. When I got close, I saw he was all swollen up. I knew he'd been very sick and in the psychiatric part of Bellevue. He said, 'I'm so glad to see you. How you been?'

"I told him fine, and he said, 'Take me for a taste.'

"We went into a bar, and I thought he'd settle down for a few, but he only had two shots. I'd heard he was so strung out he was sleeping on the stand at Birdland and that they'd had to fire him and that he owed the string section that had been backing him up twenty-five hundred dollars, which he didn't have. We talked about an hour. He said he wished people would call him for record dates like the one I'd just been on, and I told him they probably didn't because they'd think he'd want a thousand for a little old forty-two-dollar date, and he said no, he'd do it for free, just to sit in a section again and play with the other guys. Of course, he rarely had his own horn. He'd play anybody's, any old Sears, Roebuck job, so long as it had a mouthpiece and a reed. I told him I was working up at the Savoy, and he said, 'Oh, I been hearing about you, and I'm going up there to listen.' Bird had played with Jay McShann at the Savoy one of the first times he came to New York. But he never came uptown, and I never saw him again."

OCTOBER 9TH: ON THE NIGHT of June 16, 1927, a skinny, audacious seventeen-year-old saxophonist and clarinettist named Harry Carney joined Duke Ellington, Bubber Miley, Tricky Sam Nanton, Rudy Jackson, Wellman Braud, Freddy Guy, and Sonny Greer on the bandstand at Nuttings-on-the-Charles, a ballroom in Waltham, Massachusetts, and began an unrivaled stint with Ellington that lasted forty-seven straight years, that lasted, indeed, until yesterday, when Carney died, at the age of sixty-four. (After Ellington's death, Carney continued with the band, which was taken over by Ellington's son, Mercer.) One of Carney's nicknames was Youth, and his boundless stamina and pleased, persistently unworn face made it appear he would last forever. But, in fact, he died of sheer wear and tear ("The way the band never stops," he once said, "it sometimes seems that the year has at least four hundred days"). And he died, too, of bereavement, for the two men had an extraordinary relationship. They spent more time together than most married people — on bandstands, at rehearsals and recording dates, on trains, ships, and planes, and, since the late forties, driving from gig to gig in Carney's car, with Carney at the wheel and Ellington beside him, snoozing or writing music or "navigating." Carney regarded Ellington as part father,

part older brother, and Ellington treated Carney with affection-
ate jocularity. Carney responded with laughter or feigned
insult, but he lost his cool whenever Ellington, who had his
share of perversity, kept him waiting in the car too long after a
gig. Carney revered his baritone saxophone. It became an
extension of him: When he wasn't playing it he was carrying it
or cleaning it or fitting it out with a new reed. Carney
patterned his playing on Coleman Hawkins early in his life,
and he was not an innovator in the conventional sense. He
was, however, probably the first estimable jazz musician to be
hypnotized by tone, by sound. "I was always crazy about
tone," he said. "All my teachers instilled that in me. It was
always tone. Practice sustaining tones and you develop ear
pitch, you strengthen your lip muscles, you develop diaphragm
breathing, breathing from the stomach. Take a note and
sustain it from pianissimo to double forte and try to keep it
from varying pitch. And do it with and without a vibrato.
That way, you eventually develop an exact tone center."
Carney developed not only an exact tone center but a sound on
his instrument that no other baritone saxophonist has
matched. It could have housed an army. It was Wagnerian
and Churchillian. And it was one of the most beautiful musical
sounds ever devised. Carney became the foundation of the
Ellington band. He made Ellington's minor inventions sound
noble and his noble inventions sound celestial. "Sophisticated
Lady" is still with us because of the way Carney, who came to
own it, played it. Carney, for all his great staying powers,
inclined toward fragility. He said one cool fall day, "I can't
change into turtlenecks and scarves when the weather turns
and then change back, if it warms up, without getting a cold.
The same is true of putting on a hat the first time. And I can't
take a bath without getting a cold unless I go straight to bed
after. But eventually I found out from our travels around the
world that human beings can make wonderful adjustments to

climatic change. If I were just starting out, though, I'd probably suffer, but having done it so long it doesn't bother me." And it didn't. Carney probably missed only a couple of weeks at work during the half century he served his two masters.

OCTOBER 17TH: ELLINGTON'S BEST SIDEMEN became indispensable to him, and he, in turn, became indispensable to them. Few who wandered out on their own made much of a mark, and most of them eventually came back. But Sonny Greer didn't, and the band never really recovered. Greer left in 1951, after thirty years, and none of his replacements — not even the whizzbang Louis Bellson — matched him, because he had virtually grown up with the band and was an organic, root part of it. He knew what kind of backing Johnny Hodges and Cootie Williams and Tricky Sam liked, and he could tell pretty much which way their solos were going, so he could be there waiting at every turn. He knew which cymbals sounded right behind the trombones and what kind of rimshot would send Ben Webster on his way. He knew which rest to fill with a couple of thundering quarter notes on his tomtoms. Greer spoiled Ellington's horn men; they were always surprised when other drummers failed them and they had to stand on their own. Greer had class and a trim sense of melodrama. Enshrined above and behind the band in his gold-and-silver forest of chimes and cymbals and gongs and timpani, he performed an endless in-place ballet, twirling his sticks in the air, snapping his head smartly from side to side, alternating mysterious hooded expressions with diamond smiles, and reaching out to tap a cymbal as if he were knighting it. He was not much of a technician, nor was he much of a soloist, but he could make the Ellington band roar and lilt and rock. His brushwork, which had a wall-to-wall effect, was superb, and he shared Harry Carney's frenzy over tone. He got a unique sound out of a set of drums. It was precise and metallic, yet it had a loose, belling sound, an unhurrying afternoon sound. The magic of Greer's sound was such that any other drummer who sat in on his drums would get a completely different tone. Happily, Greer has emerged from a long spell of retirement and is visible five nights a week at Gregory's in a trio led by Brooks Kerr and including Russell Procope on both alto saxophone and his Barney Bigard clarinet. Greer is in his mid-seventies and is roughly the shape and size of one of his drumsticks, but he is still dapper and stylish and snappy. Tonight, Kerr stocked a set with "Scattin' at the Kit Kat," "Jeep's Blues," "Jumpin' Punkins" (Greer's old specialty), "Mood Indigo," "I Got It Bad," "Don't You know I Care or Don't You Care to Know?," and "Jump for Joy." Greer's sounds and motions — the popping eyes, the mock lunges, the imperious chin, the fly-swatting wrists — suggested that he was once again up there behind the band, making it sound like the savviest musical organization around, which, during much of his tenure, it was.

NOVEMBER 15TH: THE SECOND SEASON of George Wein's New York Jazz Repertory Company is off at Carnegie Hall. The first concert was given a week ago and the second tonight, and both were celebrations of Louis Armstrong. Altogether, forty or so Armstrong-associated tunes were played, in rough chronological order, by various small groups and a big band, all of them augmented from time to time by such Armstrong-embossed soloists as Vic Dickenson, Ruby Braff, Bobby Hackett, Ray Nance, and Taft Jordan. A lot of Armstrong's solos from the twenties and thirties (the end of the thirties was as far as the celebrations went) were transcribed and played in unison and/or harmony by two trumpet sections (one consisted of Mel Davis, Pee Wee Erwin, and Joe Newman, and the other of Bernie Privin, Ernie Royal, Newman, Jimmy Owens, and Doc Cheatham) or as solos by these men. The section work was in the main vigorous and disciplined, although it only approximated Armstrong's ingenious rhythmic calibrations. Two of the facsimile trumpet solos were marvelous — Bernie Privin's rendition of Armstrong's 1932 solo in "That's My Home," in which Privin came within a hair of catching the noble, sorrowing, bending course of Armstrong's statement, and Doc Cheatham's re-creation of Armstrong's brilliant opening muted chorus in his 1930 recording of "Sweethearts on Parade." Armstrong was got at in other ways. There were some delightful film clips, among them Dizzy Gillespie doing an extremely funny takeoff of Armstrong's handling of "I'm Confessin'," and several sequences shot at a Louis Armstrong day at the 1970 Newport Jazz Festival, during which Armstrong reminisced and then sang with Mahalia Jackson, who, before she joined him, got off a version of "Just a Closer Walk with Thee" that was filmed from the wings and afforded an extraordinarily intimate and affecting glimpse of a great performer at work. The guest soloists at Carnegie Hall applauded Armstrong by demonstrating how many first-rate, totally different trumpet players he sent on their way. We had Ruby Braff's spinning locutions in "Someday Sweetheart" and "Rosetta," Bobby Hackett's old-silver look at "Wrap Your Troubles in Dreams" and "Just a Gigolo," and Ray Nance's beautiful obbligatos behind the singer Carrie Smith in "You've Been a Good Old Wagon" and "St. Louis Blues." And to tamp it all down we heard two early Armstrong recordings — King Oliver's 1923 "Chimes in Blues," in which he took his first recorded solo, and his 1926 "Heebie Jeebies," in which he sings what is supposed to be the first recorded scat vocal.

There were soft spots in the two evenings, and the concerts could easily have been compressed into a single, streamlined affair. (Taft Jordan's imitations of Louis Armstrong were tedious when he first did them, with Chick Webb, in the thirties, and they were tedious tonight.) Yet the concerts were the most successful the New York Jazz Repertory Company has given. They brought to the fore attractive and even brilliant copies of superb Armstrong recordings that had long ago sunk out of sight and that were completely unknown to a good many in the audience. And the musicians did their archeological work with an enthusiasm and intelligence that should send us all, neophytes or not, back to the originals. Which is what a jazz repertory company should be all about.

NOVEMBER 25TH: AFTER SEVERAL FAREWELL PERFORMANCES in this country and abroad, the Modern Jazz Quartet gave its closing-out, all-sales-final concert tonight in Avery Fisher Hall. The group's previous farewell concert was given in Sydney, Australia, on July 16, and it was, as far as the group was concerned, just that. Then it was pointed out to them recently by Harold Leventhal, who produced tonight's concert, that since the quartet had started in New York it should finish in New York, and the men reluctantly agreed. Several days before the concert, John Lewis talked about the dissolution of the quartet, which had been together steadily for twenty years (it played its first gig in 1952, though) and had not had a personnel change for nineteen, which may be a record for longevity in Western music, give or take the Budapest String Quartet and the Trio de Trieste. Lewis said, "An enormous amount of fatigue had set in. We hadn't had any vacation in three years, and the road was getting to us. We were becoming too old for all those 5 A.M.s at airports. And Milt Jackson was getting restless. So we had a meeting in April, before we left for a tour of Japan, and we agreed to break up. There was never any question of hiring replacements, and we couldn't have a quartet with only two or three people. So there

was nothing for it but to agree. I think there were some little
regrets among the members toward the end, but I can't be
sure. I didn't feel that way myself. As a group, the quartet had
surpassed many goals set by other groups, and it had surpassed most of the goals it had set for itself. It's hard to
evaluate the group's contributions over-all, but specifically it's
not. There's no other vibraharpist in the world like Milt. He's
the most brilliant. What Connie Kay did was never that new,
but it was *always* platinum. And Percy Heath developed so
tremendously. He developed the most of us all. I enjoy
listening to myself as a pianist, and if I had only been the piano
player in the group and not had to conduct rehearsals and
write and arrange music I would have enjoyed playing much
more. My wife, Mirjana, plays quartet records now when I'm
in, and I see for the first time how good the group played. But
we were so busy we never thought of *how* we were doing it.
We had the luxury of playing together for so long that
everyone always knew what everyone else was going to do.
When the quartet was together, we were always wound up
musically, and now we're trying to get used to being unwound.
I still have the feeling I'm about to go out on the road again,
and I think all the time about how much I can get done here
before I do. All four of us are big gossips, and I think we miss
our rehearsals, where we used to socialize. So we've taken to
calling each other on the phone to talk, and there has even
been some visiting. But I think we were right to break up
when we did. When we started rehearsing for this concert we
hadn't played together for over four months, and I expected, I
wanted, our playing together again to feel strange and new.
But it didn't."

When the quartet started out, it gave the impression —
largely because of its occasional use of such devices as rondos
and fugues — that it had egghead leanings. But it became
clear soon enough that the group, instead of being revolution-

ary, had taken on the great task of distilling and conserving the best of what was going on around it and the best of what had gone before. It also revealed a strong distaste for musical cant, and it immediately countered through its own superb example all the dreary practices that had begun to appear in jazz (the long, windy solos, the insane tempos, the showoff rhythms, and the vacuous ensembles). By 1960, Lewis' graceful songs and the way the quartet played them had brought a new, high lyricism into jazz as well as an unprecedented degree of elegance and precision. The quartet seemed to do everything right. It dressed beautifully, comported itself onstage with dignity and sangfroid, and played consummately. And the higher its standards became the harder it swung. But unalterable excellence tends to unnerve even the most appreciative, and the longer the quartet was around the more it was said that it didn't swing, that it was effete, that it played too much fancy music, that it was lightweight — that, in short, it was a bore. Nonsense. The quartet managed nothing less than to preserve, enhance, and carry forward the lyrical and emotional heart of jazz, just as Ellington and Basie and Armstrong had done before. And it did this with an intelligence and style and wit that made its appearances occasions for recharging and restoring the spirit.

The concert tonight was like no other Modern Jazz Quartet concert I can recall. It was loose and a little wild. The solos were longer than usual, and they had a singular urgency and brilliance. The exchanges and counterpoint between Lewis and Jackson had an extraordinary gaiety and density and excitement. Kay was supercharged and (for him) quite loud, and Jackson was breathtaking throughout. Heath took a couple of extended solos, and his ensemble playing (almost inaudible the first half of the evening) was without flaw. Every facet of the quartet was on view — a host of blues, a waltz, a Spanish piece, "Summertime," a North African piece, "God

Rest Ye Merry Gentlemen," a couple of program pieces,
" 'Round Midnight," and a "Night in Tunisia" with a Jackson
break that lifted his birdlike self right off the floor.

The members of the quartet are commoners again. John
Lewis is teaching a couple of courses at City College, and will
record on his own for Columbia. Jackson is working as a
single. Kay has been recording with Paul Desmond. And
Heath, in between gigs with his brother Jimmy, has been
fishing down at Montauk. During its last year, he reports, the
quartet grossed more money than it ever had before. You can't
quit any cooler than that.

DECEMBER 13TH: A CLASSIC SINGER, Anita Ellis, has come out of
hiding after twelve years (two of them spent rehearsing) and is
appearing with the uncanny Ellis Larkins at the Bird Cage, in
Michael's Pub. She is quietly famous on two counts: She once
dubbed in the singing voices of Rita Hayworth and Vera Ellen,
and she is regarded by her admirers, one of whom is Eileen
Farrell, as possibly the best singer of her kind alive, albeit one
of the shyest and least confident. (Her arms hang little-girl
loose in front of her when she sings, and she keeps her hands
desperately clasped, and in between numbers she sometimes
tells her listeners what agony it is to stand in front of them and
perform.) Yet she is remarkably forceful and dramatic. She
has a handsome, wide-cheeked face and a halo of short, dark
hair, and the way she moves her head, opens and closes her
eyes, and aims her chin gives just the right emphasis to each
word. She is a highly skilled technician, whose intervals are
elegantly and even joyously maneuvered, and her pitch sails
down the center of each note. Her daring sense of dynamics
allows her to move with utter assurance from a high, wiry
phrase in "Porgy" to a dying shout. Her songs are hand-chosen — such standbys as "Porgy" and "Prelude to a Kiss" and

"Someone to Watch Over Me" as well as such out-of-the-way numbers as Harold Arlen's "Riding on the Moon" and "I Wonder What Became of Me," Frank Loesser's "Spring Will Be a Little Late This Year," Willard Robison's "The Four Walls and One Dirty Window Blues," and a Henry Souvaine-Johnny Mercer song from the early thirties called "Wouldja for a Big Red Apple?"

Anita Ellis in the Bird Cage is a special New York experience, once common in the city. The room is small and high-ceilinged and filled with plants, and it has glass walls that let in the night city and that seem, too, to let in the old loves and worlds and times that she tells us about so beautifully.

Ellis Larkins is accompanying Anita Ellis with such humor and imagination and sympathy that he is, in truth, a collaborator.

1975

JANUARY 30TH: THE NEXT SEVERAL DAYS will be spent celebrating Mabel Mercer's seventy-fifth birthday, which falls on February 3 and will be marked by a party on the St. Regis Roof. This afternoon, Alec Wilder talked about her. He has known her since she settled here in 1941, he has written many songs for her ("It's So Peaceful in the Country" is one), and he has come to think of her as an indispensable mother-sister-aunt figure. "I can't, I'm not sorry to say, go to Mabel's birthday party," he said. "That sort of event is just too much for me, and anyway I'm due on Grand Cayman Island in a couple of days. But I've written Mabel a letter putting it on the line. telling her *exactly* what she means to me. And I've sent her a plant, one that's in bloom now and that she can put in the ground later at her place near Chatham, upstate. When I first met her, at Tony's, on West Fifty-second Street, it was instant acceptance on my part, which is very rare, since meeting strangers has always been a threat to me. Indeed, she soon had complete control over me. I could be obstreperous in my drinking days, and if I came into Tony's noisy or wobbly, she'd give me one look and I'd find myself reproved and behaving correctly. It wasn't an angry or disapproving look; it was just a very elegant *look*. Or if I came in depressed she'd sense it immediately and sing a whole set of my songs. And I'd find myself cheered up. But then Mabel is a healer. I've gone up to visit her in the country a perfect wreck and in two days felt marvelous. It isn't that she *does* anything, that there is any laying on of hands or such. She just putters around her house, and cooks, and feeds her animals. But there is some quality, some corrective force, in her very presence. Little by little, she's improved her place. She's managed to pay off the mortgage, and when she's had a few extra pennies she's added a bathroom or a porch. So when she can't sing at all anymore she'll have her house to live in, and that's a blessing. Even better would be if some of her rich admirers — and she's had dozens — got together and set up an anonymous trust fund. But, knowing the rich — or, rather, *not* knowing the rich, despite decades of trying — that's highly unlikely.

"Mabel's singing isn't like any singing I've ever heard before. It isn't jazz singing and it isn't pop singing and it isn't classical singing. It's wholly original. Sometimes, over the years, she's sung songs I haven't particularly cared for, but I've always found myself listening. She invariably involves you: You catch her enthusiasm for certain lines she sings, and you listen for certain of her technical devices, like her changing of values on particular notes each time she sings the same song. From the very first, there was a strong feeling of normality in the rooms Mabel sang in. You'd look up and down and see an extraordinary cross-section — college professors, polite-society types, lawyers, Ivy League kids, singers and musicians, people, like Dave Garroway, who'd come bag and baggage straight from the station or airport. She'd hold whatever room she was in in her hand, and do it with sheer dignity. She never said anything when she started a set or when it was over. She sat down and sang and got out. If there was talking or laughing, she stopped singing. She didn't look at anyone, she didn't say anything.

She just stopped and waited. And when the racket subsided she started to sing again.

"In those days, we laughed a lot. We even laughed at *outré* things, as long as they had style. Mabel has a genuine sense of humor: not only does she laugh at jokes but she laughs at herself. She used to sing 'Porgy' a lot, and one night I noticed that, even with her marvelous diction, the words 'I've got my man' were coming out sounding like 'My goat my man.' When I told her, instead of asking me to go jump, as most singers would have, she laughed so hard she almost fell on the floor."

FEBRUARY 3RD: I WAS ASSIGNED at Mabel Mercer's birthday party to a table built for ten but seating sixteen. (Four hundred people bought tickets at twenty-five dollars a head, plus liquor.) Elbows perforce were pinioned, and the roast beef with potatoes and string beans was served in flying-wedge fashion. But it took a long time for the food to arrive, and before it did a white-haired, pink-faced Mabel Mercer admirer who attends all her openings and who was seated on my left passed me a note, which read:

> This reminds me of a dinner party on the Poseidon, except in the movie I seem to recall they got something to eat. Soon we will be sinking fast; the starboard lifeboats are being manned; the ship's orchestra is playing "Up a Lazy River." At 10:19 P.M., goodbye all. Vincent Astor, who used to own this hotel, would never have permitted this. Nor would he have allowed us to sit here and inhale Earl Wilson's cigar smoke (he's sitting behind us).

A short time later, Mabel Mercer arrived, and after the standing ovation a long-faced man sitting on my other side introduced himself — or re-introduced himself, for he, too, was an indefatigable Ellington follower — as Edmund Anderson and told me the following, which is the sort of almost useless information that Boswell kept track of and rightly so: that the St. Regis Roof opened in 1936, that it was given its Viennese look by the designer Joseph Urban, who had worked for Ziegfeld, that it was first called the Viennese Roof as a result, and that on the night it opened Jacques Frey and his orchestra were dressed in Viennese costumes and powdered wigs. At ten-forty-five, Donald Smith, who helped organize the birthday party, announced that the festivities would start in eight minutes. But they didn't, so Anderson went on to say that in 1938 he and Vernon Duke put on a concert on the Viennese Roof that was played by six musicians from Duke Ellington's band and fourteen musicians from the New York Philharmonic. It was called a High-Low Concert, the High being the longhair music and the Low the Ellington. Tickets were only five dollars, he added, but nobody came. Forty-two minutes after Smith's announcement, the city gave Mabel Mercer an award, and the evening officially began. Sylvia Syms and Cy Coleman sang his "The Best Is Yet to Come." Sylvia Syms was in superb voice. Jimmie Daniels, who is in his seventies, delivered "What Is This Thing Called Love?," and was followed by Thelma Carpenter, who belted out "I Can't Give You Anything but Love." Mary Lou Williams did a long, multi-tempoed "My Funny Valentine." Ruth Warrick performed, and Bobby Short did Cole Porter's "Looking at You." George Wein intoned "Thanks a Million," and Hugh Shannon got off a splendid "Down in the Depths on the Ninetieth Floor." Marian Seldes read Alec Wilder's letter to Mabel Mercer and messages from Leonard Bernstein and "Francis Albert," who sent two giant balloons in his stead. Ronny Whyte and Travis Hudson wound up the guest performances, and the manager of the hotel announced that the St. Regis Room, where Mabel Mercer has sung these past years, would henceforth be known as the Mabel Mercer Room. Mabel Mercer, resplendent in a gold-and-brown brocade gown that she made herself, came forward from her table, some of whose occupants were Mr. and Mrs. Roy Wilkins; Will Craik, a neighbor in the country; her two sisters; the singer Helen Merrill; and Charles Bourgeois, who has done more than anyone else to preserve whatever elegance is left in New York nightlife. She cut a giant cake surmounted by a replica of the chair she sits in when she performs, and then she sat down in her real chair and started to sing, and it was a wonderful time. Her voice suddenly had wings, and by the time she reached her fourteenth song, a vibrant and affecting version of Stephen Sondheim's remarkable "Send in the Clowns," the audience was rapt. She sang Alec Wilder's "While We're Young," and she closed with a rollicking "They All Fall in Love." The ovation was very long, and throughout she kept laughing and ducking her head and waving.

FEBRUARY 4TH: I TALKED WITH MABEL MERCER this afternoon, and the setting could not have been bettered by Oliver Smith, who, indeed, was at the party, along with such other notables as Alexis Smith, Arlene Francis, Hermione Gingold, and Anita Ellis. It was a friend's sixteenth-floor apartment, which looks out over the Hudson and is on the floor below the adjoining penthouses occupied in the thirties by George and Ira Gershwin. Miss Mercer was rehearsing with her accompanist, Jimmy Lyon, for her opening tonight in the Mabel Mercer Room and after she had done half a dozen songs she rested on a sofa. "The party was an honor, of course," she said. "I've happened into a lot of people's lives, and they came to say hello. And I love to have my friends love me. But I couldn't wait until it was over; the whole thing embarrassed me so. It's incredible, ridiculous to be seventy-five. It's a dream. When I was young, we used to think anyone who was that age was — well, senile. But I feel marvelous, I feel just the way I've felt all my life, give or take some arthritis pains. Heavens! I thought I'd be rusting away somewhere by this time. There are good things about getting so old: You can make mistakes and no one blames you, because they don't listen to the trills and tra-las the way they used to. So the thrush — remember when they called singers thrushes? — is croaking her way through. Even though what I do has become almost a form of reciting, every once in a while the voice comes back and surprises me, and I think, Oh, God, I didn't know I still had that!

"Nightlife is very different now from what it was in the old days. It was far more lavish then, both on the Continent and over here. Flowers and champagne flowed from the audience to the performers. And it had terrific friendliness. The same people came to Tony's night after night, and, of course, we worked until four in the morning. Sometimes the place would empty out completely at two, and then suddenly at three they'd come piling in and we'd be jammed for the last show. Then we'd go on to an after-hours place, many of which were quite respectable, with food and a decent piano. People would get up and perform. Performers love to perform for other performers. They know what you're doing, and they're the best audience you can have.

"Retire? Nonsense! How would I pay my taxes and make improvements on my house? If I stopped singing, everything would probably stop and I wouldn't be able to watch the trees grow that I'm always planting up in the country. Years ago, I collected acacia seeds in Central Park and planted them at the house, and now the trees are enormous. And I've planted Christmas trees. The first few years, I could reach up and put a star on top, and the next few years I'd get a faceful of snow when I tried, and now I'd have to jump up to the sky to reach their tops. If I don't get to see the next century in, it would be nice to sit on a cloud and watch what's going on."

*

MARCH 15TH: A COUPLE OF THINGS had become clear by the time the New York Jazz Repertory Company and The National Jazz Ensemble wound up their first seasons last year. One was that there appeared to be no single way to reproduce the jazz of the past — that, indeed, practically anything went as long as the spirit and some of the letter of the original remained intact. The other was something of a surprise. The two companies found themselves engaged in a remedial task they had not really envisioned — that of dispelling the ignorance most Americans have about their own best music. People tend to get locked into the music they grow up on; whatever comes later is threatening and foreign, and whatever came before is quaint. This insularity was particularly true of the first rock generation, which, with unwise revolutionary fervor, slammed the door on the past. But jazz musicians like Miles Davis and Buddy Rich and Joe Zawinul and Gil Evans have chipped away at the kids' armor, and, from all reports, they are beginning to pay attention. They have even had the welcome and disconcerting experience of listening to a 1927 Louis Armstrong Hot Seven for the first time and discovering that all "new" musics have to be broken in. Which is exactly where the repertory orchestras fit. By playing Jelly Roll Morton and Armstrong and early Ellington freshly and intelligently, they lift the music from the tombs of the twenties and thirties recordings. What had sounded ancient and strange so long on the old 78 r.p.m.s becomes brand-new again.

The New York Jazz Repertory Company started its second season last fall, but Chuck Israels' National Jazz Ensemble, ensconced this year at the New School, gave its first concert last week and its second tonight. The band is again sixteen strong, and there are more new faces than old. Among these are Jimmy Knepper and the towering, venerable lead trumpeter Jimmy Maxwell; two estimable young trumpeters, Danny Hayes and Tom Harrell; and Greg Herbert, an alto saxophonist who is building absorbing superstructures on Charlie Parker's foundation. Back again are the pianist Benny Aronov, the generally sufficient drummer Bill Goodwin, and the tenor saxophonist Sal Nistico. Last year, Israels opened several concerts with an ingenious, unison transcription for full band of Louis Armstrong's solo on his 1927 "Struttin' with Some Barbecue." He did so last week, but two choruses had been added — the contrapuntal interpretation of Armstrong's record by Lee Konitz and Marshall Brown, and a close approximation, delivered with gusto by Maxwell, of Armstrong's closing solo in his 1938 big-band version of the tune. From there we jumped twenty-five years to Hall Overton's arrangement of Thelonious Monk's "I Mean You." It was valuable for Herbert's well-constructed solo and for Danny Hayes' very long one. His frequent runs somewhat resemble Dizzy Gillespie's, but beyond that he has his own big tone and a fine sense of design and order. Herbie Hancock's pastel arrangement of his "Dolphin Dance" was repeated from last year, as was "Lester Leaps In," which was carried forward with fervor by Nistico and the tenor saxophonist Dennis Anderson. Both numbers had exemplary solos from Aronov. There were more original flourishes from Hayes on Dave Berger's "Twelve Tone Blues," and Knepper and Nistico were brilliant on "Donna Lee," Charlie Parker's wizard rebuilding of "Indiana." There were worthy re-creations of Ellington's "Rockin' in Rhythm," which was done last year, too, and of his 1929 arrangement of "Hot Feet," as well as of Count Basie's 1938 "Every Tub," in which Maxwell applauded Harry Edison's swaggering, ballooning bridge. "Sweet Emma," a gospel blues by Nat Adderley that was arranged by Bob Freedman in the manner of Ray Charles' small band of the fifties, had good solos by Hayes, Nistico, and Aronov. Folded into the evening about midway were four numbers built around Jim Hall, who was a guest. First came a sparkling "St. Thomas," done with the rhythm section, then Hall's big-band arrangements of "It's Easy to Remember" and his own blues "Careful," and, last and most important, an a-cappella solo by Hall on his new custom-built acoustic guitar. The solo was played without a microphone and was a long chordal meditation somewhat in the style of the pianist Keith Jarrett. In Hall's hands, the instrument was shimmering and delicate, and its sound appeared to reach every recess in the place. Perhaps the days of the electric guitar in jazz are at last numbered.

The concert tonight got off to an uneven start. The first number was Ellington's "Harlem Air Shaft," an organic, multilayered blues (with a bridge), in which the solos grow like branches from the dense ensemble. It is a kaleidoscopic little concerto, and the original recording starts at a deceptive amble, which is abruptly upset a third of the way through by three explosive "Bugle Call Rag" saxophone-section breaks, which are virtually catapulted from the ensemble by Sonny Greer's driving, crescendo snare drumming, and are then followed by Cootie Williams' three climactic trumpet statements. For some reason, drummer Bill Goodwin sat on his sticks during the breaks, which were capped bravely by Maxwell/Williams, and all the air went out of the piece. Horace Silver's "Room 608" had teeming warmup solos by Aronov and Harrell and Nistico, but Gil Evans' arrangement of "Moon Dreams," done in the late forties for Miles Davis' Nonet, never got around its narcissism. A light, speedy version of Dizzy Gillespie's "Con Alma" was played by Greg Herbert and Danny Hayes, who both *think* when they solo. Then the saxophone section, abetted by the rhythm section (just barely; the rhythm section never quite fell into place tonight), worked its way through Lee Konitz's "Subconscious-Lee," an I-can-do-it-better-than-Charlie-Parker reworking of "What Is This Thing Called Love?". The first half of the concert was closed by three numbers constructed around Roy Eldridge, who was in measured, elder-statesman fettle. He did his old Artie Shaw display number "Little Jazz," a long and beautiful slow reading of "Body and Soul" that was enlivened by the band's playing a transcription of the startling double-time passage he recorded on the same tune in 1938 with Chu Berry and Sid Catlett, and a scrambling version of Louis Armstrong's very fast rendition of "Chinatown."

The second part of the evening was made up principally of two avant-garde compositions. The first, a Tom Pierson arrangement of Wayne Shorter's 1967 "Nefertiti," was commissioned by Israels and highly praised by him — an unfailing way to put an audience on the qui vive. It was, Israels explained, full of tensions, and he was right. It is a nervous, impassioned, declamatory number, in which Nistico soloed at great length at both fast and slow speeds while the rest of the band contributed a variety of contrapuntal figures. The other modernistic effort was by Israels, and it was far more accessible. Called "Skipping Tune," because of the intervals in its attractive melody, it is based on a harmless trick: The soloists are restricted in their improvisations to the major and Lydian scales. The rest of the evening was taken up by Aronov and the ensemble trading Bix Beiderbecke's Gallicisms in a gentle and effective rendering of his piano piece "In a Mist"; a somewhat flip version of Jelly Roll Morton's "Black Bottom Stomp"; and, as encores, two repeats from last week — "Hot Feet" and "Struttin' with Some Barbecue."

It is plain, with the début of the National Jazz Ensemble, that New York's two jazz repertory companies are again pursuing their subjects in very different ways. The New York Jazz Repertory Company is offering in-depth, one-subject concerts, which have included studies of Louis Armstrong, Count Basie, Miles Davis, Jelly Roll Morton, George Russell, and Bix Beiderbecke. These have been pasted together ingeniously out of original recordings, film clips, appropriate alumni, and the usual re-creations and transcriptions. This, in effect, is a graduate-seminar approach, while the National Jazz Ensemble is using the undergraduate survey approach. (An obviously oversimplified comparison: Some of the N.J.E.'s pieces are extremely complex and some of the N.Y.J.R.C.'s pieces are kindergarten stuff.) Thus, the National Jazz Ensemble's two concerts have already refashioned Jelly Roll Morton, Louis Armstrong, early and classic Duke Ellington, classic Count Basie, bebop, hard bop, Thelonious Monk, Gil Evans, Miles Davis, and the arranging and composing of such young and unknown musicians as Dave Berger and Tom Pierson. Such a survey has unfailing appeal, and it was obvious at both concerts: Someone was invariably pleased by something — Ellington's dicty 1929 rhythms, Thelonious Monk's wrought-iron melodic lines, Gil Evans' sweeping harmonic robes. On the other hand, the New York Jazz Repertory Company seminars are, except to older, more knowledgeable jazz students, immediately forbidding. If a potential ticket buyer has never heard Morton or Beiderbecke or George Russell, the prospect of an entire evening of Morton or Beiderbecke or Russell may scare him away. For all their dissimilarities, the two repertory companies are in nonsensical competition. They subsist on some of the same fundings; they are producing basically the same music, albeit in different packages; and they are aiming at the same audiences. A suggestion: Let the two companies, short of merging, organize their scheduling so that the National Jazz Ensemble's survey course takes up the first half of next season and the New York Jazz Repertory Company's seminar course finishes it out. That way, a lot of Mus.D.s could be handed out a year from now.

MARCH 20TH: THE FIRST GREAT GATHERING of American popular singers happened between the late thirties and the early forties. Suddenly there they all were — on Fifty-second Street

and at the Blue Angel and the Village Vanguard and the Café
Societys and the Paramount, as well as on records and the
radio and in the movies. Two pecking orders, each with its
own devices and accoutrements, immediately fell into place.
In the first were such megaliths as Bing Crosby and Frank
Sinatra and Dinah Shore and Doris Day, and in the second
such quiet masters as Mabel Mercer and Billie Holiday and
Mildred Bailey and Johnny Mercer. Of the second, one of the
best and most durable was and is Helen Humes, who, it is now
plain, bears easy comparison with Mildred Bailey and Billie
Holiday. But Bailey and Holiday and most of their compeers
are dead or retired or poking around in the ruins of their
voices, while Helen Humes, freshly embarked on a long
engagement at Barney Josephson's Cookery, is singing better
than ever. That is a sufficient kindness, but she is also
invaluably sharing with us a style of singing and of performing
that is almost gone. She came out of the South of sixty years
ago, mostly self-taught and with the sounds and majesties in
her head of horn players like Dickie Wells and Jonah Jones and
of singers like Bessie Smith, whom she heard twice at the
Lincoln Theater in Louisville. It was a kind of singing that we
can barely imagine learning now. It preceded the microphone
and by necessity demanded a strong voice, Ciceronian diction,
and an outsize presence. The singer was *alone* onstage. It was
also a kind of singing that relied on embellishment and
improvisation, on an adroit use of dynamics, and on rhythmic
inventiveness. The singer jazzed his songs. Only a handful of
such singers are left, and none is better than Helen Humes.

Tonight as is his wont, Barney Josephson dimmed the lights
in the Cookery fifteen minutes before his performers were to
go on. Conversation ebbed, and that mysterious, mutually
bracing tension that exists between performers and their
audiences began. Helen Humes was seated at a table near the
front of the room, where she could greet friends and well-

wishers. She was wearing a sleeveless black gown whose halter top was emblazoned with sequins and a lot of gold brocade, and she had a white sweater around her shoulders. She is a pretty woman. Her features are regular and arranged just so, and her lifted chin italicizes them. She wears her hair in a short, dark cloud, which is lighted from beneath by her smile. Her hands and feet are small, though the rest of her is mapped out in expansive meadows, sharp drops, and roomy valleys. But extra pounds are to singers what nimble feet are to boxers; they add depth and range to the attack. Unlike many Southerners, Helen Humes has a loquacity that is frequently tempered by thought. "It's so fine to be working for Barney again," she said just after the lights had gone down. "He's brought me to New York for the first long gig I've had here since I worked for him thirty-two years ago, at Café Society Downtown. It was 1942, and I had just left Count Basie. I was tired and my health was getting bad. I was nervous with all that bus travel, so I went home to Louisville to sit around and rest. Then John Hammond called me and had me go to New York to work at Café Society, where I stayed into 1943. Then I went up to Fifty-second Street, I think at the Three Deuces, and then I was down at the Village Vanguard with Eddie Heywood. While I was there, Derby time came around and I wanted to be South, so I got Pearl Bailey to take my place for a few weeks. Well, I haven't returned to New York for any time until now, and Pearl went on from the Vanguard to the Blue Angel to Lord knows where, and she hasn't looked back since. Me, I went out to California with Connie Berry, who was a piano player. I did five seasons with Jazz at the Philharmonic. I worked in Hawaii in 1951, and in 1956 I went to Australia with Red Norvo. I went back to Australia in 1962 and again in 1964, when I stayed ten months and they tried to make me a citizen. I traveled to Europe my first time in 1962 with a raft of blues singers like Brownie

McGhee and Sonny Terry and T-Bone Walker and Memphis
Slim, and in 1967 I was at Shelly's Mannehole and Redd Foxx's
club, in Los Angeles. But Mama got sick and I went home.
When she died, not long after, I decided to quit singing, and I
took a job in a munitions factory in Louisville. I was there two
years and I made gunpowder. You had to stand on wet
concrete floors and there wasn't a lot of heat in the winter, but
I was having the best time. Being an only child, which I am,
you like crowds, you like people. Then, in 1973, Stanley Dance
came to Louisville and invited me to the Newport Jazz
Festival, but I told him I didn't know if I could sing anymore. I
was scared to death to even try. But I came up and I stayed
close to Nellie Lutcher the whole time, and she pulled me
through so good that five days after I sang at the Festival I was
on my way to France to work for four weeks. A year ago, I
went back to France and sang at Newport again and did a
week here at the Half Note.

"I was blessed in both my parents. My mother was a
schoolteacher named Emma Johnson. Her father and mother
had come from Lancaster, Kentucky. He was a full Cherokee
and a medicine man, and she was half Cherokee, half Irish. My
father was from Knoxville, Tennessee, but I didn't know much
more than that about him. He just died, at the age of
ninety-six, so I think his parents, who I never met, must have
been slaves. I was in New York doing some business when he
passed. He was in the hospital in Louisville, and he'd had a
seizure of the flu but was recovering real nice. I went over to
Jimmy Ryan's the night before I was to leave, but I felt strange.
Roy Eldridge hollered to me from the bandstand, 'Hey, Humes,
come up here and sing.' But I told him I just didn't have it in
me, and I went back to where I was stopping to go to bed, and
found out the hospital had called and my daddy had died just
when I was at Ryan's. My father was known as Judge, or J. H.,
for John Henry. He was one of the first black lawyers in

Louisville, and he was always doing something for other people. 'You have to have friends. You can't live in this world by yourself,' he'd always tell me. My mother never worked again after I came along. We had so many good times together — popping popcorn and making ice cream and playing games. When she died and I made up my mind to quit singing, I sold my piano and my record-player and my records so I wouldn't be reminded or tempted, and that was it. Or I thought it was."

Helen Humes laughed and pushed herself to her feet. She went over to the piano, which is in the center of the room. Her accompanists — Ellis Larkins on piano and Benny Moten on bass — were already warming up. She said something to Larkins, who immediately leaned back and released one of his mystical sprays of hand signals. He played several left-hand chords, and Helen Humes turned around, detached the microphone from its cradle, smiled, and, standing by the piano as easily as if she were in her living room, began "There Is No Greater Love." During the first chorus, her voice and the song kept missing one another. Her vibrato ran a little wide, she cracked a couple of notes, and her dynamics were uneven. But everything settled into place in her second chorus. She started phrases behind the beat and caught up by ramming her words together. She used melismatics brilliantly. And she worked her way back and forth quickly and cleverly between near-shouts and languorous crooning. She has a light voice strikingly reminiscent of Mildred Bailey's, but she insists that no singer, Bailey included, influenced her. Humes' voice has a dark, fervent underside, which appears when she sings the blues and which Bailey lacked. Her phrasing is hornlike. She takes daring liberties with the melody, particularly in her second choruses, and she keeps close guard on her generous vibrato. Like all pre-microphone singers, she can shout at will, and she can also slipper along just above a whisper. She is a master of rhythm. But there is nothing deliberate or contrived in her style, which has an elegant primitivism. Her next number was a shouting, medium-tempo version of "Please Don't Talk About Me When I'm Gone," and then she did an attentive "Every Now and Then," a song she delights in and renders much as it was written. "Summertime" was followed by "Birth of the Blues," complete with its verse, and a rocking — and for her — quite moody "Gee, Baby Ain't I Good to You." She kept accumulating and then sweeping away little piles of notes all through "I Can't Give You Anything But Love," and she finished her set with a dramatic reading of "If I Could Be with You One Hour Tonight."

She sat down and wrapped her sweater about her and mopped her face. Barney Josephson, wearing a handsome dark-brown Glen-plaid suit, patted her shoulder and said, "That was marvelous, Helen. Keep it up and this place will be the way it was last New Year's Eve, when people were shouting and yelling and going out of their minds over you. They wouldn't let you out the door, if you remember. It was one of the most exciting nights I can recall since I've been in this business." Helen Humes nodded to Josephson's words, and when he had finished said she felt like a rock-and-rye. "You've barely made a dent in the case we ordered for you, Helen. And you *have* to finish it. I don't think I've had an order for a rock-and-rye since World War II." Josephson gave his customary giggle and went to get her drink. She cleared her throat and banged her chest with her hand several times. "I think I still have some of that cold I toted up here from Louisville," she said. "But I feel better singing now than I ever did before. My voice used to be so clear when I was younger, and people tell me it's gotten real clear again. I'm happiest when I'm singing — particularly if I have a good accompanist like Ellis. I just sing the way I feel. Most of my songs come out differently each time, but there are some I try and do the same way each time. I've been called a blues singer and a jazz singer and a ballad singer — well, I'm all three, which means I'm just a singer. And I've always been myself. I didn't model myself on anyone when I started out. Somebody'd tell me to listen to So-and-So's record, but I'd only listen, if I listened at all, *after* I had learned the tune myself.

"I got started as a singer almost by accident. After I had graduated from high school, I took a two-year business course and got a job as a secretary in the First Standard Bank, which was the first black bank in Louisville. During my vacation, I went to stay with Margaret and Luke Stewart, in Buffalo. They were Louisville friends, and Luke was one of the greatest guitarists I ever heard. I went up there for two weeks, but I didn't get home for two years, because I took my first work in Buffalo as a professional singer. I'd been singing and playing the piano most of my life. I fiddled with the piano as soon as I was tall enough to reach the keyboard, and after I had tried the clarinet and the trumpet, which I didn't care for, I took piano lessons from a very good German teacher, who had me going in the classics. I sang in church from the time I was little, and I sang and played piano in the Sunday school Bessie Allen ran at the Booker T. Washington Center. You could learn any instrument there, and that's where Dickie Wells and Jonah Jones started. When I was fourteen, Sylvester Weaver heard me sing. He was a blues singer who had recorded on the Okeh label. He told Mr. Rockwell at Okeh about me, and Mama took me to St. Louis and I recorded 'Black Cat Moan' and 'A Worried Woman's Blues.' I believe J. C. Johnson was on the piano. A while later, I made some more records in New York, including 'If Papa Has Outside Lovin' ' and 'Do What You Did Last Night,' both of which I'd like to hear now so I could sing them again. But I never kept any of my records, because I never thought they was as good as they could have been. That was all the recording I did then, except the Okeh people asked me would I like to go on tour. But Mama said no.

"I worked at the Spider Web, in Buffalo, and then over at the Vendome Hotel, where I was with Al Sears' band. He's retired now and doesn't do *nothin'* but play golf. I must have been in Buffalo a year, and then I went on to Schenectady, where I did my first radio program, with two white girls, and on to Albany and Troy. I went home after that, and a few months later I rejoined Al Sears at the Cotton Club in Cincinnati. This was in 1937. One night, Count Basie stopped in and offered me a job. He said he'd pay me thirty-five dollars a week, but I was already making that without having to travel, and Basie wasn't much yet anyway, so I said no. Well, Al Sears *did* go on the road, and we ended up at the Renaissance Ballroom, in Harlem, where John Hammond heard me, and this time I *did* join Basie. Billie Holiday had just left him, and I went with the band at the Famous Door, on Fifty-second Street, in 1938. That was when Basie really exploded, and when he had Buck Clayton and Dickie Wells and Lester Young and Jo Jones. I didn't have any trouble being the only woman in the band. I did my singing and went home and read a book and went to sleep. When we went on the road down South, the chances were good we wouldn't be allowed to eat in any decent place, so I started doing the cooking. I had my pots and my hot plate with me, and I cooked backstage. When I'd left the band and was at the Café Society, the phone would ring and it would be somebody from the band passing through, and he'd say, 'Hey, Humes, this is So-and-So. What you got cookin', honey?' Jimmy Rushing was my best friend in the band. He was full of fun and had stories in his head twenty, thirty years old. We'd sit on the bandstand together and he'd tell me things and we'd start laughing, and Basie would get mad. Later, when I was in L.A., Jimmy'd call when he was in town and I'd cook and we'd spend the day eating and drinking and playing cards and laughing."

Ellis Larkins and Benny Moten were in the middle of an

intermission set, and Helen Humes paused to listen for several minutes. "This is the first time I ever worked with Ellis — the first time I ever *met* Ellis — and he is something else," she said. "People told me before, 'Look out for Ellis, he's difficult.' But he's all right. Since I don't have anybody in my family left to look after, I might as well spend the rest of my time singing. But I'll keep Mama and Papa's house in Louisville. Thank heavens a neighbor recently moved into it to keep an eye on it! Down there in the summer, the little boys in the neighborhood make a path through my yard going after the peaches on my three peach trees. They come early in the morning and call up, 'Miss Helen, my mama wants to make me a cobbler, so can I pick some peaches?' One little boy came back and back and finally a tattletale told me, 'Miss Helen, he selling those peaches.' I've had a very happy life, and I wouldn't do it otherwise. I even got married once and survived. I married a Navy man in 1952, but I haven't seen him since 1960. He wanted to settle in Japan, and I told him, 'Fine, and I'll be right here if you ever come back.' I don't even know where he is now. I haven't made all the money some people think I have, but anytime my friends are in distress and if there's anything I can do for them, I do it. I guess I'm like my father that way, and I guess he was like *his* father that way. At least, that's what Mama always told him."

APRIL 1ST: FOR FORTY YEARS, Count Basie, a shy, matter-of-fact man who believes that life should not be tampered with, has hoped that no one would notice him up there at the piano. So he has played his lilting, instructional four-bar introductions, his drifting-through-the-moonbeams eight-bar bridges, and his occasional furtive solo choruses, and then disappeared into the engine room of his band to plant a ferocious, deep-register left-hand chord here, a cluster of high right-hand chords there, and in general to stoke and stir his musicians. But long ago, between 1938 and 1942, he recorded a dozen or so numbers with just a rhythm section, and no one has ever forgotten. There at last was Basie's remarkable and unique piano playing! It had wit, a nice obliquity, a flawless command of time, unceasing inventiveness, grace, and a singular American originality. What Hemingway had done for American prose Basie was doing for American music. Even so, the recordings were not as good as they seemed. The earlier ones were clogged by repetitive tempos and by a lot of boogie-woogie, which was the rage, and the later ones had a stiff, rather aimless quality. One had perforce to make do with Basie in his big-band setting and with the hope that he would eventually be coaxed into a recording studio for another solo outing. But all that happened was that Basie's piano playing got better and better. He refined what seemed perfect. His playing became more subtle rhythmically and melodically. His touch got increasingly silvery. He grew wittier and even more unpredictable. More than ever, one could listen and say, "Ah, he will play such-and-such a chord now or such-and-such a note," and be dead wrong. Suddenly Basie was seventy years old, and things looked gloomy. It was Beethoven never making it to the quartets, Joyce setting aside "Finnegans Wake," Ellington quitting after "Creole Love Call." Then, in May of last year, Norman Granz, the impresario, got Basie into a studio with just Ray Brown on bass and Louie Bellson on drums, and produced "For the First Time: The Count Basie Trio" (Pablo). Basie is relaxed, sure, funny, inventive, and brilliant. Part of the reason is his accompaniment, which was ingenious on Granz's part. Brown is a great and sympathetic bassist, and Bellson has taste, good time, and technique to spare. And both clearly relish working with Basie. Moreover, Basie's other self, the guitarist Freddie Greene, is not on hand, and this turns out well, too. Basie is freed rhythmically and harmonically from Greene's steady chop-chop-chop accompanying chords, and time and again he delightedly fills in nooks and crannies that Greene would have seen to. Even the selection of materials is enlightened. There are two medium-fast takes of "Lady Be Good," the second slightly faster than the first. Both applaud the melody and settle into telegraphic odes. There is a funny, rocking "I'll Always Be in Love with You," and an almost hustling version of "As Long As I Live," a tune that is customarily handled in a slow, extended hum. But Granz has pulled off another miracle: Basie plays organ on two numbers. The first, "Blues in the Church," is a slow blues that opens and closes with superb Brown solos accompanied by Basie moans and cries, and that includes in between an assortment of chords, tremolos, and those breezes-in-the-trees that only Basie manages on the organ. The second organ piece is a tongue-in-cheek version of the dreadful "Song of the Islands," which Basie mastered memorably with his band in 1939. Best of all on the record are its four piano blues. "Baby Lawrence" (or Laurence, as the matchless, lamented dancer preferred) is very fast and has swatches of Fats Waller stride piano. "Royal Garden Blues" is medium and choice; the grand old tune has rarely received a treatment that is at once mischievous and dead serious. "Pres" is an easy tribute to Lester Young. And "Blues in the Alley" is an extraordinary slow blues that consists of eight choruses of silences, probing lower-register single notes, riffling chords, and a pervasive mood that is as sad as it is elegant. It is one of the great recorded blues.

APRIL 7TH: PIANO PLAYERS are doubly blessed. Unlike fiddle and wind players, they don't wear out (Artur Rubinstein, Earl Hines, Eubie Blake), and they play an endlessly variegated instrument. The piano, especially in jazz, can be anything. It can be a full band or a consummate solo instrument. It can be a guitar or a bank of percussionists. It can rhapsodize as fulsomely as a string section or release single-note melodic lines that course like the wind. It can define the bones of harmonic thought. It can uniquely support and point up the human voice. It can, in its lowest registers, produce mysteries and majesties only a tuba can rival. It can even produce, when cleverly manipulated, notes that technically do not exist — blue notes and interstitial notes, those elusive non-notes jazz musicians invented. Yet the piano is a comparatively easy instrument, and as a result there's scarcely been room for all the jazz piano players. This overcrowding has been particularly discouraging for those special and delicate pianists whom Count Basie once called the "poets of the piano." Everything about them tends to be delicate — their attack, their touch, the construction of their solos, their very careers, which are often thwarted by a lack of recognition, by timidity, by poor timing, or by the discovery that there are easier ways to make a living. Consider Walter Norris. His name has been in the air in New York for years, but the only place he has worked any length of time is that non-place the Playboy Club. He was mentioned briefly in Leonard Feather's "Encyclopedia of Jazz" (born in 1931, in Little Rock; went to Los Angeles and worked with Stan Getz, Zoot Sims), but he is not in the most recent edition. There is a full-page photograph of him — thin, dark, gesticulating — in a documentary book about West Coast jazz by William Claxton, but no text. He played on Ornette Coleman's first recording, but few people remember. He has been with the Thad Jones-Mel Lewis band a year, but it plays here only one night a week when it is not on the road. But Norris' turn has come. A while ago, he told Bradley Cunningham, the sheltering and sagacious owner of Bradley's, that he is now "ready" to come out by himself. So he opened tonight at Bradley's, with the bassist George Mraz, for a week. He is a remarkable pianist. He has clearly listened to Art Tatum, but he has also listened to Bud Powell and Teddy Wilson and Debussy and Ravel. His touch is even and light. He uses his considerable technique beautifully: his arpeggios, which whip and coil, have logic and continuity; his double-time dashes are parenthetical and light up what they interrupt; his long single-note passages continually pause and breathe; no tempo rattles the clarity of his articulation, which has a private, singing quality. He is an adventuresome and oblique pianist who likes to start his numbers with inside-out phrases, who likes to bang the heads of his harmonies together. His slow ballads are singular; they continually tap at the hull of the melody, testing its soundness, cheering its beauties. Tonight, Norris made "Falling in Love with Love" sound lean and swinging, and he tested every inch of "Everything Happens to Me." "Cherokee" has always had a Hi-ho-Silver quality, but he made it soar rather than race. He made "Maple Leaf Rag," which can be immovable, swing from within. He played a medium-tempo blues that had a swaying, waltzlike quality. And he got "Lover Man" out of the swoon Billie Holiday left it in thirty years ago. Norris' decision to come out is correct, but he should have made it sooner.

MAY 3RD: CECIL TAYLOR packing them into the Five Spot for three solid weeks! Cecil Taylor playing *encores* to get off the stand! Cecil Taylor — iconoclast, super-avant-gardist, mysterioso pianist — a matinée idol! Incredible but true. When Taylor first came up, the thought of such acclaim would have caused jigging hilarity. After four years at the New England Conservatory, he was a classically trained pianist who improvised. He was Bartók or Stravinsky or Berg sitting at a piano and knocking out twenty or thirty choruses, which had a remote but unmistakable jazz flavor. There was nothing accessible or even specially attractive about his music. It

operated completely on its terms; to join in, the listener did the
work. Little has changed about Taylor. He is still tiny and
muscular and solemn, and he still performs like a wrecking
crew. He stabs and pounds and hammers the keyboard. His
enormous glissandos skid so heavily one expects the keys to
remain flattened. He plays staccato arpeggios so fast they
become ribbons of sound. His arms are blurred pistons, and he
rocks in wild irregular circles. He comes very close to making
visual music. And so his new popularity is suddenly under-
standable. His music, though totally dissimilar in content and
construction, has all along been a forerunner of electronic
music, of hard rock, and so has his way of performing it. The
music around him has simply caught up to Taylor, and
everything he does is now apposite. One can easily imagine
turning on to Taylor, drifting down through his polyrhythms
and dense harmonic tongues, through his massive chords and
thundering arpeggios. Taylor's first number tonight at the Five
Spot was the first set, and it lasted almost an hour and twenty
minutes. It was vintage Taylor and it consisted of several
immense Taylor solos spelled by somewhat shorter statements
by the alto saxophonist Jimmy Lyons, an indefatigable cohort
of Taylor's and an eclectic who spins out variations on the
thoughts of John Coltrane and Ornette Coleman and Eric
Dolphy. Perhaps Taylor's instrument no longer matters. He
has become obsessed with blocks of sound, with sequoias of
sound, and if he could not produce on the piano what he hears
in his head, he would do it by other means. He would gather
about him whales and jets and cascades, and make them sing
and roar and crash. And we'd listen.

MAY 6TH: "TAKE ME, warts and all!" Norman Granz seemed to
keep crying out in the fifties, when his one-man jazz empire
was pumping away night and day. And so we did, suffering his

Jazz at the Philharmonic concerts, with their interminable
solos and drum battles and tenor-saxophone histrionics, on the
chance that Roy Eldridge or Charlie Parker or Lester Young
might play a great solo; suffering the endless records by Ella
Fitzgerald and Oscar Peterson on the chance that next week
Granz might release a priceless session by Ben Webster and
Harry Edison or by Eldridge and an Ellington contingent;
suffering his compulsive prolixity, his "This, then, is this, then"
liner notes, so that we wouldn't miss the occasional pearl. It
was the LP recording that went to Granz's head. He recorded
entire concerts, and simulated jam sessions in which one
number might last over half an hour. He recorded all those
musicians who grew up in the three-minute cage of the old
78-r.p.m. recordings, musicians who came to do everything in
three minutes — smoke a cigarette, eat a sandwich, drink a
drink. But their minds and imaginations tended to wander and
grow diffuse when they were turned loose in the endless
pastures of the LP recording. Brevity was beauty to them, a
way of life impossible and unwise to try and unlearn. But
impresarios do not grow rich by being sensitive and sensible.
In 1953 and 1954, Granz got Art Tatum into a recording studio
for three or four sessions and told him to play whatever he
wanted at whatever tempo he liked for whatever length of time
seemed right. Tatum forthwith produced almost two hundred
numbers, and a veritable selected works of Art Tatum was
released. The albums have long been out of print, but Granz,
after a fifteen-year hiatus in his activities in this country, is
making records again, and one of his first acts has been to
reissue one hundred and twenty-one of the Tatum solos in a
thirteen-volume set called "The Tatum Solo Masterpieces"
(Pablo).

There is an expensive and important aura about all these LPs
in their box. The expense (about sixty dollars at Goody's) is
real, but the importance is an illusion. There is nothing

startling or major here. The albums simply contain Tatum piano solos that range from two minutes to almost seven minutes in length and that unsurprisingly average around four minutes. The material is familiar and includes retreads of such Tatum display pieces as "Humoresque" and "Elegy" and "Danny Boy" as well as such Tatum-owned ballads as "Willow Weep for Me," "Moonglow," "Stompin' at the Savoy," "Begin the Beguine," and "Love for Sale." The albums take over nine hours to listen to, and if one dives in for a couple of hours at a time, several disconcerting things become clear about Tatum as he is here. He seems to have lost his sense of proportion and design. Many of the numbers move in fits and starts and have lumps and gaps and irregularities. A statement of the melody is interrupted (and so virtually destroyed) by one of Tatum's celebrated, out-of-tempo Earl Hines whirlpools. A passage of driving, on-the-beat improvisation suddenly dissolves into arpeggios and glissandos and grandstanding harmonies. A number abruptly ends after two choruses or rambles on indefinitely. (Compare the flawless pointillism of Teddy Wilson, who is so often wrongly thought of as a lesser Tatum.) Tatum never had much taste, and it is all but gone here. He gives straight rhapsodic treatments to "Deep Purple" and "Night and Day" and "Without a Song" — which have cried out since the day they were written for a little derring-do and deviltry from their interpreters. And he attempts to take apart and rebuild such melodic edifices as "Willow Weep for Me" and "The Man I Love," the last of which turns into the only bad Tatum performance I can recall. Finally, his clichés become unavoidable for the first time. Here is the glissando that leads coyly into an in-tempo passage; the swirling, meaningless, befogging arpeggios, a Sargasso Sea of arpeggios; the busy ad-lib passage in which he keeps rushing up to and backing off from the beat. He rarely surprises us rhythmically or dynamically or with his improvisations, which tend to conceal rather than enhance. One must blame Granz for putting this flawed Tatum before the public and then magnifying him. He got to Tatum just three years before his death, when the great engines were beginning to run down. He also recorded him in the wrong way, for Tatum was a born showoff who was not particularly happy by himself in a recording studio. And Granz asked too much of him: better thirty beauties than over a hundred flawed effusions.

But there *are* stunning numbers in the set. "Come Rain or Come Shine" is Tatum near his best. It has a marvelous ad-lib chorus, full of reverent and exquisite harmonies, improvised passages that are serious and graceful extensions of Arlen's tune, and a climax that oddly celebrates two moods — cheerfulness and fleeting gloom. "Tea for Two" is joyous parody that moves at top speed and has an in-tempo, out-of-tempo section that is a rococo masterpiece. "Blue Lou" is short, stripped-down, and full of business. "Please Be Kind" has a chorus in which the rhythm sways from side to side in slow motion. "I'm Comin' Virginia" is wild and irreverent and crowded with extraordinary harmonies. "Isn't It Romantic" has a brilliant double-time explosion, and "Aunt Hagar's Blues" is a merciless ribbing of the blues, a form that Tatum — bored? embarrassed? jumpy over its empty harmonic expanses? — invariably poked fun at. And "Jitterbug Waltz" is ingenious simply for the off-center way that Tatum places his notes during his statement of the melody.

Norman Granz set out to build Tatum (and himself) a monument in his Tatum solo recordings. But how was he to know that twenty years later the extraordinary LP called "God Is in the House" would appear, and that it would be full of material recorded by Tatum mainly in Harlem after-hours clubs in the early forties, when he was at his peak — an album, indeed, that eclipses much of the rest of Tatum's recorded output? But perhaps it doesn't matter to Granz, if one is to

believe his introductory note to "The Tatum Solo Masterpieces": "The most important and satisfying work I ever had
was the Tatum project — imagine! Having Art Tatum all to
myself, an audience of one, doing almost 200 songs for me."

MAY 24TH: THREE MORE New York Jazz Repertory Company
concerts have trudged by. The first, given in mid-April, was a
history of jazz, made up of snippets from earlier concerts. It
began with a ragtime number for small band, "St. Louis
Tickle," and ended with big-band impressions of Ornette
Coleman, John Coltrane, and Miles Davis. Two noteworthy
things happened. The remarkable Bob Wilber summoned up
the clarinettists Omer Simeon and Frank Teschemacher with
superb, intuitive readings of their solos on Jelly Roll Morton's
recording of "Shreveport Stomp" and Red Nichols' of
"Shimme-Sha-Wobble," and then gave an uncanny demonstration of how Johnny Hodges played "Warm Valley" on the
soprano saxophone. And later on there were some superb film
clips, among them the Billie Holiday and the Thelonious Monk
sequences from "The Sound of Jazz," and a hitherto unknown
segment made in 1951 and showing a swollen Charlie Parker
and a thin Dizzy Gillespie playing "Hot House." The next
N.Y.J.R.C. concert, early in May, presented first-rate re-creations of the Savoy Sultans and Lucky Millinder's Blue Rhythm
Band. The Sultans had nine pieces and served as the house
band at the Savoy Ballroom between 1937 and 1946. The
group had derivative soloists and purely functional arrangements, but it swung so hard, night in and night out, that it
caused continual disarray among the bands it spelled. Millinder's band lasted from 1934 to 1943, and is chiefly memorable
as an ongoing on-the-job training program through which
passed Red Allen, J. C. Higginbotham, Sandy Williams, Harry
Edison, Clyde Hart, Ellis Larkins, Dizzy Gillespie, Frankie

Newton, and the whole John Kirby band, Russell Procope excepted. (Kirby had Charlie Shavers, Buster Bailey, Procope, Billy Kyle, and O'Neil Spencer.) The pianist in the N.Y.J.R.C. orchestra throughout the evening was Patti Bown, who appears to be another of Basie's poet-pianists. Her solos were inventive and even a little scary (she can go Cecil Taylor one better), and her accompanying was swinging and subtle and prickly. Tonight's repertory concert turned out to be the last of the season, and it was devoted to stride piano. The best moments were provided by Eubie Blake, Claude Hopkins, Dick Wellstood, and Brooks Kerr. Kerr played a rhapsody written by Willie the Lion forty years ago and a good 1913 Luckey Roberts piece, "Pork and Beans." The subtle and harmonically adroit Claude Hopkins, who is not a stride pianist but a swing pianist, played soft and sliding versions of "I Would Do Anything for You" and "Three Little Words." Wellstood lamentably dodged in and out, but his single solo number, "Snatches," was adept and funny. Eubie Blake delivered a little Blake, a little Gershwin, and another Luckey Roberts. Again he shamed us by holding aloft a standard of warmth and proficiency and joy that little contemporary music can match.

Brooks Kerr reminded us along the way that Duke Ellington died a year ago tonight, and then played and sang an Ellington trifle called "Ain't Nothin' Nothin' Baby Without You." Ellington's presence has become, if anything, a little larger than it was in life. One still runs into him all over town: on West Fifty-fifth Street, walking uphill from Fifth Avenue to City Center with his careful, rocking old man's gait; on the stage at Carnegie Hall, dipping his head and doing his funny finger-popping bit; steaming along in a cab and seated beside the surprised driver, who sneaks looks at Ellington's working clothes — a ratty sweater and an old bandanna wrapped around his head; at the Rainbow Grill, where he took a small group from the band to play for dancing in the summer of

1967, and where, during intermission, he would sit at his table and talk, his eyes shining and laughing, his voice threading its cool, gracious way through his hand-chosen words, his gestures like flags.

JUNE 25TH: THAT SMALL, RARE GROUP of lyric trumpet players who came up in the thirties (nurtured, in the main, by Louis Armstrong, Roy Eldridge, and Red Allen) is just about gone. It included Emmett Berry, Buck Clayton, Shorty Baker, Doc Cheatham, Joe Thomas, Bill Coleman, Sidney de Paris, Frankie Newton, and Harry Edison. Only Coleman and Cheatham and Edison are still working. Coleman lives in Europe, Cheatham in New York, and Edison on the West Coast. Edison will be sixty this year, but his playing — particularly on a new recording, "Basie Jam" (Pablo) — has lost none of its subtlety and sureness and swing. His career has been uncomplicated. He came out of Columbus, Ohio, and, after a spell with Alphonso Trent, joined Lucky Millinder. He left Millinder and went with Count Basie in the late thirties, and stayed until 1950. Then he moved to California, where he has worked in the studios and for Norman Granz and Basie and Buddy Rich, had his own small groups, and played a thousand obbligatos for various singers. (Most of those muted, plaintive, calling-in-the-hills sounds in the background of Frank Sinatra's records in the sixties are Edison.) The origins of Edison's laconic style are not as clear. He is frequently said to have passed through Roy Eldridge's umbra, but one suspects that he also listened to Red Allen's legato statements with Fletcher Henderson and to Frankie Newton. In any case, his style was set by the time he reached Basie, and it hasn't changed. Edison constantly plays with time. He loafs behind the beat on medium and fast numbers, and on very slow ones he goes into unaggressive double-times. He is fond of silence and he plays almost as many rests as he does notes. He is also fond of striking the same note like a bell over and over again. He likes to bend notes, in a mocking, slurred way, the way Billie Holiday did in the late thirties. And his sense of dynamics is dramatic: He will inflate and deflate a single note within the space of a beat. He has a majestic tone, which seems to continually overflow. Those famous booming legato bridges he'd take with Basie's band always suggested an old gent shouting into his first telephone.

Edison is in excellent condition on "Basie Jam," which is just that. Count Basie, on both piano and organ, has Edison, Zoot Sims and Eddie Davis, J. J. Johnson, Irving Ashby, Ray Brown, and Louis Bellson, and they jam their way through five blues of varying speeds. Edison is remarkable on the slow "Hanging Out," where he hits one note twelve times in a row, sounds like Frankie Newton, pulls a complex run out from under us, and bends a variety of notes every conceivable way. He plays a fine halftime open-horn solo on the very fast "Freeport Blues," and a good muted one on "One-Nighter." But everyone is exemplary on "Basie Jam," in particular Zoot Sims, who opens his solo on "One-Nighter" with a short double-time phrase of such beauty and perfection one is forced to go back again and again to marvel at its construction. Perhaps Edison inspired it; he favors such *mots* himself.

June 27th: The first day of the twenty-first Newport Jazz Festival (and the fourth Newport Jazz Festival-New York) consisted of a repeat of the Bix Beiderbecke concert given on April 3 by the New York Jazz Repertory Company and a jam session by a dozen members of the company's orchestra. These last included Patti Bown and Billy Taylor (piano), Chris White and Lisle Atkinson (bass), Alphonse Mouzon and Freddie Waits (drums), Zoot Sims, Eddie Daniels, and Cecil

Payne (saxophone), Jimmy Owens, Chet Baker, Charles Sullivan, and Waymond Reed (trumpet), and Garnett Brown and John Gordon (trombone). The session, held in Carnegie Hall at eleven-thirty tonight, was discursive and showy. Payne and Daniels offered more notes than the ear could hold, and so did Brown and Atkinson, whose solos had a look-at-me quality. But there were corrective efforts. The drummers, alternately and in tandem, were often funny, Chet Baker took a light-boned solo on "Softly as in a Morning Sunrise," and Patti Bown was a mischievous wonder. She is an intense performer whose constant motions suggest an almost spent top and who is as much at home within the solos of others as she is within her own. Her accompaniment forms a secondary, self-effacing solo — a set of cheering and cautionary notes that push and steer the soloist. Her own improvisations are hard-swinging précis of longer, more elaborate statements — one suspects — that she edits in her head. In her solo on "Oleo," she managed to suggest a parody of stride piano, limning and applauding its outlines and rhythms without ever quite stating them. She worked so hard, in fact, that she provoked Billy Taylor, who followed her, into the strongest solo I've heard him play in twenty years.

The Beiderbecke celebration, offered earlier in the evening at Carnegie, was widely overpraised its first time around. Two bands, representing the Wolverines and Jean Goldkette, caught much of the gentleness and clarity of his playing, but they ignored the driving, almost demonic side that countless in-person observers have testified to and that appears in his recording of "Barnacle Bill the Sailor." Jimmy McPartland, John Glasel, Franc Williams, and Warren Vaché handled his solos, in unison or separately, and only Vaché was truly on the mark. He can play Beiderbecke note for note, but he makes the notes sound as if *he* had invented them. There were other unexpected benefits. A young bassist and tubist, Vince

Giordano, played Adrian Rollini's formidable bass-saxophone parts in "Since My Best Gal Turned Me Down," "At the Jazz Band Ball," "Goose Pimples," and "Royal Garden Blues" with a booting looseness, and he also appeared in two numbers in which Joe Venuti, Zoot Sims, and Bucky Pizzarelli re-created Venuti's old recording group The Blue Four. This new group, which only indirectly had to do with Beiderbecke, played "China Boy" and a blues, and it had a texture (just about gone in jazz) and drive and joy that were unmatched during the evening. Dill Jones and Marian McPartland wandered through three of Beiderbecke's curious, circular piano pieces, and for half the evening Bill Rank and Speigle Willcox, Goldkette alumni, joined in. One more cavil: The tempos were much too slow in "Goose Pimples," "Way Down Yonder in New Orleans," and "I'm Comin' Virginia."

JUNE 28TH: GOSPEL SINGING IS JAZZ gussied up and dressed in the clothes of the Lamb. Gospel singers use jazz phrasing and rhythms and inflections, and they often use them outrageously. They bend notes almost in two, they growl like bears, they jam six syllables into a single note, and they play hob with the beat. And jazz musicians brought up on church music have returned the compliment by dipping into these marvelous excesses. (Ray Charles is built on church music.) But everybody borrows from gospel now, for the music has moved well out into the secular (and white) world in the last couple of decades, and is even performed in night clubs and on days other than Sunday. The gospel program put together by Tony Heilbut for the early Carnegie Hall concert tonight was almost all first-rate. A film that showed us part of Mahalia Jackson's spectacular (and final) Newport performance in 1970 was shot mainly from below, and it had the surrealistic effect of making her head seem truly in the heavens. Two of Mahalia's teachers followed — Sallie Martin, who is seventy-nine and still sings in an enormous, looming contralto, and Thomas A. Dorsey, who is seventy-six and began as an accompanist for Ma Rainey. One of Mahalia's best disciples, Dorothy Love Coates, sang four numbers. But the evening belonged to a sixty-year-old singer named Claude Jeter, who was born in Montgomery, Alabama, and now lives in New York. Jeter is the most astonishing gospel singer — and one of the most astonishing singers — I have ever heard. Most gospel singers favor white and weight, but Jeter is thin and owlish and bespectacled, and he wears close-cropped hair and dark business suits. He could pass the plate easily, but his singing is deceptively housed. He sings mainly in falsetto now — a rich falsetto in the area of a countertenor. His phrasing is startling. He begins a passage quietly and on the beat, pauses a beat, and abruptly shouts the next syllable, bending it half an octave and growling in a way that summons up the millennium-announcing days of Cootie Williams. Then, silent and still, he quickly searches the audience for the effects of such shocking music, and slips into his next phrase. His sense of time is ecstatic: It rivals Billie Holiday's, and it explains a great deal about Ray Charles'. He sang the "Battle Hymn of the Republic" slowly, and after he had broken his cries over us again and again, the possessed were on their feet and shouting, and the hall was rocking. And his two other numbers were equally commanding. The remainder of the evening was given over to the J. C. White Singers, who have helped Max Roach with some of his onstage sociological treatises; a good quartet, the Sensational Nightingales; and Marion Williams, who began with the late Clara Ward.

Mr. Suave (Benny Carter) and Mrs. Sexy (Maria Muldaur) gave the second concert at Carnegie tonight. They appeared for the first time in New York late last fall, and caused talk on both sides of the popular-music fence. What was Muldaur, a thirty-two-year-old pop-rock-country singer, doing with a *jazz* band, and what was Carter, a sixty-seven-year-old monument of the music, doing accompanying Muldaur? Carter says Muldaur has tremendous potential, and Muldaur says she loves working with Pop Carter, no matter what his age. (Actually, Carter is carrying forward a minor and honorable tradition in jazz. Countless first-rate jazzmen have helped of-the-moment singers by playing behind them and have gone unscathed.) Carter began the concert by leading a ten-piece New York pickup band that included Danny Stiles, Hank Jones, Frank Wess, Bucky Pizzarelli, and Grady Tate through four instrumentals. "Doozie" had fine solos by Stiles and Pizzarelli, who, in his two choruses, unexpectedly brought Charlie Christian to life. Hank Jones offered a slow, crystal "The Very Thought of You," and Carter played luxurious versions of "Green Dolphin Street" and "The Shadow of Your Smile." None of his primness was evident, and his celebrated style — the stepping, descending patterns, the bowing melodic figures, the cool sense of time — moved past with ease and grace.

Muldaur gave the second half of the concert. She came onstage with her ringlets and small, pretty child's face and began scaling an unending series of bumps out into the hall. One's immediate reaction was that she should be spanked and sent to bed. But she's too old for that, and too old for the way she sings. She has a light voice, a cork voice, and an intuitive, little-girl way of phrasing. One hears Mildred Bailey, and once in a while there is an attractive cracked quality in her voice, but the rest is raggedy and waifish. She puts on a good visual show, though, and it was painless to watch her bump and wiggle through "Lover Man" and "Squeeze Me" and "Gee, Baby Ain't I Good to You" and "It Don't Mean a Thing if It Ain't Got That Swing." But it was far better to train the radar on Carter's arrangements behind her. Their sumptuous harmonies and roomy saxophone figures were beautiful.

JUNE 30TH: YESTERDAY, FOUR MEMBERS of Bob Crosby's Bobcats were reunited on several ferryboat rides up the Hudson, and during the evening, at Carnegie Hall, the big bands of Buddy Rich and Harry James formed booming parentheses around the Ruby Braff-George Barnes quartet. The four old Bobcats were brother Bob, Yank Lawson, Eddie Miller, and Bob Haggart, and the four supporting non-Bobcats were Chuck Folds (piano), Johnny Mince (clarinet), George Masso (trombone), and Ron Traxler (drums). Miller has spent little time in the East. He is a missing link who belongs somewhere between Lester Young and Bud Freeman. He has Young's balsa tone and Freeman's homemade rhythmic attack. But his ballads are singular. He got off two during the one-o'clock boat ride — "Sophisticated Lady" and "Dream" — and they were crooning marvels. He keeps his vibrato down, he hugs the melody, and he moves steadily along just this side of bathos.

Buddy Rich opened the concert last night with eight blasters and a heavy, subaqueous drum solo, and it was closed by Harry James, who, in the evening of his career, is turning into a crazy-kid trumpet player. His solos on several blues had a nerviness and swagger one used to hear in a seventeen-year-old third trumpeter who had just come on the band. The Braff-Barnes quartet is a complex of high invention, precision, and big egoes, and when it is in balance there is no better group in jazz. But last night Braff was down (his runs didn't jell and his timing seemed slack), and Barnes was up (his seesaw rhythms were in abeyance and his melodic lines were relaxed and spacious).

Tonight, we were offered four organists at Carnegie (Don

Lewis, Jack McDuff, Rhoda Scott, Larry Young) and two bands at the Roseland Ballroom. The organ concert was a commercial for the Hammond Organ people, who subsidized it, and the dance was part concert, part dance. The concert was given by Miyami and his New Herd, a billowing, derivative Japanese band that played both American standards and Japanese folk material. An explanatory narrative was read before each number, which was like returning your neighbor's lawnmower with a note telling him how to work it. Count Basie, surrounded by his customary glistening bottleworks, provided the excellent dance music.

JULY 1ST: THE FESTIVAL WENT INTO GEAR today, and we had, as we will have through Saturday, two concerts at seven-thirty and two at eleven-thirty. The first concert at Avery Fisher was the annual celebration of American popular song, and it went askew during the beginning set, or what there was of it. Zoot Sims and Jim Hall were scheduled to play George Gershwin, and they did get through "Embraceable You," "Someone to Watch Over Me," and "The Man I Love." Then, having taken up their allotted twenty minutes, they obeyed orders and left the stage. It was the waiter removing your mousse when your head is turned. The two men are strikingly sympathetic musically, and their mutual aesthetic composure had just begun to show in "The Man I Love." Hall and Sims reshaped it and reshaped it again, and the results were superb. The audience was already leaning into their next number, a certain masterpiece — and they were gone. The misdeed was unwittingly compounded by Cy Coleman, who cheerfully played and sang twice as many numbers, and by Helen Humes, who delivered six Fats Wallers and a blues sweetly and well. Johnny Hartman, struggling with his intonation, celebrated Duke Ellington by singing two Ellingtons, one Billy Strayhorn,

one Kurt Weill, a blues, and "On a Clear Day." Chet Baker, in
company with a five-piece group, played three Rodgers and
Hart songs in an overly jazzy way. But Margaret Whiting,
serene and statuesque, brought the proceedings to a lyrical
close with more than half a dozen Harold Arlen songs. She is a
very good singer — a straight, knowledgeable, lilting singer
— and she gave Arlen his due.

The second concert at Avery Fisher was taken up by Miles
Davis, and there was little that was new in his first number and
set, which lasted close to an hour. Davis went electric years
ago, and he was surrounded onstage by amplifiers and electronic instruments. He played several solos, muted and open,
electrified and not, and everything was as of old — the clams,
the beseeching tone, the melodic, free-time passages, the
seeming disjointedness, and the incessant effort to get through
to whatever it is musically that he has been trying to get
through to for the past twenty years. By the time I arrived at
Carnegie to hear the program of solo pianists, Harold Mabern,
Bernard Peiffer, and Barry Harris had slipped by and Dorothy
Donegan, got up in a tight silver lamé gown that gave her a
striped-bass effect, was giving "Tea for Two" what for. She
was followed by Roland Hanna, Cedar Walton, John Lewis,
and Eubie Blake, all of whom were afflicted by concertitis.

Thunder from the musical left: The *Times* reported this
morning that the avant-gardists are running a mini-festival
downtown and that they are disgruntled about the Festival.
Juma Sultan, a percussionist, is quoted: "In our view, Newport
has never been a jazz festival. It has never shown an interest
in presenting a true cross-section of the music, but has been
concentrated on the popular and established musicians, ex-
cluding the community." The Festival this year appears to be
conservative, but every imaginable type of jazz has been heard
during its four years in New York. The new-thing jazz Sultan
is pushing has never gained much of an audience (it bombed

thoroughly at the Festival in 1973), and neglect has become its tradition. Barely a music, it is hard, humorless, uncompromising, and sociological, and much exposure would destroy it.

JULY 2ND: SULTAN SHOULD CHERISH his music's isolation and perseverance. It has not, as is often the case with musical avant-gardes, withered away or degenerated into straight pop. Look at Chuck Mangione and Gato Barbieri, who split the early concert at Avery Fisher tonight. Both have had vague avant-garde reputations, but now they've become the Glenn Miller and Artie Shaw of the present. Mangione wears funny clothes — a red felt hat, a short shirt that reveals his belly button, and leather pants. He writes attractive melodies, and plays them in a lush way. Barbieri wears funny clothes, too: a white suit and a black, wide-brimmed gangster hat. He uses a continually rasping tone and long-held, slowly revolving notes, and once in a while he peppers his music with chants or gaucho shouts.

Stan Getz and various associates, past and present, gave the late concert at Avery Fisher. Charlie Byrd, on acoustical guitar, set down four numbers, the best of them "Top Hat, White Tie, and Tails" and "Undecided." Jimmy Rowles, preserved in his own amber, played three slow ruminations ("Poor Butterfly," "Prelude to a Kiss," and "My Buddy"), in which each note had trouble getting free of the preceding one, and was joined by Getz for three slightly jauntier efforts. Gary Burton, equipped with four mallets and his shimmering vibraharp, erected twin towers of sound, which were full of aluminum chords, brilliant circular phrases, and washing, ad-lib rhythms. Their motion was perpendicular. Getz reappeared, and he and Burton played a couple of hands of "Here's That Rainy Day." Getz brought on his present group (Al Dailey on piano, Clint Houston on bass, Billy Hart on drums) for two numbers, and then Heloisa Gilberto, the new wife of João Gilberto, did a Gilberto and "Joost Wan ov Dose Tings." Mabel Mercer, battling Getz's somewhat strident obbligatos, sang four perfect numbers. The masters of ceremonies were Marian McPartland and Alec Wilder, who, seated at a table at stage right, looked as if they were stuck in the library on a lovely Saturday afternoon.

JULY 3RD: PEDALING BACKWARD, the day went like this: Cleo Laine and Johnny Dankworth gave the late concert at Avery Fisher. Dankworth, who would have made a good second alto saxophonist with Alvino Rey, played eight numbers with a New York pickup band (Danny Stiles, Frank Wess, Jimmy Nottingham, etc.) and then accompanied Cleo Laine, who opened her sample box and offered us E. E. Cummings, Spike Milligan, Shakespeare, Bessie Smith, "My Bill," a blues, and "On a Clear Day." A quartet named Oregon started the early concert at Avery Fisher, and its members took turns on guitar, piano, trumpet, sitar, tabla, violin, French and English horn, oboe, conga drums, bass, triangle, flute, and bass clarinet. Their music is Western "classical" streaked with East Indian music. They were followed by Keith Jarrett, who played four of his magical, rolling gospel-and-blues numbers. First, as is his wont, he stood, then he crouched, and finally he sat down like this:

Thelonious Monk, for so long seemingly imperishable, has been in semi-retirement, but he brought on a quartet made up of Paul Jeffrey on tenor saxophone, Larry Ridley on bass, and Thelonious, Jr., on drums. Monk himself has worn away, and so has his playing. He is thin and gray, and he sounded as he did thirty-five years ago. All the eccentricities have vanished, leaving a straight, modern-sounding chord-based pianist. Gone are the stringy runs, the spasmodic rhythms, the splayed chords, and the nervous humor. It was almost as if Monk were telling us that he had been putting us on all these years and that he had finally tired of the joke. Jeffrey was surprisingly eloquent and forceful.

The day started with a bang. Zoot Sims appeared with a quintet at the last of the free noonday concerts that have been given this week on the northwest corner of Sixth Avenue and Fifty-first Street. The group included a revivified Jimmy Rowles, the trumpeter Marky Markowitz, the bassist Major Holley, and Mike DiPasqua on drums. Sims was buoyant, and so was Markowitz, an old big-band trumpeter who plays with a wasteless assurance and frequent nods in the direction of Rex Stewart and Roy Eldridge.

JULY 4TH: ON THE OCCASION of the hundred-and-ninety-ninth anniversary of Independence, George Wein decided to open his own Hall of Fame, and here are the first lucky entrants: Bobby Hackett, Jabbo Smith, Barney Bigard, Vic Dickenson, Joe Venuti, Red Norvo, Teddy Wilson, Earl Hines, Milt Hinton, and Jo Jones. All were at Avery Fisher to play the early concert, and all were presented with plaques by John Hammond, who in turn was presented with one by George Wein. Two dozen numbers were played, and the proceedings, unlike most all-star ragbags, were orderly, intelligent, and frequently sterling. Of particular note: a 1942 film clip of the Ellington band, in which "C Jam Blues" was played by Ray Nance, Rex Stewart, Barney Bigard, Tricky Sam Nanton, Ben Webster, and Sonny Greer, the last of whom got off a neat, racketing solo; a clip from the "Sound of Jazz" in which a band made up of Stewart and Red Allen, Pee Wee Russell, Vic Dickenson, Coleman Hawkins, Milt Hinton, and Jo Jones played "Rosetta." Back to live action: two Dickenson solos on his own "I'll Cry" and "Constantly"; beautiful Norvo versions of "I Surrender Dear" and "Tea for Two" (Norvo, stationed off to one side of the stage, said later he felt as if he were playing in a sidecar); Earl Hines doing his own "Monday Date" and "Blues in Thirds"; three superior Teddy Wilson solos, with matching Jones brushwork; a willowy Bobby Hackett "Body and Soul," with superlative accompanying Jones high-hat (old man Jo was in superb form all evening); a burning Joe Venuti "Sweet Georgia Brown"; and a witty duet by Hinton and Jones. Unfortunately, Jabbo Smith didn't play. He appeared onstage during an ensemble and made the motions, but nothing came out. He was reportedly overcome with emotion. Never mind; better to leave undisturbed those dazzling solos he recorded in the late twenties and early thirties.

Over to Carnegie Hall at eleven-thirty to catch Sylvia Syms, who was jammed into a Lionel Hampton parade. She was accompanied by Mike Abene on piano, Randy Brecker, Jay Leonhart, and Panama Francis, and the best of her six songs were "As Long As I Live" and "More Than You Know." Then back to Avery Fisher to see if Sonny Rollins would shake off the queer paralysis that stage appearances seem to induce in him. He didn't. He played very little during his six numbers, and he used a husky Gato Barbieri tone and an odd mode of repeated notes and phrases. When the audience applauded, he rocked back and forth near the microphone and uttered strings of "Thankyouthankyouthankyou." But Rollins' idiosyncracies have never fooled anyone; he remains the wizard of living saxophonists.

JULY 5TH: THERE WILL BE THREE more Hudson River ferryboat rides tomorrow and a big soul-soap bash out at Nassau

Coliseum. So, to all intents and purposes, today is the last day of the Festival. The seven-thirty Avery Fisher concert began with a dark horse named Tania Maria. She is a small-faced, strongly built Brazilian singer and pianist, and she was accompanied by Helio on bass and Boto on drums. She sings in Portuguese, and none of her five songs was familiar, but it didn't matter. She has an urgent, precise hammering voice, and her singing is unbelievably close. There are no spaces, no chinks, no chances for her phrases to stand back and be admired. Her piano playing moves parallel to her singing and then fuses with it when she scat-sings. Where did this marvelous, fiery jazz come from? One hears in it suggestions of Carmen McRae and Ella Fitzgerald and Anita O'Day, but little else. Were the Brazilians singing and playing such music a hundred years ago? Did jazz really come up the Amazon?

After Tania Maria, I went over to Carnegie to catch Woody Herman's current Thundering Herd. It was like all the Thundering Herds he's had in the last fifteen years — young (three members had just been plucked from that extraordinary musical orchard, North Texas State), strident, forceful, and good. Stan Kenton occupied the second half of the program. Vast and tired and grandeur-ridden, he sat through most of the set while his boys Wagnered their way through "My Funny Valentine" and "All The Things You Are," a show-off blues, and some Latin edifices built around Candido, the rubbery conga drummer. The second concert at Carnegie started with Bill Watrous and his Manhattan Wildlife Refuge, and during the four numbers I heard Watrous demonstrated again that he is doomed for the rest of his life to try and domesticate a virtuosity that enables him to do anything on the trombone that comes into his mind and do it perfectly.

Sarah Vaughan was in residence at Avery Fisher for the late show, and during her second half she joked with Percy Heath, her bassist for the night, sang "Moonlight in Vermont" and "Poor Butterfly" and "Mean to Me" and a dozen other songs, rocketed time and again from her lowest register to her highest and from her highest to her lowest, gave lesson after lesson in melodic calligraphy, swallowed whole sets of lyrics alive, and stamped the word "rococo" on every one of our foreheads.

Earlier in the day, James T. Maher, the distinguished observer of American music, said that he was weary of the prolixity and density of so much contemporary jazz. It was becoming Brahmsian, and it reminded him of years ago, when, suddenly tiring of listening to symphonic music, he had turned with relief and pleasure to chamber music, where he could breathe again. He said that much the same thing had happened at the Hall of Fame concert. He also wondered where the plethora of notes jazz musicians play these days end up and whether the space there is unlimited.

JULY 8TH: GEORGE WEIN sang his annual postprandial blues in the *Times* today. Of the thirty-one events presented during the Festival, five sold out and six had houses ninety-per-cent full. The rest fell below seventy-five per cent, which Wein considers his break-even figure. (Wein did not point out that half a dozen concerts were protected by various fundings.) As a result, he said, he will probably cut down the number of concerts next year, thus eliminating, one hopes, such non-crowd-drawing dross as the organ concert, Dave Brubeck, Stanley Turrentine, Jon Lucien, Ramsey Lewis, and Bobbi Humphrey. But the Festival has been shrinking since its second year in New York (it is impossible to believe that he had *two* concerts in Yankee Stadium in 1972), and he will most likely return to the format that worked so well for so long at Newport — seven concerts spread over four days. The *Times* did not mention two improvements in the Festival — the almost complete disappearance of m.c.s and the streamlining of the concerts themselves. Many presented only two attractions, and many lasted under three hours. There is a classic

directness about life in New York, and perhaps Wein's subur-
ban Boston romanticism is at last bowing to it.

OCTOBER 10TH: BY 1940, the pursuit of American primitivism
in this country was well under way (collecting folk art,
collecting black jazz musicians, recording Appalachian folk-
singers, writing dialect novels), and one of its choicest finds
was the drummer Zutty Singleton, who died this July, at the
age of seventy-seven. Between the late thirties and the early
forties, Singleton, steadily visible at Nick's or the Village
Vanguard or Jimmy Ryan's, was one of the mascots of the
Brooks Brothers set. He played its private parties, and he
played the Sunday-afternoon jam sessions at Ryan's, where
the tapping of white buck shoes was thunderous. He played a
session on the St. Regis Roof that was broadcast to Britain,
which was ecstatically told by the announcer, Alistair Cooke,
that Singleton was the "greatest colored drummer alive."
Singleton was an ingratiating performer. His ceaseless motions were puppetlike. His head rolled from side to side and
his eyelids fluttered like butterflies. His arms seesawed, and he
lunged to the right or the left for a choked-cymbal stroke or a
tomtom beat. He played with a cheerful mock ardor, and the
instant he finished a number his broad smile came out like the
sun. What chiefly held his admirers were his snare-drum rolls,
which were beautiful. They flowed like cream on marble, and
he used them everywhere — for background figures with the
afterbeat emphasized, for press rolls in slow tempos, and in his
solos, which often consisted of an unbroken roll that rose and
fell, that shouted and whispered. For all that, Singleton was a
patchy drummer who had barely enough technique to get by.
He never learned to use a high-hat properly, his time was often
unsteady, and his solos were predictable. His style came to a
standstill around 1930, and it would have been unkind to
compare him, ten years later, with such contemporaries as Sid

Catlett and Jo Jones and Chick Webb. But Singleton was a fountainhead, and fountainheads are beyond cavil. He presided over drumming in Chicago during the late twenties and early thirties, when he worked with Louis Armstrong and Earl Hines, and from out of his shadow came drummers like Catlett and Gene Krupa and Lionel Hampton. He was a short, round, beamish man, an ingenuous, pleased country boy whose beginnings now seem Arcadian: "I was born in Bunkie, Louisiana," he once said. "My grandmother worked for a Dr. Hayes there, and when my mother was seventeen my grandmother summoned her up from New Orleans, where she was living with an aunt. My mother used to go to the local grocery store, which was owned by a man named E. E. Singleton. It looked like they got together. It looked like they got together, and that's how I appeared. He must have been in his thirties. I saw him just twice. He came to our house one night when I was six. He'd been hunting, and he had a lot of game. The other time, Viny Monroe, who'd been my midwife, came by and said, 'Come on, boy, I'm going to take you by your daddy's store.' She did, and those were the two times I saw him. Of course, the house we lived in he bought for my mother."

NOVEMBER 4TH: THE FIRST STYLE PRIMITIVE ARTISTS like Singleton hit on is their single experiment. Their technical limitations prohibit further experimentation and allow only a certain amount of growth, which generally takes the form not of expansion but of an intensification of what they already are. Primitive artists feed on themselves. An excellent instance is Erroll Garner. Garner's career is now thirty years old, and he has been an enormous success. He has become even more lofty than the Modern Jazz Quartet was in its best years. He plays mainly in concert halls, he takes plenty of time off to count his huge royalties from "Misty," long a standard, and he rarely bothers to record anymore. So Columbia has done us a service by restoring to print the old, workaday Garner in "Erroll Garner." It contains twenty-one numbers made between 1950 and 1956, when Garner was in mint form, and much of it is brilliant.

There are degrees of originality, and Garner's is of the highest. He long ago listened to Art Tatum and Earl Hines and Mary Lou Williams, and some of his long-armed single-note melodic lines go on and on like Bud Powell, but the rest is Garner. (He has never studied his instrument and cannot to this day read music.) His originality has proved irresistible, even to those from whom he once learned and who now learn from him. His style is melodramatic, swinging, emotional, and often startling. No pianist has had a more daring sense of dynamics. Here is what he does with his volume knob on a typical number: He delivers his outrageous, mini-symphonic introduction at a shout, pauses a split second, and drops into a soft, barely audible embellishment of the melody. The El has passed and you can hear the breeze in the ailanthus again. When he reaches the first bridge, he turns the volume up slightly, and turns it down again for the last eight bars. He then lets loose a brief, noisy concentration of chords (a satellite that has spun off his introduction), cuts the sound to a whisper, and goes into a full chorus of improvisation that grows gradually louder and ends in massive chords. But Garner's dynamics are perverse. His loudest passages are often his least inspired, while his softest are often his most affecting. One has to continually lean into his music to catch its best moments. Garner's style has other refreshing quirks. In place of oompah figures or tenths or clusters of offbeat chords in the left hand, he plays on-the-beat guitar chords — *rump rump rump rump* — that amount to his own rhythm section and that make the bass and drums he invariably carts around superfluous. And he is a remarkable ballad player. He uses a lot of loud pedal and an almost impenetrable foliage of chords and tremolos. Then, just as one is beginning to despair

of seeing daylight again, he releases the loud pedal and goes
into a quiet, on-the-beat improvisation — a device that surprises the listener, cuts the sugar, and immediately knocks the
piece into shape. Like Fats Waller and Tatum, Garner has a
strong comic streak. He spoofs certain songs, and occasionally he gets off sharp, funny parodies of other pianists. And, in
the mysterious manner of so many Eastern pianists, he cannot
take the blues seriously.

The delights of the Columbia reissue include a very fast
"Lover," spelled out in astonishingly mellifluous single-note
lines, lines that *hustle;* wild, seemingly where-am-I? introductions in "Love for Sale," "Can't Help Lovin' Dat Man," and
"Music, Maestro, Please"; a funny "Dancing in the Dark," full
of rich, lisping Eddie Duchin chords; a bowling, blowing
"Avalon"; a superbly lush (then lean) reading of his ballad
"Dreamy"; an eight-minute "Man I Love," in which he extracts
all the melodic juice before doubling the tempo and playing a
remarkable melody-based improvisation; and a jumping, jolly
"Honeysuckle Rose." Most jazz musicians use the composer's
work as a stepping-off place for what they pray will be an even
better composition. But Garner does not. Listen to how he
gladdens the melodies of "Man I Love" and "Lover" and "I
Never Knew," how he heightens and freshens them and makes
them sing.

Garner revealed during his most recent New York appearance that he is following the course of all great primitives. His
playing is more intense and prolix. His celebrated introductions often swell into steaming, complete compositions. His
dynamics are even more dramatic. His tremolos are veritable
hanging gardens, and his single-note lines cascades. But one
has a dream about Garner. How fine it would be to hear him
with a small band of his choosing, just jamming and lyricing
along. It might ease the weight of his crown as well as produce
some lightning music.